Communications
in Computer and Information Science   1882

Rationale

The CCIS series is devoted to the publication of proceedings of computer science conferences. Its aim is to efficiently disseminate original research results in informatics in printed and electronic form. While the focus is on publication of peer-reviewed full papers presenting mature work, inclusion of reviewed short papers reporting on work in progress is welcome, too. Besides globally relevant meetings with internationally representative program committees guaranteeing a strict peer-reviewing and paper selection process, conferences run by societies or of high regional or national relevance are also considered for publication.

Topics

The topical scope of CCIS spans the entire spectrum of informatics ranging from foundational topics in the theory of computing to information and communications science and technology and a broad variety of interdisciplinary application fields.

Information for Volume Editors and Authors

Publication in CCIS is free of charge. No royalties are paid, however, we offer registered conference participants temporary free access to the online version of the conference proceedings on SpringerLink (http://link.springer.com) by means of an http referrer from the conference website and/or a number of complimentary printed copies, as specified in the official acceptance email of the event.

CCIS proceedings can be published in time for distribution at conferences or as postproceedings, and delivered in the form of printed books and/or electronically as USBs and/or e-content licenses for accessing proceedings at SpringerLink. Furthermore, CCIS proceedings are included in the CCIS electronic book series hosted in the SpringerLink digital library at http://link.springer.com/bookseries/7899. Conferences publishing in CCIS are allowed to use Online Conference Service (OCS) for managing the whole proceedings lifecycle (from submission and reviewing to preparing for publication) free of charge.

Publication process

The language of publication is exclusively English. Authors publishing in CCIS have to sign the Springer CCIS copyright transfer form, however, they are free to use their material published in CCIS for substantially changed, more elaborate subsequent publications elsewhere. For the preparation of the camera-ready papers/files, authors have to strictly adhere to the Springer CCIS Authors' Instructions and are strongly encouraged to use the CCIS LaTeX style files or templates.

Abstracting/Indexing

CCIS is abstracted/indexed in DBLP, Google Scholar, EI-Compendex, Mathematical Reviews, SCImago, Scopus. CCIS volumes are also submitted for the inclusion in ISI Proceedings.

How to start

To start the evaluation of your proposal for inclusion in the CCIS series, please send an e-mail to ccis@springer.com.

Andreas Holzinger · Hugo Plácido da Silva ·
Jean Vanderdonckt · Larry Constantine
Editors

Computer-Human Interaction Research and Applications

5th International Conference, CHIRA 2021
Virtual Event, October 28–29, 2021
and 6th International Conference, CHIRA 2022
Valletta, Malta, October 27–28, 2022
Revised Selected Papers

 Springer

Editors
Andreas Holzinger
Medical University Graz
Graz, Austria

Jean Vanderdonckt
Université Catholique de Louvain
Louvain-la-Neuve, Belgium

Hugo Plácido da Silva
IT - Institute of Telecommunications
Lisbon, Portugal

Instituto Superior Técnico
Lisbon, Portugal

Larry Constantine
Madeira Interactive Technologies Institute
Funchal, Portugal

ISSN 1865-0929   ISSN 1865-0937 (electronic)
Communications in Computer and Information Science
ISBN 978-3-031-41961-4   ISBN 978-3-031-41962-1 (eBook)
https://doi.org/10.1007/978-3-031-41962-1

This Springer imprint is published by the registered company Springer Nature Switzerland AG
The registered company address is: Gewerbestrasse 11, 6330 Cham, Switzerland

Preface

The present book includes extended and revised versions of a set of selected papers from the 2021 and 2022 editions of CHIRA - The International Conference on Computer-Human Interaction Research and Applications. CHIRA 2021 was exceptionally held as online event, due to COVID-19, and CHIRA 2022 was held in Valletta, Malta as a hybrid event.

CHIRA 2021 received 48 paper submissions from 20 countries, of which 4% were included in this book. CHIRA 2022 received 37 paper submissions from 17 countries, of which 17% were included in this book.

The papers were selected by the event chairs and their selection is based on a number of criteria that include the ratings and comments provided by the program committee members, the session chairs' assessment and also the program chairs' global view of all papers included in the technical program. The authors of selected papers were then invited to submit a revised and extended version of their papers having at least 30% new material.

The purpose of the International Conference on Computer-Human Interaction Research and Applications (CHIRA) is to bring together professionals, academics and students who are interested in the advancement of research and practical applications of interaction design & human-computer interaction. Four parallel tracks were held, covering different aspects of Computer-Human Interaction, which were Human Factors and Information Systems, Interactive Devices, Interaction Design and Adaptive and Intelligent Systems.

The papers selected to be included in this book contribute to the understanding of relevant trends of current research in Computer-Human Interaction Research and Applications, including: User-Centered Interaction Design Patterns, User Experience Design, Multimedia and Multimodal Interaction, Interaction Design Modelling, Haptic and Tangible Devices, Accessible and Adaptive Interaction, User Behaviour Analysis, User Experience Evaluation, Modelling Human Factors, Mobile Computer-Human Interaction, Machine Learning, Information Retrieval, Human-Centered AI and Design and Evaluation.

We would like to thank all the authors for their contributions and also the reviewers who have helped to ensure the quality of this publication.

October 2022

Andreas Holzinger
Hugo Plácido da Silva
Jean Vanderdonckt
Larry Constantine

Organization

Conference Co-chairs

Larry Constantine	Madeira Interactive Technologies Institute, Portugal
Andreas Holzinger	Medical University Graz, Austria

Program Co-chairs

CHIRA 2021

Hugo Plácido da Silva	IT - Instituto de Telecomunicações, Portugal

CHIRA 2022

Hugo Plácido da Silva	IT - Instituto de Telecomunicações, Portugal
Jean Vanderdonckt	Université Catholique de Louvain, Belgium

Program Committee

CHIRA 2021

Iyad Abu Doush	American University of Kuwait, Kuwait
Christopher Anand	McMaster University, Canada
Nizar Banu P. K.	Christ University, India
John Brooke	Independent Researcher, UK
Eric Castelli	LIG Grenoble, France
Christine Chauvin	Université de Bretagne Sud, France
Ahyoung Choi	Gachon University, Republic of Korea
Yang-Wai Chow	University of Wollongong, Australia
Cesar Collazos	Universidad del Cauca, Colombia
Arzu Coltekin	University of Applied Sciences and Arts Northwestern Switzerland, Switzerland
Lizette de Wet	University of the Free State, South Africa

Joerg Doerr	Fraunhofer Institute for Experimental Software Engineering, Germany
Andrew Duchowski	Clemson University, USA
Achim Ebert	University of Kaiserslautern, Germany
Vania Estrela	Universidade Federal Fluminense, Brazil
Peter Forbrig	University of Rostock, Germany
Diego Gachet	European University of Madrid, Spain
Valentina Gatteschi	Politecnico di Torino, Italy
Gheorghita Ghinea	Brunel University London, UK
Toni Granollers	University of Lleida, Spain
Martin Hitz	Alpen-Adria-Universität Klagenfurt, Austria
Sadanori Ito	National Institute of Information and Communications Technology, Japan
M.-Carmen Juan	Instituto Ai2, Universitat Politècnica de València, Spain
Adi Katz	Sami Shamoon College of Engineering, Israel
Gerard Kim	Korea University, Republic of Korea
Josef F. Krems	Chemnitz University of Technology, Cognitive and Engineering Psychology, Germany
Gerhard Leitner	Alpen-Adria-Universität Klagenfurt, Austria
Wen-Chieh Lin	National Chiao Tung University, Taiwan, Republic of China
Eurico Lopes	Escola Superior de Tecnologia, Instituto Politécnico de Castelo Branco, Portugal
Michael Lyons	Ritsumeikan University, Japan
Lorenzo Magnani	University of Pavia, Italy
Federico Manuri	Politecnico di Torino, Italy
Frédéric Mérienne	Arts et Métiers ParisTech, France
Daniel Mestre	Aix-Marseille University/CNRS, France
Neema Moraveji	Stanford University, USA
Giulio Mori	Institute of Information Science Technologies, Italy
Lia Morra	Politecnico di Torino, Italy
Max Mulder	TU Delft, The Netherlands
Max North	Kennesaw State University, USA
Francisco Rebelo	ITI/LARSys and University of Lisbon, Portugal
Andrea Resmini	Halmstad University, Sweden
Laura Ripamonti	Università degli Studi di Milano, Italy
Andrea Sanna	Politecnico di Torino, Italy
Frédéric Vanderhaegen	University of Valenciennes, France
Gualtiero Volpe	Università degli Studi di Genova, Italy
Kanliang Wang	Renmin University of China, China
Marcus Winter	University of Brighton, UK

Diego Zapata-Rivera   Educational Testing Service, USA
Juergen Ziegler   University of Duisburg-Essen, Germany
Floriano Zini   Free University of Bozen-Bolzano, Italy

CHIRA 2022

Iyad Abu Doush   American University of Kuwait, Kuwait
Christopher Anand   McMaster University, Canada
Nizar Banu P. K.   Christ University, India
John Brooke   Independent Researcher, UK
Eric Castelli   LIG Grenoble, France
Christine Chauvin   Université de Bretagne Sud, France
Cesar Collazos   Universidad del Cauca, Colombia
Arzu Coltekin   University of Applied Sciences and Arts
                               Northwestern Switzerland, Switzerland
Lizette de Wet   University of the Free State, South Africa
Joerg Doerr   Fraunhofer Institute for Experimental Software
                               Engineering, Germany
Vania Estrela   Universidade Federal Fluminense, Brazil
Jesus Favela   CICESE, Mexico
Peter Forbrig   University of Rostock, Germany
Gheorghita Ghinea   Brunel University London, UK
Toni Granollers   University of Lleida, Spain
Martin Hitz   Alpen-Adria-Universität Klagenfurt, Austria
M.-Carmen Juan   Instituto Ai2, Universitat Politècnica de València,
                               Spain
Adi Katz   Sami Shamoon College of Engineering, Israel
Wen-Chieh Lin   National Chiao Tung University, Taiwan,
                               Republic of China
Federico Manuri   Politecnico di Torino, Italy
Daniel Mestre   Aix-Marseille University/CNRS, France
Lia Morra   Politecnico di Torino, Italy
Max North   Kennesaw State University, USA
Francisco Rebelo   ITI/LARSys and University of Lisbon, Portugal
Laura Ripamonti   Università degli Studi di Milano, Italy
Carsten Röcker   Fraunhofer IOSB-INA, Germany
Andrea Sanna   Politecnico di Torino, Italy
Markku Turunen   Tampere University, Finland
Frédéric Vanderhaegen   University of Valenciennes, France
Gualtiero Volpe   Università degli Studi di Genova, Italy
Marcus Winter   University of Brighton, UK
Floriano Zini   Free University of Bozen-Bolzano, Italy

Additional Reviewers

CHIRA 2021

Yi-Jheng Huang	Yuan Ze University, Taiwan, Republic of China
Asif Ali Laghari	Sindh Madressatul Islam University, Pakistan
Chun-Shu Wei	National Yang Ming Chiao Tung University, Taiwan, Republic of China

Invited Speakers

CHIRA 2021

Albrecht Schmidt	Ludwig-Maximilians Universität München, Germany
Pattie Maes	MIT, USA
Anton Nijholt	University of Twente, The Netherlands

CHIRA 2022

Abigail Sellen	Microsoft Research Cambridge, UK
Karen Holtzblatt	InContext Design, USA
Alan Dix	Swansea University, UK

Contents

Music Tangible User Interfaces and Vulnerable Users: State of the Art and Experimentation

Adriano Baratè[1], Helene Korsten[2], Luca A. Ludovico[1(✉)],
and Eleonora Oriolo[2]

[1] Laboratory of Music Informatics (LIM), Department of Computer Science,
University of Milan, via G. Celoria 18, Milan, Italy
{adriano.barate,lucaa.ludovico}@unimi.it
[2] Department of Computer Science, University of Milan,
via G. Celoria 18, Milan, Italy
{helene.korsten,eleonora.oriolo}@studenti.unimi.it
https://www.lim.di.unimi.it

Abstract. Tangible user interfaces (TUIs) let users manipulate digital information with their bodies and perceive it with their senses. This concept can be applied to the control of digital musical instruments and, in a more general context, music-oriented devices. Specifically addressing vulnerable users, namely people in a condition of cognitive and/or physical impairment, this paper presents the state of the art about music TUIs and describes an experiment conducted on a small group. The methodology consisted in building user-tailored experiences to let participants acquire basic musical skills with a hands-on approach implemented through an ensemble of digital instruments. The achieved results included both the improvement of music competencies in vulnerable users and the acquisition of soft skills.

Keywords: Music · Tangible user interfaces · Computer-supported education · Educational vulnerability · Social disadvantage · Accessibility · Educational poverty

1 Introduction

A relevant research question in the field of sound and music computing concerns if and how technology can bridge the gap between musical activities (including learning, composition, performance, etc.) and physical and cognitive users' impairments.

The scientific literature shows that digital technologies can help in a number of ways: for example, a computer-based system can substitute and/or augment a standard musical instrument [22,33,43], pave the way for unleashing creativity [47,48,60], provide alternative interfaces suitable to overcome impairments [31,35,51], and encourage the development of music-related skills [5,10,54]. According to [45], music teaching through information technology can also affect

A. Holzinger et al. (Eds.): CHIRA 2021/2022, CCIS 1882, pp. 1–25, 2023.
https://doi.org/10.1007/978-3-031-41962-1_1

behavior relating to learners' online learning attitudes, music learning motivation, and learning engagement. The ubiquity of portable devices (notebooks, tablets, smartphones, etc.), equipped with ad-hoc hardware accessories, suitable software tools, and easy-to-use interfaces, can represent a solution even in vulnerable contexts.

Please note that disability and aging are not the only factors that hamper the development of musical skills; also conditions of social disadvantage may constitute a barrier [14,36,46].

Music is learned and taught in multiple ways depending on the socio-cultural contexts in which learning occurs, and musical activities should be culturally responsive and meaningful so as to respond to diverse learning contexts [13]. Critical aspects such as user-friendliness, usability, accessibility, affordability, and suitable use of multimodality must be considered.

In this work, we propose the use of tangible user interfaces both as musical instruments to use in conjunction with traditional ones and as an orchestra. The goal of the experimentation we conducted was to foster musical expressiveness and interaction between users in conditions of social disadvantage. Participants were characterized by cognitive and/or physical impairments or they had a background of educational poverty.

The key research questions we aim to answer are:

RQ1. Can tangible user interfaces encourage the acquisition of basic musical skills in socially-distressed subjects?
RQ2. Can an ensemble of music tangible user interfaces foster soft skills such as socialization and cooperation among peers?
RQ3. Can these results be measured or somehow assessed?

In the following, we will try to answer these questions. To this end, the present work is organized as follows: Sect. 2 will define the concept of tangible user interface (TUI) and provide the state of the art; Sect. 3 will focus on music TUIs; Sect. 4 will describe the experimental activities, including some previous experiences, the details of project "Note Digitali", and the experimental setting; Sect. 5 will focus on the results achieved and propose possible strategies to measure users' performances; finally, Sect. 6 will draw the conclusions.

Please note that this paper is an extension of the work presented at the 5th International Conference on Computer-Human Interaction Research and Applications (CHIRA 2021) [12].

2   Tangible User Interfaces

Tangible user interfaces (TUIs) replace the graphical user interfaces (GUIs) typical for user interaction in computing systems with real physical objects. The key idea is to give digital information a physical form and let these physical forms serve as a representation and control for digital information. A TUI lets users manipulate digital information with their bodies and perceive it with their senses. One of the pioneers in tangible user interfaces is Hiroshi Ishii, a professor at MIT who heads the *Tangible Media Group* at the MIT Media Lab. His particular vision for TUIs, called *Tangible Bits*, is to give physical form to digital information, making bits directly manipulable and perceptible [40]. *Tangible Bits* pursues the seamless coupling between physical objects and virtual data.

TUIs aim to overcome some limitations posed by classic computer interaction, offering intuitive ways to build complex structures, manipulate parameters, and connect objects. TUIs use physical forms that fit seamlessly into a user's physical environment, giving physical form to digital information and taking advantage of haptic-interaction skills [41]. All physical objects can potentially be a part of a digital user interface [39]. For example, if an object, which is part of a TUI, is moved or put in a specific position, a digital signal will be sent from either the tangible object itself or from another device that senses the object.

Currently, there are different research areas and applications related to TUIs. For instance, tangible augmented reality implies that virtual objects are "attached" to physically manipulated objects; in tangible tabletop interaction, physical objects are moved upon a multi-touch surface; moreover, physical objects can be used as ambient displays or integrated inside embodied user interfaces.

Since TUIs make digital information directly manipulatable with our hands and perceptible through our peripheral senses, this approach can be particularly effective for young [68] and disadvantaged users [1,17,28].

One of the scenarios where TUIs are particularly effective is gamification. Focusing on recovering from physical impairments, games can be used to increase the motivation of patients in rehabilitation sessions. Motivation is one of the main problems evidenced in traditional therapy sessions, often hampered by the repetitive nature of exercises. Most studies show that effective rehabilitation must be early, intensive, and repetitive [16,59]. As such, these approaches are often considered repetitive and boring by the patients, resulting in difficulties in maintaining their interest and in assuring that they complete the treatment program [59]. On the other hand, due to their nature, games can motivate and engage the patients' attention and distract them from their rehabilitation condition. On one side, they require some motor and cognitive activity, and, on the other, they can offer feedback and levels of challenge and difficulty that can be adapted to the patients' skills. We can see similar advantages in the development of domain and soft skills for other categories of impaired users.

Serious games are an option that provides learning combined with entertainment. The locution "serious games" refers to playful activities that provide training and physical or mental exercise in a fun and enjoyable way [25]. These games can be not only a way to prevent the feeling of loneliness [24], but they can also enable social interaction [30]. During the last decades, digital games have become a popular leisure activity.

A quite obvious field of application for tangible interfaces is the overcoming of visual impairment through gamification [49,55,58]. Different forms of physical impairment have been addressed as well.

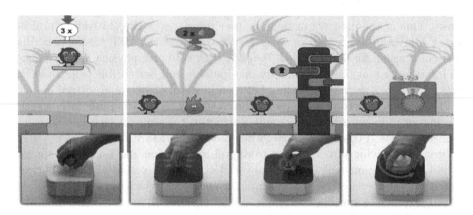

Fig. 1. The user interface and some gestures supported by *Handly*. Images were taken from [65].

For example, *Handly* is an integrated upper-limb rehabilitation system for persons with neurological disorders [65]. *Handly* consists of tangibles for training four-hand tasks with specific functional handgrips and a motivational game. The system consists of four tangible training boxes, which each present one essential grip and associated hand task: push-pull, squeezing, knob turning, and key turning (see Fig. 1). *Handly* combines tangibles specifically designed for repetitive task-oriented motor skill training of typical daily activities with serious gaming, thus offering a comprehensive approach. *Handly* focuses on therapy for various neurological disorders that can cause functional disabilities in the hands.

Segara is an integrated hand rehabilitation system for patients with rheumatoid arthritis (RA) very similar to *Handly* [69]. *Segara* consists of tangibles for training six tasks with Interactive functional handgrips and a motivational serious game (see Fig. 2). It shows that a system combining games and tangibles to enhance hand rehabilitation is feasible and highly appreciated by patients.

Resonance is an interactive tabletop artwork that targets upper-limb movement rehabilitation for patients with an acquired brain injury [26]. The artwork consists of several interactive game environments, which enable artistic expression, exploration, and play. *Resonance* provides uni-manual and bi-manual game-like tasks and exploratory creative environments of varying complexity geared toward reaching, grasping, lifting, moving, and placing tangible user interfaces on a tabletop display (see Fig. 3). Each environment aims to encourage collaborative, cooperative, and competitive modes of interaction for small groups of co-located participants.

NikVision is a tangible tabletop based on a user-centered design approach for the cognitive stimulation of older people with cognitive impairments and dementia problems in nursing homes [18]. The general experiences of the users when working with the tangible tabletop were assessed and applied to the design of new cognitive and physical stimulation activities. From these experiences, guidelines for the design of tangible activities for this kind of user were extracted

Fig. 2. The user interface and some examples of activities with *Segara*. Images were taken from [69].

Fig. 3. The user interface and a play session of *Resonance*.

for the design and evaluation of tangible activities that could be useful for other researchers. *NIKIVision*'s game activities are specially designed for the elderly and have different levels of difficulty and audio feedback. The list of activities includes:

– *Clothes Activity*—Based on the daily task of getting dressed, users interact with the tabletop by using different objects with realistic drawings of pieces of clothing and letters. Fine motor skills are addressed when users have to pick up the two-dimensional objects to place them on the tabletop;

- *Shapes Activity*—Users have to select the indicated geometrical shapes and situate them on the box displayed on the tabletop;
- *Roads Activity*—Focusing on upper-half motor skills, users have to move the object on the tabletop surface by following a virtual road, also avoiding physical obstacles in the most difficult levels. The objects with which the users interact are different handles designed to stimulate different kinds of grabbing actions.

It is worth remarking that, when the applications are not explicitly conceived for impaired users, gamification can also pose critical issues. For example, Smith and Abrams [63] explore the issue of access to digital technology by using the lens of accessibility. More specifically, this paper considers the needs of all learners, including those who identify as disabled, and raises important inquiries about equity and access to technological instructional materials. Notably, online courses enhanced with gamification elements present potential access barriers and challenges to learners who identify with auditory, cognitive, neurological, physical, speech, or visual disabilities.

3   Tangible User Interfaces for Music

Music TUIs apply the concept of tangible interfaces to the music field. As demonstrated by the scientific literature and a number of commercially-available applications, TUIs are being profitably used in musical performances and music therapy.

A tangible interface provides the user with a physical way to interact with music and sound parameters. In this sense, the advent of digital technologies paved the way for innovative and original approaches. Music TUIs can play a number of roles: for example, synthesizers to generate sound, sequencers that perform audio samples and mix them together, remote controllers for music and sound parameters, or interfaces for music-related games.

A key concept is the one of *music embodiment*: it can be defined as a corporeal process that enables the link between music as an experienced phenomenon and music as physical energy [44]. This process focuses on the cognitive relationship that ties musical subjects and objects, an idea critically analyzed and reworked by Schiavio and Menin [61].

Music TUIs are a technological means able to support and encourage music embodiment, thus breaking down the barriers that hinder musical creativity and expressiveness, especially in young people and impaired performers. On one side, a tangible interface offers a physical way to interact with music and sound parameters, somehow recalling the kind of interaction of traditional musical instruments; on the other side, it can simplify the process, e.g., making it more accessible and intuitive.

In the following, we will mention some musical applications (Sect. 3.1) and then we will focus on the *Kibo*, namely the device that we adopted in our experimentation (Sect. 3.2).

3.1 Musical Applications of TUIs

Many music TUIs are based on *fiducial markers*, or simply *fiducials*, namely objects placed in the field of view of an image-recognition system with functions of control, user input, reference, or measure. Examples of fiducials include:

- 2D markers, e.g. barcode systems or pictograms [29];
- basic 3D geometrical shapes, e.g. multi-faceted cubes [57];
- 3D printed objects, e.g. diorama models of musical instruments [4].

For example, the principle of fiducials is fully exploited in the *Reactable*, a digital musical instrument developed by the Music Technology Group at the Universitat Pompeu Fabra in Barcelona [42]. The *Reactable* employs fiducials to generate and control music and sound parameters. This device has a tabletop tangible user interface formed by a round translucent table used as a backlit display. Special blocks called *tangibles* (see Fig. 4) can be placed on the table and moved by the user according to the intended result; their geometrical and spatial characteristics are detected in real time by the image-recognition system, that, in turn, pilots the virtual modular synthesizer to create music or sound effects. Currently, there are two versions of the *Reactable*: *Reactable Live!* and *Reactable experience*. The former is a smaller, more portable version designed for professional musicians. The latter is more similar to the original *Reactable* and suited for installations in public spaces.

Another fiducial-based framework for music is *D-Touch* [20], which defines a class of tangible media applications implementable on consumer-grade personal computers. *D-Touch* fiducial markers for music-performance applications are shown in Fig. 5.

BeatBearing is a do-it-yourself (DIY) project.[1] This tangible rhythm sequencer is made of a computer interface overlaid with the grid pattern of metal washers and ball bearings. The system is controlled by an Arduino micro-controller.

Many working prototypes have been described in the scientific literature.

In 2001, Paradiso *et al.* reviewed some initiatives based on magnetic tags, including *Musical Trinkets*, an installation based on tagged objects publicly exhibited first at SIGGRAPH 2000 and, several months later, at SMAU in Milan [52].

In 2003, Newton-Dunn *et al.* described a way to control *Block Jam*, a dynamic polyrhythmic sequencer using physical artifacts [50]. The idea of a tangible sequencer addressing the preparation and improvisation of electronic music is also the foundation of a more recent platform called *mixiTUI*. [53].

Modular sound synthesis is addressed by the *Spyractable* described in [56]. This platform reconfigures the functionality of the *Reactable* and redesigns most features, adjusting it to a synthesizer's needs.

---

[1] https://www.jameco.com/Jameco/workshop/JamecoFavorites/beatbearing-rhythm-sequencer.html.

Fig. 4. The fiducial markers of the *Reactable*. The picture is taken from [23].

Fig. 5. The fiducial markers of *D-Touch*. The picture is taken from [20].

The *MusicCube*, described in [2], is a wireless cube-like object that lets users physically interact with music collections using gestures to shuffle music and a rotary dial with a button for song navigation and volume control. In 2008 Schiettecatte and Vanderdonckt presented *AudioCubes*, a similar product consisting in a distributed cube interface for sound design [62].

Fig. 6. The fiducial markers of *TuneTable*. The picture is taken from [32].

Finally, it is worth mentioning the *TuneTable* [67], a platform based on programmable fiducials for music coding (Fig. 6). This approach was assessed in a computational musical tabletop exhibit for the young held at the Museum of Design, Atlanta (MODA). Workshop activities had the goal of promoting hands-on learning of computational concepts through music creation.

For a more up-to-date and comprehensive review of music TUIs in the scientific literature, please refer to [8].

3.2 Kodaly *Kibo*

The *Kibo* by Kodaly is a wooden board presenting eight unique geometric shapes that can be inserted into and removed from suitable slots. This device, also sensitive to pressure variations on single tangibles, returns the dynamic response of a polyphonic acoustic instrument.

The main control over music parameters is realized through a set of 8 easily-recognizable tangibles, shown in Fig. 7. Each object has a different shape fitting in a single slot. Tangibles present symmetry properties so that they can be rotated and flipped before being inserted in their slots. They have a magnetic core, consequently, they can be also stacked one on top of the other. The body of the *Kibo* contains a multi-point pressure sensor that allows the detection of the insertion and removal of tangibles. The characteristics of the sensor make the instrument both extremely sensitive and very resistant. Concerning the former aspect, it is sufficient to bring a tangible closer to the body to trigger a reaction; similarly, the gentle touch of fingers over an already plugged tangible is recognized as a pressure variation. Concerning robustness, the *Kibo* has been designed to tolerate strong physical stresses, like punches and bumps. A distinctive feature is the possibility of detecting pressure variations over tangibles.

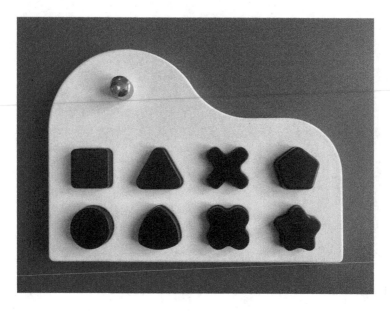

Fig. 7. The *Kibo*'s body and tangibles.

The *Kibo* can be connected via Bluetooth or USB to iOS and macOS devices running a proprietary app, that acts both as a synthesizer and a configuration center. Windows and Android operating systems are also supported via third-party drivers.

The communication between the controller and the app occurs by exchanging standard MIDI 1.0 messages. The MIDI engine integrated into the app supports up to seven *Kibo* units simultaneously, without perceivable latency. Being a fully compatible controller, the *Kibo* can also be integrated into any MIDI setup without the intervention of the app as a mediator.

In addition to the advantages of any music TUI, the *Kibo* was chosen for the "Note digitali" project because this device simplifies the establishment of a network of musical instruments working together like an orchestral ensemble [3].

Moreover, the app natively embeds three operating modes that are particularly useful in educational, rehabilitative, and therapeutic fields [9]:

1. *Musical Instrument Mode*—In this scenario, *Kibo*'s tangibles are usually mapped onto pitches. Associations between shapes and notes can be customized; in this way, the device is not bound to a fixed association (e.g., a C-major scale), but it supports key changes, other scale models, non-standard note layouts, etc. Through suitable processing of MIDI messages, a single key could also trigger multiple musical events, e.g. custom chords or arpeggios. The metaphor of a keyboard controller is further extended by the *aftertouch* effect, namely the possibility to detect pressure variations over tangibles after note attacks;

2. *Beat Mode*—In this scenario, tangibles are mapped onto single percussive instruments. The pressure sensor, presenting a high level of resistance to strong mechanical stresses but also a noticeable sensitivity, allows effects ranging from hard mallet beats to delicate brush rubbing. With respect to the previous one, such an operating mode greatly simplifies the interaction and makes the performance more intuitive for beginners; for example, the melodic and harmonic dimensions of music are absent, and a number of musical parameters (e.g., the release time for notes) are ignored;
3. *Song Mode*—In this scenario, the *Kibo* is employed as a controller to trigger already available music loops. Tangibles are associated with mutually synchronized but independent tracks, like in a multi-track environment. When tangibles are inserted, the corresponding tracks are activated; when they are removed, tracks are muted (but they keep running silently, so as to preserve global synchronization). This type of interaction with music content is particularly suitable to engage users who are not able or do not wish to create their own music.

The reconfigurability of the *Kibo*, coupled with the adoption of standard communication protocols, enables numerous heterogeneous scenarios. Multiple *Kibo* units in an ensemble can be set to cover distinct note ranges and timbres, or even to work in different operating modes, thus providing the teacher with great flexibility. Additional operating modes could be easily implemented by assigning other meanings, even extra-musical ones, to the MIDI messages generated by the *Kibo* via ad-hoc software interfaces.

4 Experimentation

4.1 Background

The current proposal is rooted in some previous music-therapy experiences conducted by the same working group with the help of digital technologies, as documented in [7,11]. Also in that case, the idea was to employ a computer-based interface in order to overcome the physical and cognitive impairments that often hamper musical activities in users with disabilities. Such a goal only partially overlaps the one of the "Note Digitali" project; in fact, in the scenario described below, not only impairments but also conditions of social disadvantage will be considered.

Other key differences with respect to the aforementioned experiences must be remarked. First, from a technical point of view, human-computer interaction did not occur through a music TUI but through the *Leap Motion* controller, an optical hand-tracking module able to detect and capture the movements of the user's hands with great accuracy [66]. The applicability of such a device to music recalls the concept of "air" musical instruments, i.e. virtual instruments employing depth cameras or other sensor systems to implement an interaction paradigm based on performing gestures in the air, without touching a physical interface [34]. Examples have been documented and discussed in [21,27], and

[64]. Conversely, the "Note Digitali" project (discussed later) employs the *Kibo*, the music TUI described in Sect. 3.2. Clearly, this kind of interface completely changes the human-computer interaction paradigm.

Moreover, in previous experiences, the musical performance mainly involved only the impaired user – interacting through the *Leap Motion* controller – and the therapist – playing a traditional instrument. The social aspects typical of making music together were limited to the relationship between a single learner and his/her educator. Conversely, the proposal detailed below will focus on peer-to-peer interaction between multiple performers, whereas the main roles played by the instructor will be to explain, help, and propose musical activities.

The scientific literature reports other experiences of ensemble playing on digital instruments. For example, the aspects of human interaction and communication in a digital music ensemble have been addressed by Hattwick and Umezaki [37,38]; Ben-Tal and Salazar proposed a new model for collaborative learning based on the connections between the technological tools and the social frameworks in emerging digital music collectives [15]; Cheng investigated the development of musical competency in a laptop ensemble [19].

With respect to other similar initiatives, our proposal presents novel features regarding the expressiveness of the selected digital device, the availability of a fine-tuned learning environment, and the attention paid to affective and emotional aspects. These characteristics will be better clarified in the next sections.

4.2   The "Note Digitali" Project

The initiative described in this work was launched in response to "Call 57" by *Fondazione di Comunità di Milano - Città, Sud Ovest, Sud Est e Adda Martesana ONLUS*. In this framework, the project "Note digitali" (in English: digital notes) provided the common umbrella to host different activities dealing with music and disadvantaged people. The project involved three partners:

1. *Laboratorio di Informatica Musicale* (Laboratory of Music Informatics), Department of Computer Science, University of Milan. Established in 1985, it is one of the most relevant Italian research centers dealing with sound and music computing;
2. *Casa di Redenzione Sociale* (House of Social Redemption), Milan. Founded in 1927, this institution has been conducting activities in both the social and cultural fields, specifically addressing problems linked to the context of the northern suburbs of Milan: fragmentation of the social fabric, widespread educational poverty, and lack of public spaces;
3. *Fondazione Luigi Clerici*, Milan. In operation since 1972, this foundation offers vocational courses and apprenticeship initiatives, also for adult and impaired students. The mission is to create a network able to integrate education and organizational skills in collaboration with public and private authorities, local institutions, trade associations, and social organizations.

The project was conceived as an experiment of cultural citizenship where music turns into a means of self-empowerment and social cohesion. The goals included providing basic musical competencies and skills, fostering creativity, and, above all, encouraging interaction and socialization in vulnerable participants. The expected results included the promotion of participation in the sociocultural life of the community by people with different types of disabilities, the perception of music as a means of aggregation, and self-empowerment, namely the self-discovery for the participants of their skills and abilities.

4.3   The Experimental Setting

Workshop activities were conducted in small groups under the guidance of an experienced tutor in a time span from December 2020 to May 2021.

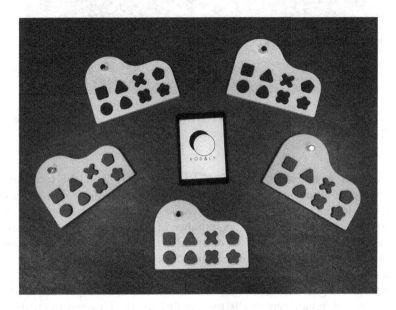

Fig. 8. The hardware equipment used during the experimental activity: five *Kibo* units and an *Apple iPad*. The picture is taken from [12].

The basic hardware equipment used during the experimental activity included 5 *Kibo* units connected to an Apple iPad via Bluetooth Low Energy (BLE), as shown in Fig. 8. The room where most activities took place was also equipped with traditional and digital musical instruments, such as drums and an electric piano (Fig. 9). This setting provided the tutor with many options, including the exclusive use of *Kibo* units (with or without the direct involvement of the tutor) and mixed performances with traditional instruments, specifically the piano and the ukulele. In the latter scenario, the tutor was the only performer enabled to play a non-digital instrument. Most participants had no previous music knowledge, so the function of the tutor was basically to explain musical concepts and guide learners toward an autonomous performance.

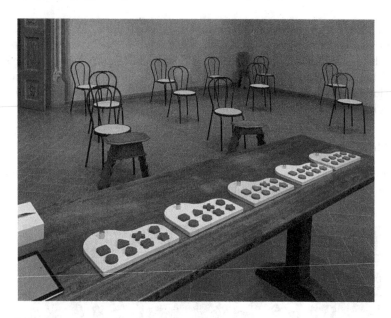

Fig. 9. The classroom where workshop activities took place. The picture is adapted from [12].

The current technical limitations of BLE currently limit the total amount of *Kibo* units simultaneously connected to a single mobile device: the maximum amount is 7. In the case of an expanded *Kibo* orchestra, such a constraint can be overcome by employing a higher number of devices suitably configured to communicate with a subset of *Kibo* units. Moreover, these TUIs can be used as standard MIDI controllers, thus operating in conjunction with other compatible hardware equipment.

As the participants admitted to the workshops were expected to present different types of impairment or distress conditions, the idea was to create small and homogeneous groups. Participants were subdivided into teams made of 4 people, in order to guarantee, on one side, a number of peers sufficient to foster social interaction and, on the other, let the tutor easily supervise and guide the experience. The tutor had background experiences both in music therapy and in digital music technologies.

Participants belonged to 3 categories:

1. young students aged 12 to 18 with psycho-social support needs;
2. adults aged 25 to 50 with cognitive and/or physical impairment;
3. children with special needs (in particular due to dyslexia, dyspraxia, and dyscalculia) aged 7 to 10.

The total number of participants was 20 (12 males, 8 females). They formed 5 teams: 2 teams (8 participants, 2 females) for the first category, 2 teams (8

Table 1. The detailed program of the workshop [12].

Unit	Task	Description
1	1.1	Presentation of participants and pre-test
	1.2	Introduction to the *Kibo* and its features
	1.3	The *Kibo* and piano interactive performance
	1.4	All participants playing the same rhythmic pattern
2	2.1	Theoretical fundamentals of melody and rhythm
	2.2	Playing a short piece as an ensemble
	2.3	Writing and reading a simplified score
3	3.1	Theoretical fundamentals of harmony and timbre
	3.2	Playing a piece with different musical instruments
	3.3	Making music together with a *Kibo* ensemble
4	4.1	Playing a song mixing *Kibo*'s operating modes
	4.2	Music improvisation inspired by paintings

participants, 4 females) for the second category, and 1 team (4 participants, 2 females) for the third category.

Each 4-people team attended a complete cycle made of 4 didactic units. Units were administered once a week and lasted 2 h each. In this way, any cycle was completed in the time span of one month.

Table 1 shows the program of each educational cycle, divided into units and tasks. Depending on the characteristics of the team (age, type of impairment, previous music knowledge, level of attention, etc.), some adjustments were made on the fly by the tutor in order to fine-tune the educational activities. The basic idea was to drive learners along two parallel growth paths: on one side, improving their musical skills by gradually introducing new dimensions (rhythm, melody, harmony, timbre); on the other side, encouraging their interaction aptitudes through music (listening to the tutor's performance, playing alone, playing with the tutor, playing in an ensemble, playing together and improvising in front of an audience). Some tasks implied theoretical investigations and other tasks focused on practical activities.

The adoption of a music TUI was fundamental for breaking down the initial barriers (physical impairments, lack of instrumental practice, sense of insecurity or shame) and letting participants be involved in a musical performance in a very limited amount of time.

It is worth underlining the relevance of some tasks. Task 2.3 implied the ability to translate a sequence of musical events (possibly available in Common Western Notation format) into a sequence of pictograms referring to fiducials. In this way, learners were pushed to develop soft skills (teamwork, problem-solving, etc.) and the ability to reason abstractly. Task 3.3 asked participants to perform a music piece together by playing different roles: two leading voices, a rhythmic base, and a harmonic accompaniment. This task encouraged synchronization abilities, information exchange, and peer-to-peer cooperation. Finally, Tasks 4.1 and 4.2 explored the field of music improvisation, both mixing already available materials and playing freely under the influence of visual artworks. In the latter case, the portability of the system (the *Kibo* units and the tablet) was a key aspect to conduct such an experience in a museum with a collection of paintings.

5 Discussion

Before addressing the research questions posed in Sect. 1, it is worth reporting some general considerations about our experimentation.

The first observation concerns the choice of the device. The *Kibo* proved to be a good solution from many points of view, from technical aspects (e.g., easy device connection and communication) to physical ones (e.g., user-friendliness and robustness). Unfortunately, it is not an affordable product. At the moment of writing, in Italy, this device is sold for 900 to 1000€. Building an ensemble of *Kibo* units, including the need to have an Apple mobile device, is not a low-budget operation. From this point of view, a mixed approach that includes other traditional or digital instruments can help.

Concerning organizational aspects, a team composed of up to 5 participants was a good compromise. Conversely, the presence of a single tutor in the class-room did not guarantee fluid conduct of educational activities. In fact, she had to explain theoretical concepts, play an instrument, support impaired users, and, sometimes, even solve technical issues simultaneously.

The 2-h length for lessons was adequate and generally appreciated by partic-ipants, but the number of didactic units per cycle should be increased in order to better cover the high number of subjects. For instance, the intriguing rela-tionship between music and visual arts was confined to Task 4.2, but it could become the focus of a whole educational cycle.

Finally, in our experimentation teams were not formed according to previous musical knowledge but considering social conditions and impairments. On one side, this choice facilitated the cooperation between users sharing similar prob-lems and the consequent fine-tuning of the program, but, on the other side, it merged people with different expectations into a single team. The *Kibo*, as well as many other music-oriented TUIs, is a facilitator for people with no music knowl-edge, but its limited possibilities can easily cause boredom and disengagement in more skilled users.

5.1 Answering Research Question 1

RQ1 aimed to investigate the applicability of a TUI-based approach to the acqui-sition of basic musical skills in vulnerable learners. This research question focused on individual experience, acquisition of knowledge, and development of music-related skills.

From classroom observations and user feedback, the *Kibo* proved to be a suitable tool to let users with no previous knowledge develop *musical intelli-gence*, namely abilities in the field of perception and autonomous production of music. The results achieved by all participants, including very young as well as impaired ones, included the ability to understand the main dimensions of music (melody, rhythm, harmony, timbre), recognize variations in some parameters (e.g., dynamics, tempo, instrumentation), and autonomously reproduce a simple tune. These achievements have been assessed through the instructor's observations.

If compared with the pre-workshop situation, the best results have been obtained by those participants who presented both physical and cognitive impairments (specifically, the second team of the second category). The members of this team had started from a lower level of knowledge, whereas other participants had recently studied music at school. Moreover, using an enabling technology was the only opportunity for them to make music, and, in most cases, this workshop was their first active musical experience. For these reasons, their reaction to the use of a TUI was enthusiastic. Figure 10 shows a wheel-chaired participant and a blind participant.

Fig. 10. A physically-impaired and a visually-impaired user making music with the *Kibo* in the context of the "Note Digitali" project.

Another observation is more tightly related to the specific features of the *Kibo*. The geometric shapes of the fiducials proved to be suitable both to overcome visual impairments (tangibles were easily recognizable to the touch and pluggable into the slots) and cognitive ones (sequences of shapes were easy to remember also in case of memory deficit or inability to read a score).

5.2   Answering Research Question 2

One of the goals of the workshop was to emphasize a series of soft and transversal skills through the creation of shared musical performances. RQ2 aims to assess this kind of non-musical achievement.

Making music together as an ensemble requires the development of social skills, encourages cooperative aptitudes, and promotes the ability to listen to the other and perform in front of an audience.

For most teams cooperation did not represent a problem, rather it encouraged relations and strengthened the ties inside each group. For the first team, conversely, playing together was a real challenge. Let us recall that the members were children aged 12 to 14 with a difficult background, coming from a context of social fragility and educational poverty. The problems encountered with them were mostly behavioral: respecting others, listening without talking over, and playing the instruments at the right time. Luckily, the engagement due to making music together and the interest in the playful interface of the *Kibo* let them overcome internal conflicts and focus on a common goal.

The adoption of a TUI also encouraged problem-solving and abstraction skills, which are two key aspects of computational thinking. The problem to solve was how to reinvent a music score suitable both for people with no music knowledge and for impaired users. The solution was to translate music notation into *Kibo*'s symbols (see Fig. 11).

Fig. 11. A music sheet for *Kibo* with fiducial symbols added by hand.

The cooperation of each team member was fundamental for completing Task 3.3. Learners had to form a small musical ensemble where everyone should play an important part. The tutor guided the process so as to promote personal abilities without causing frustration in participants. Each team was able to apply the principles of self-regulation, also thanks to the distinguishing features of the TUI in use. For example, a blind girl who demonstrated a great, unexpected sense of rhythm could perform her part using the *Kibo* in Beat Mode; two young students autonomously decided to share the leading voice of a piece by playing it in turn in Instrument Mode; and less skilled users were able to participate taking benefit from the Song Mode.

More time would have been helpful to consolidate this work, but all the learners understood the meaning of working together and actively contributing to the achievement of a shared purpose.

5.3   Answering Research Question 3

RQ1 and RQ2 were answered through qualitative assessment. Conversely, RQ3 focuses on quantitatively-measurable results.

The necessary premise concerns the main goal of the project "Note Digitali", which was not intended to provide participants with specific musical skills but to let them interact and express themselves in a creative way. From this point of view, even if some activities addressed musical education (see Tasks 2.1 and 3.1), the development of music-related competencies was a sort of desirable side effect. For this reason, users' performances have not been recorded or tracked from a numerical point of view, even for those activities implying a predefined pattern to be reproduced (see Tasks 1.4, 2.2, and 2.3). Nevertheless, this operation could be easily performed by a computer-based system.

The most critical issue does not concern how to obtain values from a music TUI but how to assess the musical skills based on those values. In fact, as clarified in [6], the objective evaluation of users' performances in music is not a trivial task.

First, for an activity with very strict time constraints, the influence of delays in gesture acquisition, signal propagation, and recording can be a decisive factor. Suffice it to say that tolerable delays in digital audio workstations are in the range of 2 to 5 ms. Conversely, the BLE protocol itself can introduce undesirable lags. Clearly, slight delays would not influence the quality of performance as perceived by human players, above all if beginners or amateurs, but they would influence the automatic assessment by a computer system.

In addition, giving a score to a performance that diverges from the expected one is intrinsically complex. Music is made of many interconnected aspects – melody, rhythm, harmony, timbre, expression, etc. – and even a mistake involving a single dimension could have multiple interpretations. For example, detecting a 0.1s offset on a regular pattern of beats at a low metronome (e.g., 60 bpm, with each beat lasting 1s) would not be critical, but the same value measured on a smaller rhythmical value and at a higher metronome (e.g., 180 bpm) would have a much higher impact. This problem could be solved by using a relative instead of an absolute criterion to measure errors. But what about a melodic pattern where the performer is regularly 1 note ahead or an octave below? Even more so when participants are amateur musicians who suffer from some form of impairment that hampers their performance from a cognitive or physical point of view.

In conclusion, answering RQ3 is technically possible, but its feasibility depends on the context. It would be interesting to conduct this kind of analysis on music students from a conservatory or in a professional orchestra, whereas it makes little sense in a scenario where music expression is mainly intended to foster inclusion and break down barriers.

6   Conclusions

This paper elucidates the notable accomplishments achieved through the organization of ensemble playing sessions utilizing a music TUI, particularly concerning the augmentation of musical aptitude, social interaction skills, and soft skills among vulnerable users.

Unsurprisingly, the implementation of a music TUI proves instrumental in resolving the customary accessibility predicaments encountered by physically impaired individuals when engaging with conventional musical instruments. Within the ambit of the documented experiment, the majority of participants presented motor impairments, while a subset of these individuals also experienced visual impairments. For such users, a TUI serves as an essential enabling technology, facilitating their participation in musical performances. Many participants experienced the joy of playing music for the first time, fostering a collaborative environment. Overall, the experience yielded highly positive outcomes, evoking enthusiastic responses from the learners.

Furthermore, a TUI possesses the capacity to bridge the divide between cognitive impairments and a comprehensive understanding and engagement with various musical dimensions. In this context, the proficiency to read and memorize musical scores assumes nontrivial significance. Remarkably, not only were these impediments successfully surmounted, but the participants even managed to generate new musical scores, owing to the implementation of a simplified language and a gamification approach.

In summary, it became evident that engagement can push the boundaries of users, enabling them to achieve unprecedented outcomes. Employing a music TUI, with the guidance of a skilled tutor, fosters engagement and effectively diminishes initial barriers, thereby alleviating the sense of frustration frequently encountered by disadvantaged users, which often hampers their musical creativity and expressive capabilities.

It is important to note that the TUI not only serves as an empowering technology for impaired users who are unable to play traditional instruments, but it also stimulates creativity and facilitates musical expressiveness even after a relatively brief exploration period.

Acknowledgments. This project has been funded by "Bando 57", a call promoted by *Fondazione di Comunità di Milano - Città, Sud Ovest, Sud Est e Adda Martesana ONLUS*. The authors wish to acknowledge their project partners: *Casa di Redenzione Sociale di Milano* (in particular, Luigi Codemo) and *Fondazione Luigi Clerici di Milano* (in particular, Federica Monguzzi). The authors also thank *Cooperativa Sociale Cura e Riabilitazione Onlus* for the support offered to impaired users.

References

1. Aljaam, J., Jaoua, A., AlHazbi, S., Hasnah, A., Karime, A., Elsaddik, A.A.: An assistive computerized system with tangible user interfaces for children with moderate intellectual and learning disabilities. Int. J. Emerg. Technol. Learn. (iJET) **6**(2011) (2011)

2. Alonso, M.B., Keyson, D.V.: Musiccube: making digital music tangible. In: CHI 2005 Extended Abstracts on Human Factors in Computing Systems, CHI EA 2005, pp. 1176–1179. Association for Computing Machinery, New York (2005). https://doi.org/10.1145/1056808.1056870

3. Amico, M.D., Ludovico, L.A.: Kibo: A MIDI controller with a tangible user interface for music education. In: Lane, H., Uhomoibhi, J., Zvacek, S. (eds.) Proceedings of the 12th International Conference on Computer Supported Education (CSEDU 2020), vol. 1, pp. 613–619. CSEDU, SCITEPRESS - Science and Technology Publications, Lda., Setúbal (2020). https://doi.org/10.5220/0009805206130619

4. Avanzini, F., Baratè, A., Ludovico, L.A.: 3D printing in preschool music education: opportunities and challenges. Qwerty - Open Interdisc. J. Technol. Cult. Educ. **14**(1), 71–92 (2019)

5. Avanzini, F., Baratè, A., Ludovico, L.A., Mandanici, M.: A computer-based approach to teach tonal harmony to young students. In: Lane, H., Uhomoibhi, J., Zvacek, S. (eds.) Proceedings of the 11th International Conference on Computer Supported Education (CSEDU 2019), vol. 1, pp. 271–279. SCITEPRESS - Science and Technology Publications, Lda. (2019)

6. Avanzini, F., Baratè, A., Ludovico, L.A., Mandanici, M.: A web platform to foster and assess tonal harmony awareness. In: Lane, H.C., Zvacek, S., Uhomoibhi, J. (eds.) CSEDU 2019. CCIS, vol. 1220, pp. 398–417. Springer, Cham (2020). https://doi.org/10.1007/978-3-030-58459-7_19

7. Baratè, A., Elia, A., Ludovico, L.A., Oriolo, E.: The leap motion controller in clinical music therapy. a computer-based approach to intellectual and motor disabilities. In: McLaren, B.M., Reilly, R., Uhomoibhi, J., Zvacek, S. (eds.) Proceedings of the 10th International Conference on Computer Supported Education (CSEDU 2018), Funchal, Madeira, Portugal, 15–17 March 2018, pp. 461–469. SCITEPRESS - Science and Technology Publications, Lda., Setúbal (2018)

8. Baratè, A., Korsten, H., Ludovico, L.A.: A multidimensional-taxonomy model for music tangible user interfaces. Multimodal Technol. Interact. (2023)

9. Baratè, A., Korsten, H., Ludovico, L.A.: A music tangible user interface for the cognitive and motor rehabilitation of elderly people. In: Constantine, L., Holzinger, A., Silva, H.P., Vanderdonckt, J. (eds.) Proceedings of the 6th International Conference on Computer-Human Interaction Research and Applications (CHIRA 2022), pp. 121–128. SCITEPRESS - Science and Technology Publications, Lda. (2022)

10. Baratè, A., Ludovico, L.A.: An open and multi-layer web platform for higher music education. J. e-Learn. Knowl. Soc. 16(4), 29–37 (2020). https://doi.org/10.20368/1971-8829/1135356

11. Baratè, A., Ludovico, L.A., Oriolo, E.: Investigating embodied music expression through the leap motion: experimentations in educational and clinical contexts. In: McLaren, B.M., Reilly, R., Zvacek, S., Uhomoibhi, J. (eds.) CSEDU 2018. CCIS, vol. 1022, pp. 532–548. Springer, Cham (2019). https://doi.org/10.1007/978-3-030-21151-6_25

12. Baratè, A., Ludovico, L.A., Oriolo, E.: An ensemble of tangible user interfaces to foster music awareness and interaction in vulnerable learners. In: Constantine, L., Holzinger, A., Silva, H.P. (eds.) Proceedings of the 5th International Conference on Computer-Human Interaction Research and Applications (CHIRA 2021), pp. 48–57. SCITEPRESS - Science and Technology Publications, Lda. (2021). https://doi.org/10.5220/0010653400003060

13. Barton, G., Riddle, S.: Culturally responsive and meaningful music education: multimodality, meaning-making, and communication in diverse learning contexts. Res. Stud. Music Educ., 1321103X211009323 (2021). https://doi.org/10.1177/1321103X211009323

14. Bates, V.C.: Equity in music education: back to class: music education and poverty. Music Educ. J. **105**(2), 72–74 (2018)

15. Ben-Tal, O., Salazar, D.: Rethinking the musical ensemble: a model for collaborative learning in higher education music technology. J. Music Technol. Educ. **7**(3), 279–294 (2014)

16. Burke, J., McNeill, M., Charles, D., Morrow, P., Crosbie, J., McDonough, S.: Augmented reality games for upper-limb stroke rehabilitation. In: 2010 Second International Conference on Games and Virtual Worlds for Serious Applications, pp. 75–78 (2010). https://doi.org/10.1109/VS-GAMES.2010.21

17. Carreño-León, M., Sandoval-Bringas, J.A., Alvarez-Robles, T., Cosio-Castro, R., Estrada Cota, I., Leyva Carrillo, A.: Designing a tangible user interface for braille teaching. In: Stephanidis, C., Antona, M., Gao, Q., Zhou, J. (eds.) HCII 2020. LNCS, vol. 12426, pp. 197–207. Springer, Cham (2020). https://doi.org/10.1007/978-3-030-60149-2_16

18. Cerezo, E., Bonillo, C., Baldassarri, S.: Therapeutic activities for elderly people based on tangible interaction. In: ICT4AWE, pp. 281–290 (2020)

19. Cheng, L.: Musical competency development in a laptop ensemble. Res. Stud. Music Educ. **41**(1), 117–131 (2019)

20. Costanza, E., Shelley, S.B., Robinson, J.: Introducing audio D-TOUCH: a tangible user interface for music composition and performance. In: Proceedings of the 6th International Conference on Digital Audio Effects (DAFX-03), London, UK, 8–11 September 2003 (2003)

21. Dahl, L.: Comparing the timing of movement events for air-drumming gestures. In: Kronland-Martinet, R., Aramaki, M., Ystad, S. (eds.) CMMR 2015. LNCS, vol. 9617, pp. 3–21. Springer, Cham (2016). https://doi.org/10.1007/978-3-319-46282-0_1

22. d'Alessandro, N., Tilmanne, J., Moreau, A., Puleo, A.: Airpiano: a multi-touch keyboard with hovering control. In: Berdahl, E., Allison, J. (eds.) Proceedings of the International Conference on New Interfaces for Musical Expression, pp. 255–258. Louisiana State University, Baton Rouge (2015). https://doi.org/10.5281/zenodo.1181434. http://www.nime.org/proceedings/2015/nime2015%5F261.pdf

23. Dance Music Northwest: The awesome instrument you've never heard of: Reactable (2015). https://www.dancemusicnw.com/awesome-instrument-youve-never-heard-reactable/

24. De Carvalho, R.N.S., Ishitani, L., Nogueira Sales De Carvalho, R., et al.: Motivational factors for mobile serious games for elderly users. In: Proceedings of XI SB Games, pp. 2–4 (2012)

25. Dörner, R., Göbel, S., Effelsberg, W., Wiemeyer, J. (eds.): Serious Games. Springer, Cham (2016). https://doi.org/10.1007/978-3-319-40612-1

26. Duckworth, J., et al.: Resonance: an interactive tabletop artwork for co-located group rehabilitation and play. In: Antona, M., Stephanidis, C. (eds.) UAHCI 2015. LNCS, vol. 9177, pp. 420–431. Springer, Cham (2015). https://doi.org/10.1007/978-3-319-20684-4_41

27. Fan, X., Essl, G.: Air violin: a body-centric style musical instrument. In: NIME, pp. 122–123 (2013)

28. Farr, W., Yuill, N., Raffle, H.: Social benefits of a tangible user interface for children with autistic spectrum conditions. Autism **14**(3), 237–252 (2010)

29. Fiala, M.: Artag, a fiducial marker system using digital techniques. In: 2005 IEEE Computer Society Conference on Computer Vision and Pattern Recognition (CVPR 2005), vol. 2, pp. 590–596 (2005). https://doi.org/10.1109/CVPR. 2005.74

30. Fonseca, X., Slingerland, G., Lukosch, S., Brazier, F.: Designing for meaningful social interaction in digital serious games. Entertain. Comput. **36**, 100385 (2021)

31. Frid, E.: Accessible digital musical instruments—a review of musical interfaces in inclusive music practice. Multimodal Technol. Interact. **3**(3), 57 (2019)

32. Furness, D.: Prospective memory in normal ageing and dementia. Digital Trends (2016). https://www.digitaltrends.com/cool-tech/tunetable/

33. Gabrielli, L., Välimäki, V., Bilbao, S.: Real-time emulation of the clavinet. In: ICMC (2011)

34. Godøy, R.I., Haga, E., Jensenius, A.R.: Playing "Air Instruments": mimicry of sound-producing gestures by novices and experts. In: Gibet, S., Courty, N., Kamp, J.-F. (eds.) GW 2005. LNCS (LNAI), vol. 3881, pp. 256–267. Springer, Heidelberg (2006). https://doi.org/10.1007/11678816_29

35. Gorbunova, I., Voronov, A.M.: Music computer technologies in computer science and music studies at schools for children with deep visual impairment. In: 16th International Conference on Literature, Languages, Humanities & Social Sciences (LLHSS-18), Budapest, Hungary, 2–4 October 2018, pp. 15–18 (2018)

36. Harrison, K.: The relationship of poverty to music. Yearbook Tradit. Music **45**, 1–12 (2013)

37. Hattwick, I.: Face to face, byte to byte: Approaches to human interaction in a digital music ensemble. University of California-Irvine, MFA (2011)

38. Hattwick, I., Umezaki, K.: Approaches to collaboration in a digital music ensemble. In: NIME 2012 Proceedings of the International Conference on New Interfaces for Musical Expression, pp. 466–469 (2012)

39. Ishii, H.: Tangible bits: beyond pixels. In: Proceedings of 2nd International Conference on Tangible and Embedded Interaction, TEI 2008, pp. xv–xxv. Association for Computing Machinery (2008). https://doi.org/10.1145/1347390.1347392

40. Ishii, H.: The tangible user interface and its evolution. Commun. ACM **51**(6), 32–36 (2008). https://doi.org/10.1145/1349026.1349034

41. Ishii, H., Ullmer, B.: Tangible bits: towards seamless interfaces between people, bits and atoms. In: Proceedings of the ACM SIGCHI Conference on Human Factors in Computing Systems, pp. 234–241 (1997)

42. Jordà, S.: The reactable: tangible and tabletop music performance. In: CHI 2010 Extended Abstracts on Human Factors in Computing Systems, pp. 2989–2994 (2010)

43. Ko, C.L., Oehlberg, L.: Touch responsive augmented violin interface system ii: integrating sensors into a 3d printed fingerboard. In: Michon, R., Schroeder, F. (eds.) Proceedings of the International Conference on New Interfaces for Musical Expression, pp. 166–171. Birmingham City University, Birmingham (2020). https://doi.org/10.5281/zenodo.4813300, https://www.nime.org/proceedings/2020/nime2020%5Fpaper32.pdf

44. Leman, M., et al.: Embodied Music Cognition and Mediation Technology. MIT press, Cambridge (2008)

45. Li, J., Wu, C.H., Lin, T.J., Chang, R.J.: Determinants affecting learner's behaviour in music education applying information technology. In: Proceedings of the 11th International Conference on Computer Supported Education, vol. 2: CSEDU, pp. 424–431. INSTICC, SciTePress (2019). https://doi.org/10.5220/0007734404240431

46. McAnally, E.A.: General music and children living in poverty. Gener. Music Today **26**(3), 25–31 (2013)
47. Mellor, L.: Creativity, originality, identity: investigating computer-based composition in the secondary school. Music Educ. Res. **10**(4), 451–472 (2008)
48. Morreale, F., De Angeli, A., Masu, R., Rota, P., Conci, N.: Collaborative creativity: the music room. Pers. Ubiq. Comput. **18**(5), 1187–1199 (2014)
49. Najjar, A.B., Alhussayen, A., Jafri, R.: Usability engineering of a tangible user interface application for visually impaired children. Hum.-Centric Comput. Inf. Sci. **11**(14), 891–921 (2021)
50. Newton-Dunn, H., Nakano, H., Gibson, J.: Block jam: a tangible interface for interactive music. J. New Music Res. **32**(4), 383–393 (2003)
51. de Oliveira, P.A., Lotto, E.P., Correa, A.G.D., Taboada, L.G., Costa, L.C., Lopes, R.D.: Virtual stage: an immersive musical game for people with visual impairment. In: 2015 14th Brazilian Symposium on Computer Games and Digital Entertainment (SBGames), pp. 135–141. IEEE (2015)
52. Paradiso, J.A., Hsiao, K.y., Benbasat, A.: Tangible music interfaces using passive magnetic tags. In: Proceedings of the 2001 Conference on New Interfaces for Musical Expression, NIME 2001, pp. 1–4. National University of Singapore, SGP (2001)
53. Pedersen, E.W., Hornbæk, K.: mixitui: a tangible sequencer for electronic live performances. In: Proceedings of the 3rd International Conference on Tangible and Embedded Interaction, pp. 223–230 (2009)
54. Pesek, M., Vučko, Ž, Šavli, P., Kavčič, A., Marolt, M.: Troubadour: a gamified e-learning platform for ear training. IEEE Access **8**, 97090–97102 (2020)
55. Pires, A.C., et al.: A tangible math game for visually impaired children. In: The 21st International ACM SIGACCESS Conference on Computers and Accessibility, pp. 670–672 (2019)
56. Potidis, S., Spyrou, T.: Spyractable: a tangible user interface modular synthesizer. In: Kurosu, M. (ed.) HCI 2014. LNCS, vol. 8511, pp. 600–611. Springer, Cham (2014). https://doi.org/10.1007/978-3-319-07230-2_57
57. Rabbi, I., Ullah, S.: 3D model visualization and interaction using a cubic fiducial marker. In: De Paolis, L.T., Mongelli, A. (eds.) AVR 2014. LNCS, vol. 8853, pp. 381–393. Springer, Cham (2014). https://doi.org/10.1007/978-3-319-13969-2_28
58. Ramos Aguiar, L.R., Álvarez Rodríguez, F.J.: Methodology for designing systems based on tangible user interfaces and gamification techniques for blind people. Appl. Sci. **11**(12), 5676 (2021)
59. Rego, P.A., Moreira, P.M., Reis, L.P.: Architecture for serious games in health rehabilitation. In: Rocha, Á., Correia, A.M., Tan, F.B., Stroetmann, K.A. (eds.) New Perspectives in Information Systems and Technologies, Volume 2. AISC, vol. 276, pp. 307–317. Springer, Cham (2014). https://doi.org/10.1007/978-3-319-05948-8_30
60. Riley, P., Alm, N., Newell, A.: An interactive tool to promote musical creativity in people with dementia. Comput. Hum. Behav. **25**(3), 599–608 (2009)
61. Schiavio, A., Menin, D.: Embodied music cognition and mediation technology: a critical review. Psychol. Music **41**(6), 804–814 (2013). https://doi.org/10.1177/0305735613497169
62. Schiettecatte, B., Vanderdonckt, J.: Audiocubes: a distributed cube tangible interface based on interaction range for sound design. In: Proceedings of the 2nd International Conference on Tangible and Embedded Interaction, TEI 2008, pp. 3–10. Association for Computing Machinery, New York (2008). https://doi.org/10.1145/1347390.1347394

63. Smith, K., Abrams, S.S.: Gamification and accessibility. Int. J. Inf. Learn. Technol. **36**, 104–123 (2019)

64. Tarabella, L.: Handel, a *Free-Hands* gesture recognition system. In: Wiil, U.K. (ed.) CMMR 2004. LNCS, vol. 3310, pp. 139–148. Springer, Heidelberg (2005). https://doi.org/10.1007/978-3-540-31807-1_11

65. Vandermaesen, M., De Weyer, T., Feys, P., Luyten, K., Coninx, K.: Integrating serious games and tangible objects for functional handgrip training: a user study of handly in persons with multiple sclerosis. In: Proceedings of 2016 ACM Conference on Designing Interactive Systems, pp. 924–935 (2016)

66. Weichert, F., Bachmann, D., Rudak, B., Fisseler, D.: Analysis of the accuracy and robustness of the Leap Motion controller. Sensors **13**(5), 6380–6393 (2013)

67. Xambó, A., et al.: Experience and ownership with a tangible computational music installation for informal learning. In: Proceedings of the Eleventh International Conference on Tangible, Embedded, and Embodied Interaction, pp. 351–360 (2017)

68. Xu, D.: Tangible user interface for children - an overview. In: Proceedings of the UCLAN Department of Computing Conference. Citeseer (2005)

69. Zhao, X., et al.: Segara: Integrating serious games and handgrip for hand rehabilitation in rheumatoid arthritis patients. In: The 9th International Symposium of Chinese CHI, pp. 101–104 (2021)

Mitigating the Spread of Misinformation Through Design

Safat Siddiqui$^{(\boxtimes)}$ and Mary Lou Maher

University of North Carolina, Charlotte, NC, USA
{ssiddiq6,M.Maher}@uncc.edu

Abstract. This paper presents a novel approach to mitigating the spread of misinformation by presenting social media design principles based on users' interaction tendencies. The focus of our design principles is to provide new design affordances to make the truth louder. This research leverages users' high and low interaction tendencies to amplify truth by increasing users' interactions with verified posts and decreasing their interactions with unverified posts. The paper describes a theoretical basis and 3 design principles, and presents an analysis of participants' responses to the design principles. In addition, this paper investigates users' views on sharing and preference for platform-based incentives. The results show that users with lower interaction tendencies share verified information more when they receive additional interaction support. Furthermore, due to the interaction tendencies, users exhibit opposite preferences for platform-based incentives that can encourage their participation in making the truth louder. Users with high interaction tendencies prefer incentives that highlight their presence on the platform, and users with low interaction tendencies favor incentives that can educate them about the impact of their participation on their friends and community.

Keywords: Fake news · Misinformation · Intervention · Mitigation · Interaction · Design principle · Social media

1 Introduction

This paper presents a shift in focus for the mitigation of fake news that has the goal to encourage social media users to share more credible information rather than solely relying on stopping the spread of misinformation. Misinformation, one type of fake news that refers to unintentional spreading of false information, is responsible for increasing polarization and the consequential loss of trust in science and media [18]. To reduce the spread of misinformation, social media platforms are removing the accounts that spread misleading information and the posts that contain false information. In addition to that effort, platforms are introducing new indicators that facilitate the process of getting contextual information about posts that have questionable veracity. The purpose of the

© The Author(s), under exclusive license to Springer Nature Switzerland AG 2023
A. Holzinger et al. (Eds.): CHIRA 2021/2022, CCIS 1882, pp. 26–50, 2023.
https://doi.org/10.1007/978-3-031-41962-1_2

indicators is to assist users' information verification process while consuming or before sharing the information with other users. Though the intention of these indicators is to minimize the spread of questionable content [24,34,38], the design aspects do not address users' interaction behaviors to leverage the interaction tendencies in distributing credible information. In this paper, we present users' active-passive interactions tendencies as the basis for design and provide 3 principles of designing social media interaction that combat fake news with a focus on making the truth louder on social platforms.

A focus on making the truth louder on social platforms means that the interaction designs nudge users toward distributing credible information and limiting the spread of unverified information. Nudges, in the form of suggestions or recommendations, intend to steer users' behaviors in particular directions without sacrificing users' freedom of choices [1,42]. We identify that users' interaction abilities on social media can be described in the range from active to passive - active users have a strong tendency to interact with content and other users, whereas passive users have the tendency to refrain from interactions [6,12,44]. Users' interaction behaviors could transform overtime. Shao [35] has suggested that users initially consume content and eventually start participating on the platform and produce content. The Reader-to-Leader Framework [29] indicates the evolution of a user from a reader to a leader. This paper builds on our understanding of the active-passive continuum presented in [12,29,35] to develop a theoretical basis for nudging user behavior to adopt the 2 target interaction behaviors that combat fakes news by making the truth louder:

- **Target behavior 1 (TB1):** Users interact to increase the spread of verified and credible information.
- **Target behavior 2 (TB2):** Users interact to reduce the spread of unverified and questionable information.

We present 3 principles for designing social media interaction that are grounded on users' active-passive tendencies and intend to increase users' likeliness of performing the 2 target behaviors. The design principles are inspired by the Fogg Behavior Model (FBM) [10] that suggests a change of behavior happens when individuals have 2 factors: 1. the ability to change the behaviors and 2. the motivation to change the behaviors and overlays 3 types of prompts, 1. Signal, 2. Facilitator, and 3. Spark. In our design principles, the factor 'ability' refers to individuals' interaction tendencies and the factor 'motivation' refers to individuals' motivation to contribute in making the truth louder. The 3 design principles of social media interaction for combating misinformation are:

1. **Awareness on Making the Truth Louder:** The goal of this design principle is to remind users and nudge their attention to perform the target behaviors that can make the truth louder. This design principle is inspired from the Signal prompt in FBM [10] and appeals to social media users who possess high ability to perform the behaviors and high motivation to contribute to making the truth louder.

2. **Guidance on Making the Truth Louder:** The goal of this design principle is to provide users the necessary interaction supports for performing target behaviors that lead to making the truth louder. This design principle is inspired from the Facilitator prompt in FBM [10] and appeals to social media users who have low ability to perform the target behaviors but possess a high motivation to contribute to making the truth louder.

3. **Incentive on Making the Truth Louder:** The goal of this design principle is to provide incentives and encourage users to perform the target behaviors that can make the truth louder. This design principle is inspired from the Spark prompt in FBM [10] and appeals to social media users who have the ability to perform the interaction behaviors but are not highly motivated to participate in making the truth louder.

This paper investigates the effect of interaction design on the user across the active-passive continuum when the design adopts the awareness principle and provides factual information about the content. Similarly, this study investigates the effect of a design on the users across the active-passive spectrum that adopts the guidance principle and provides additional interaction support to increase users' participation in combating misinformation. This research is not a UI contribution; instead, the UI is used to study the responses of users to the design principles for personalized interaction-focused intervention. Finally, this research explores how the users across the active-passive continuum show preferences for the platform-based incentives that a design adopting the incentive design principle can utilize. The findings of these investigations can identify the effective design principles that can be applied to develop personalized interaction-focused interventions to amplify the truth on social platforms.

The organization of this paper is as follows: Sect. 2 presents the related work and describes how the design principles contribute to the research on combating fake news. In Sect. 3, we discuss the differences between active and passive users' interaction behavior and describe the connection of users' interaction tendencies with the target behaviors that can make the truth louder. Section 4 presents the 3 design principles, provide prototypes to explain the principles and discusses the existing social media interventions in the lens of these design principles. Section 5 describes the experimental design conducted to investigate users' responses to three design principles and Sect. 6 presents the effect of 3 principles on users with different interaction tendencies and shows the experiment results.

2   Related Work

Social media companies are taking steps to reduce the spread of fake news, such as misinformation (unintentional misleading information) and disinformation (intentional misleading information). They develop algorithms and work with third parties to detect fake content and the accounts who spread those fake information [31,32]. Platforms such as Facebook and Twitter remove fake content and the accounts that display inauthentic activities [13,33]. To reduce the spread of unverified information, the platforms demote flagged posts and the content that are detected to be spam or clickbait [3,8]. In the research communities, a wide range of algorithms have been developed to detect fake information by analyzing textual features, network structure, and developing propagation models [17].

Despite the ongoing development of sophisticated algorithms, misleading information is still posted and spread on the platforms. Researchers have investigated effective ways of correcting the misinformation that has already spread, and identified the negative effects of fake information on individuals due to cognitive biases, such as confirmation bias, continued influence, backfire effect [18,19,22]. Studies have been conducted to understand how users seek and verify the credibility of news on social media [4,9,23,43], how they interact with misinformation [11], why and how users spread fake news [2,21,39,40]. Those investigations provide a broader context of the problem of fake news spreading on social media and add value in developing communication and mitigation strategies for platform-based interventions.

The platform-based interventions create indicators that assist users in making informed decisions on their choices of information consuming and information sharing on the platform. For example, Facebook provides an information ('i') button that shows details about the source website of an article, and places 'Related Articles' next to the information that seems questionable to the platform [15,38,41]. Twitter warns users about the information that could be misleading and harmful, and directs users to credible sources [34]; Twitter also introduces a community-driven approach, Birdwatch, to identify misleading information on the platform [7]. In addition to the platform-based attempts, there exist browser extensions [5,27] and media literacy initiatives [14,30] to assist users in identifying the credibility of content.

However, the primary focus of existing design interventions is to communicate to users about the credibility of the content. In this paper, we shift the focus to create intervention designs that consider the difference between active and passive users and are adaptive to individual's interaction tendencies. Preece et al. [29] have also suggested the importance of various interface supports to increase participation more generally, where our focus is on increasing participation to make the truth louder. We provide 3 design principles for the UX researchers to explore the design ideas with respective design goals and address users' active-passive tendencies to increase users' participation for combating fake news.

3   Target Behaviors for the Users with Different Interaction Tendencies

To make the truth louder, our design principles focus on promoting 2 target behaviors for social media users possessing interaction tendencies ranging from active to passive. In this section, we present the relationship between 2 target behaviors and users' interaction tendencies on social platforms.

3.1   Users' Interaction Tendencies on Social Platforms

Social media users have different interaction tendencies on social platforms. Some users play an active role by participating in various interactions, such as posting comments, sharing content and creating their own content and posts, uploading photos and videos. These users are known as active users [6,16]. Chen et al. [6] identified 25 active users' interactions on social media and categorized those into 4 dimensions: Content Creation, Content Transmission, Relationship Building, and Relationship Maintenance. Conversely, some social media users do not like to interact with social media that produces a digital footprint - they are known as passive users [12,25]. Passive users prefer to seek information and entertainment on social platforms and they are more involved in the interactions that are required to consume information - that type of interactions can be identified as Content Consumption. According to [35], users first consume content, then start participating and become the members who can produce content. Shao's [35] suggestion indicates that users are initially involved in the interactions related to content consumption, and over time, users start using interaction items related to the dimension of relationship building, relationship maintenance, and content transformation. When users develop relationships with other users and get habituated to interacting with content, they proceed using interaction items related to content creation.

The passive and active users have different preferences towards the interaction dimensions because of their interaction tendencies [12,44]. Though the users are similar in the dimension of content consumption, the interaction preference between active and passive users starts to differ in other dimensions of interactions, such as content creation and content transmissions. In comparison to active users, passive users have less preference for interaction items that are not related to content consumption. The design affordance that helps users to get context and verify information are related to the interactions of content consumption dimension, where interaction preferences between active and passive users remain similar. We focus on the interactions of content transmissions where active users are more likely to participate than passive users and provide 3 design principles of social media interaction adaptive to users' interaction tendencies.

3.2   Difference Between Users' Abilities to Perform the Target Behaviors

The ability to perform the 2 target behaviors will be different for the users due to their interaction tendencies. Active and passive users on social media demonstrate the opposite ability because of their online interaction tendencies, making target behavior 1 (TB1) easier for active users but difficult for passive users, and target behavior 2 (TB2) easier for passive users but difficult for active users.

The ability to contribute to the spread of verified information (TB1) demands interactions with content and other social media users - such ability is high for the active users but low for the passive users. Due to active users' natural inclination, they are habituated to perform high levels of interactions, such as sharing information with other users, making comments, or sending love/like reactions to the content - these interactions contribute to the distribution of verified information. But passive users hesitate to perform such interactions and have low levels of interactions on social platforms, which makes adopting the target behavior 1 challenging for passive users.

In contrast, limiting the spread of unverified information (TB2) is easier for passive users to adopt compared to active users as it requires users to interact less with the unverified content. For target behavior 2, passive users get an advantage as they have the general tendency to interact less with social media content. However, active users have to be reflective about their activities on social platforms so that they do not interact with any unverified content because of their natural behavioral tendencies, which makes adopting target behavior 2 harder for active users.

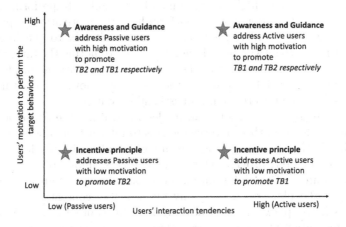

Fig. 1. The design principles addresses the differences between active and passive users to perform the target behaviors [36].

The design principles address the differences between active and passive users' online interaction tendencies to direct their interactions to make the truth louder on social media, as illustrated in Fig. 1. Active users have high interaction abilities, and passive users have low interaction abilities. As users' interactions (e.g., shares, comments, likes) on social platforms lead to the distribution of the content in that platform, the principles intend to assist active users in adopting the target behavior to interact only with the credible information and not to interact with unverified or questionable information. Similarly, the principles intend to support passive users to increase their interactions with credible information that can make the truth louder on social platforms.

4   Design Principles that Address Users' Interaction Tendencies

We present 3 design principles that address users' interaction tendencies: Awareness, Guidance, and Incentive on making the truth louder. In this section, we describe the design principles that appeal to the users of different levels of interaction abilities and motivation, and discuss the existing design interventions in reference to these principles.

4.1   Awareness on Making the Truth Louder

The purpose of the Awareness design principle is to assist social media users in recognizing verified and unverified content that appears in their social media feeds and remind users to perform the target behavior that can make the truth louder. This design principle is a Signal prompt in the FBM [10] that is effective for individuals who have high motivation and high ability to perform the target behavior. When active users on the platform have the motivation to participate in making the truth louder, they can respond positively to the intervention designs that follow the Awareness design principle promoting the target behavior 1. Likewise, passive users can respond easily to the interventions that follows the Awareness design principle to promote the target behavior 2 - requesting limited interactions with the unverified and questionable content.

Most of existing interventions can be described using the Awareness design principle as the focus of these interventions is to inform users about the context and validity of the information. For example, social media platforms, such as Facebook and Twitter, provide related fact-checkers' information so that users can get the context of the information. Facebook shows an indicator to related articles when the platform detects any questionable content [38,41]. Twitter warns users if the platform identifies any harmful content [34]. The accuracy nudging intervention [26] draws users' attention to the accuracy of the content, and NudgeFeed [5] applies visual cues to grab users' attention to the credibility of the information source - whether the information source is mainstream or non-mainstream. These platform-based interventions educate users about the context of the information when users are involved in content consumption interactions. Some interventions, such as Facebook, alert users when they interact to share any questionable content [38]. These interventions follow the Awareness design principle as the purpose is to make users aware of the context before they share the information on social media.

To describe the Awareness design principle, we present a design prototype that promotes the target behavior 1, illustrated in Fig. 2. The prototype use the standard signifiers 'Like', 'Comment', and 'Share' buttons of Facebook that signal users can perform interactions to like the information, make comments about that information, and share that information with other users. The credible information in Fig. 2. is collected from [26] study, and we add 'More information about this link' and 'Related Articles' sections that assist users in getting the context of the content. Figure 2. follows the Awareness design principle that uses texts in the 'More information about this link' section to communicate with users about the credibility of information and information source, and have related fact-checked articles in 'Related Articles' section to provide more contextual information. This prototype focuses on informing the active users about context of the information so that the subset of active users who posses the motivation to contribute in making the truth louder become aware to share the verified information.

Fig. 2. Prototype describing the Awareness design principle for promoting target behavior 1 [36].

4.2   Guidance on Making the Truth Louder

The purpose of the Guidance design principle is to simplify the interactions for the users to increase their ability to interact on social platforms and educate users about the interactions that can lead to the distribution of credible information and limit the spread of unverified harmful information. This design principle is a Facilitator prompt in the FBM [10] that is effective for individuals who have high motivation but low ability to perform the target behaviors. This design principle focuses on promoting target behavior 1 among passive users by simplifying the interaction steps for them that assist their interactions for distributing credible information. Likewise, this design principle can promote target behavior 2 among the active users by designing interaction and affordance that assist them limiting their interactions with unverified content.

To describe the Guidance design principle, we present a design prototype that promotes the target behavior 1 by simplifying sharing interactions, illustrated in Fig. 3. The prototype follows the Guidance design principle that increases users' interaction ability with credible information by reducing the number of interaction steps required for sharing credible information. The Share button has the biggest impact on digital footprints as this functionality allows users to share the information with the users of their network; the Comments and Like buttons have smaller digital footprints compared to that. Facebook includes different sharing options, such as share publicly or privately, and users get those sharing options when they press the share button. In addition to the affordance presented in Fig. 2, this prototype has different sharing options upfront and reduces the number of interaction steps for sharing. The prototype includes the privately sharing option to facilitate the motivated passive users' interactions toward the credible information. As passive users have a natural inclination to avoid digital footprint, the motivated passive users will feel comfortable sharing credible information privately to their friends rather than sharing publicly with the whole network. The prototype also includes additional 2 sharing options that enable users to share the verified fact-checked information with a single step of interaction. The design can apply visual cues on those buttons or use text to guide users about the interactions that lead to the distribution of credible information on the social platform.

Fig. 3. Prototype describing the Guidance design principle for promoting target behavior 1 [36].

4.3   Incentive on Making the Truth Louder

The purpose of Incentive design principle is to encourage and motivate users to orient their interaction behavior in a direction that can make the truth louder on the platform. The Incentive design principle is a Spark prompt in the FBM that is proven effective for the individuals who have the high ability but low motivation to perform the target behaviors. This design principle can prompt the less motivated active users to perform target behavior 1 and the less motivated passive users to perform target behavior 2.

To describe the Incentive design principle, we present a design prototype that promotes the target behavior 1 by providing users badges, illustrated in Fig. 4. The concept of 'Community Service Badges' can demonstrate a way to incentivize social media users to increase their motivation for performing the target behaviors. When users perform social media interactions for making the truth louder, they will receive badges. The platform can add benefits to the badges, such as prioritizing the content posted by users who have the badges, suggesting other users to follow the individuals who hold the badges due to the contribution in distributing credible information. Such platform-based benefits can attract active users to become reflective about their social media interactions and perform interactions only with credible information.

The platform-affordances can communicate with users and encourage them to participate in making the truth louder as a part of their responsibilities for creating personal, social, and societal impacts. Figure 4 includes the text *"Please participate in distributing credible information; your friends may benefit"* to communicate with social media users and inspire their motivation. As the community service badges indicate individuals' effort to make the truth louder on social platforms, the badges can gather positive impressions from other social media users, which can attract the platform's active users to attain the badges. The platform-based interventions can identify useful information and harmful information by relying on the fact-checking services and assist users in developing the interaction habits by rewarding them with the badges.

Fig. 4. Prototype describing the Incentive design principle for promoting target behavior 1 [36].

5   Study Design and Data Analysis

This section describes a survey design conducted on Amazon Mechanical Turk from November 30 to December 12, 2021, which has 2 experiment conditions: control and treatment. The control condition adopts the awareness design principle, and the treatment condition adopts the guidance design principle. This section explains the designs used in 2 conditions and the questionnaire to gather insights into the incentive design principle. This section describes the study tasks for the 2 conditions, the participants' recruitment process, and the study's social media usage and data analysis approach.

5.1   Participants

We collected 1075 responses and randomly assigned participants into two design conditions: Condition A (control condition) was the baseline condition typical of most social media platforms, and Condition B was the treatment condition in which we encouraged interaction with verified news and discouraging interaction with unverified news. The inclusion criteria were that participants should be

18 years of age or older, use social media at least 3 times a week, read Covid-19 Vaccine-related news, be located in the US. In the survey, we included 2 additional questions to check participants attention while completing the survey. We eliminate the survey records that have incorrect responses for these two attention-check questions. In addition, we remove the records that have not finished answering all the questions and have incomplete responses. In the control condition, there are 503 participants (M: 286, F: 211, O: 6; avg age: 38, SD: 11, min: 20, max: 71). In the treatment condition, there are 503 participants (M: 305, F: 195, O: 3; avg age: 38, SD: 11, min: 20, max: 89).

5.2   Content Selection

The news items in this study focus on the topic of the Covid-19 vaccine and address the helpful and harmful aspects of the vaccine in regard to individuals' health and society. We carefully selected headlines with minimal political overtones so that the study invokes fewer political biases. Initially, we selected 60 verified and unverified headlines from politifact.com, a well-known 3rd party fact-checking journal that distinguishes true and false information posted on social media. The politifact.com journal politifact labels the posts as one of the 6 categories: True, Mostly True, Half True, Mostly False, False, and Pants on Fire. We rely on these labels to determine the factual position of the post. We selected 8 health-focused headlines - 4 labeled as True and 4 labeled False by the politifact.com journal.

5.3   Study Tasks for Awareness Design Principle

The awareness design principle aims to inform participants of the factual position of the post they are seeing. The presentation of the headline as a social media post adopts the awareness design principle discussed in Sect. 4. Figure 5 shows an example of the design used in the control condition when the headline is unverified. Participants can see the headline in plain text; we do not include the source of the headline or any image to reduce biases. To inform the participants about the factual position of the headline, we use the information icon "(i)" and the text message "This information is determined as False by politifact.com [28]. We added another section named' Related Articles' to give the participants additional information about the headline. The 'Related Articles' section includes the fact-check headline of an article and supports the label (False or True) determined by politifact.com [28]. A similar design pattern is used for the verified content. We have finalized the designs for the survey study by addressing feedback from the participants in pilot studies.

The design includes three basic interaction functionalities: Like, Comment, and Share - these functionalities are the most common interaction facilities provided by the platforms. The Like button allows users to react to the post, and users use the Comment button to express opinions about the post. The Share button allows users to spread the headline on the platform. After showing participants the headlines, we ask them the question: "What actions would you like to

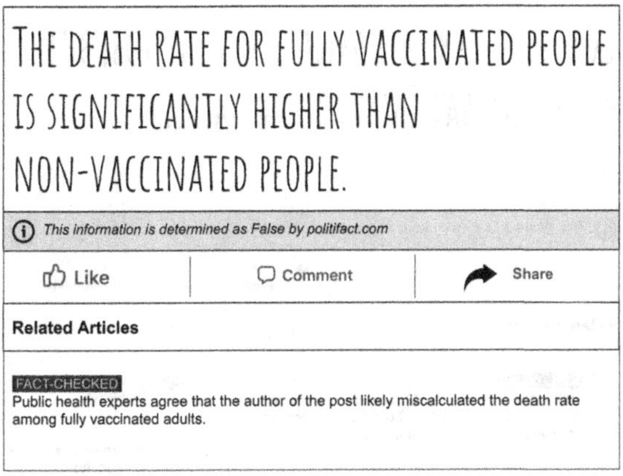

THE DEATH RATE FOR FULLY VACCINATED PEOPLE IS SIGNIFICANTLY HIGHER THAN NON-VACCINATED PEOPLE.

ⓘ *This information is determined as False by politifact.com*

👍 Like | 💬 Comment | ➤ Share

Related Articles

FACT-CHECKED
Public health experts agree that the author of the post likely miscalculated the death rate among fully vaccinated adults.

Fig. 5. Design and interaction functionalities of the awareness principle applied to unverified headline (control condition).

take?" and provide them with 4 multiple options: 1. Press 'Like' button, 2. Press 'Comment' button, 3. Press 'Share' button, and 4. Take no action. The study task is inspired by the news sharing task used in [24, 26, 45], where participants see news headlines and are asked to decide whether they would share the headline on social media or not. On the contrary, our study task asks participants to decide which interaction functionalities they would like to use if they see the headlines (i.e., post) on their social media.

5.4   Study Tasks for Guidance Design Principle

The guidance design principle aims to assist users in spreading credible information. The design that adopts the guidance principle for verified posts provides two post-sharing functionalities to share the verified posts, as illustrated in Fig. 6. Users can share the verified posts publicly or privately. Additionally, the design provides two article-sharing functionalities that allow participants to share the related fact-checked information. Participants can share the fact-checked article publicly or privately. The observations during the pilot studies inform the design decisions of publicly and privately sharing functionalities - participants tend to utilize the publicly and privately sharing functionalities in different scenarios. Thus, the design includes these two functionalities to assist users in sharing more credible information.

The design for unverified posts that adopts the guidance principle provides two article-sharing functionalities to spread credible information related to the unverified posts. As illustrated in Fig. 7, participants receive the interaction functionalities to share the fact-checked article publicly or privately. The design also keeps the traditional post-sharing functionality that users can utilize to share unverified posts. However, the post-sharing functionalities when the posts are unverified do not include the privately or publicly sharing functionalities and do

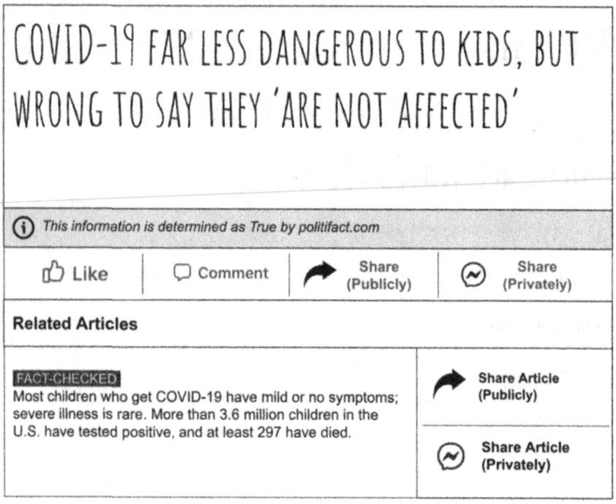

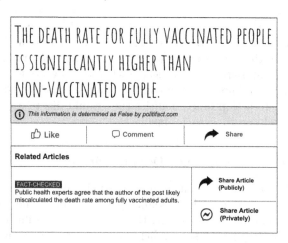

Fig. 6. Design and interaction functionalities applied to verified headline in the guidance principle (treatment condition).

THE DEATH RATE FOR FULLY VACCINATED PEOPLE IS SIGNIFICANTLY HIGHER THAN NON-VACCINATED PEOPLE.

Fig. 7. Design and interaction functionalities of the guidance principle applied to unverified headline (treatment condition).

not assist participants in sharing unverified posts. We have finalized the designs for the survey study by addressing feedback from the participant of the pilot studies in several iterative process.

Before the study tasks begin in the treatment condition, the survey describes the functionalities of the additional sharing buttons presented in the study. After showing the participants the headlines, the questionnaire asks: "What actions would you like to take?" and provides participants with multiple options to select interactions presented with the headlines. Participants receive # options when posts are unverified: 1. Press 'Like' button, 2. Press 'Comment' button, 3. Press 'Share' button, 4. Press 'Share Article (Publicly)' button to share Related Article,

5. Press 'Share Article (Privately)' button to share Related Article, 6. Take no action. When posts are verified, participants see 2 post-sharing options: Press 'Share (Publicly)' button to share social media post and Press 'Share (Privately)' button to share social media post, instead of the Press 'Share' button option.

5.5   Questionnaire for Incentive Design Principle

The incentive design principle focuses on users' platform-based incentives and motivation that can increase participation in combating misinformation. This section describes the questionnaire designed to gather insights regarding users' preferences for the platform-based incentive across the active-passive continuum. The questionnaire includes questions regarding participants' motivation to participate and their level of trust in fact-checking journals and correlates the responses with the interaction decisions across the active-passive continuum. All these questions are presented as the study's post-task questionnaire.

Four kinds of platform-based incentives are identified during the rounds of pilot studies: 1. Getting badges, 2. Getting followers, 3. Content prioritization, and 4. Receive information regarding the impact. The observation during the pilot studies reveals that individuals might be encouraged to participate in combating misinformation if platforms offer them badges, help them gain followers, prioritize their content and inform them how their participation helps their community. Table 1 shows the statements used in the survey study so that the research can investigate users' preference for the platform-based incentives due to their active-passive interaction tendencies.

Table 1. The platform-based incentives and corresponding statements.

Platform-based incentives	Statements of the incentive
Getting badges	"The platform gives me badges that inform other users about my contribution for combating misinformation."
Getting followers	"The platform suggests other users to follow my account as I contribute in combating misinformation."
Content prioritization	"The platform prioritizes my posts to other users as I contribute in combating misinformation."
Receive information regarding the impact	"The platform shows me how I am helping my friends and community by participating in combating misinformation."
Other	"Other"

The questionnaire collects information regarding individuals' level of motivation to contribute to combating misinformation that requires participating in spreading credible information and reducing the spread of misinformation. In the post-task questionnaire, participants are asked to rate their level of agreement with two statements: 1. "I like to contribute to sharing verified and helpful information on social platform." and 2. "I like to contribute to reducing the spread of unverified and harmful information on social platform." For those two statements, participants can choose their agreement using one of the options: Disagree, Somewhat Disagree, Neither agree nor disagree, Somewhat Agree, Agree.

The questionnaire collects information regarding individuals' levels of trust in the fact-checking journals as the interventions present the factual positions determined by these journals. In the post-task questionnaire, participants are asked to rate their agreement with the statement: "When judging the credibility of a news article, I trust information from the fact-checking journals (e.g., Politifact.com)." Participants are allowed to rate their level of agreement using the options: Disagree, Somewhat Disagree, Neither agree nor disagree, Somewhat Agree, Agree.

5.6   Social Media Usage Questionnaire

The survey includes 5 questions related to participants' social media usage tendencies. The self-reporting questions collect information on how individuals spend their time on social platform: whether they like to create content, spread content, or consume content. We collect information about how likely participants what to spend their time on building or maintaining relationships with other social media users. These 5 questions are developed from the the Active-Passive (AP) Framework presented in [37]. Table 2 shows the social media questionnaire used in this study. Unlike the previous studies [24,26,45] that collect certain information regarding users' social media usage, this study is designed to utilize the social media usage questionnaire to determine users' interaction tendencies in the active-passive continuum of the AP Framework [37].

Table 2. Social media usage questionnaire to determine users' active-passive tendencies.

Interaction dimension	Corresponding statement for the dimension
Content creation	On social media, I spend time creating my own content (e.g., posting tweets, status, articles, photos, videos)
Content transmission	On social media, I often share information (e.g., retweet, share content created by others)
Relationship building	On social media, I spend time on relationship building (e.g., create group/event, join group/event, sending messages to non-friend)
Relationship maintenance	On social media, I spend time on relationship maintenance (e.g., commenting on content, chatting with friends)
Content consumption	On social media, I spend time browsing content created by others

5.7   Data Analysis

To find the clusters of users in the active-passive continuum, we applied the K-means clustering algorithm [20] on users' social media usage responses. We represent each response as a five-dimensional vector as participants provided their levels of agreement for five statements. We convert the options: Agree, Somewhat Agree, Neither Agree or Disagree, Somewhat Disagree, and Disagree into the numeric values 4, 3, 2, 1, 0, respectively - the higher numeric value indicates the higher agreement with the statement. After converting users' responses to the social media usage questionnaire into 5-dimensional numeric vectors, we train the k-mean algorithm on that vector representation. We apply the elbow method to find the optimum number of clusters.

The clustering algorithm identifies 3 clusters of participants. We calculate the number of decisions taken for each interaction by the participants of 3 clusters. As the participant numbers in the 3 clusters are different, we calculate the percentages of decisions taken for each interaction across the 3 participant clusters. We used Chi-square analysis to find how the participants across the 3 groups utilized the interaction functionalities and tested the statistical significance. For the decisions of each interaction option, we apply the chi-square to test whether the interaction decisions across 3 groups are independent or related to each other. As we perform the independence test for 3 categories, the degrees of freedom (df) are (3-1) = 2. We hypothesize that there exists a difference in the interactions across the 3 categories, and the null hypothesis is that there is no difference. When the p-value of the chi-square test is less than 0.05, we reject the null hypothesis and accept the alternative hypothesis.

6   Results

This section describes how 3 clusters of participants have emerged on the active-passive continuum from participants' responses to the social media usage questionnaire. Then, the section presents how the participants in these 3 clusters use the basic interaction functionalities such as like, comment, and share for verified and unverified posts. Afterward, this section shows the participants' interaction differences between control and treatment conditions.

6.1   Three Clusters of Users on the Active-Passive Continuum

Three clusters of users have emerged from the analysis of the participants (N=1006) responses to the social media usage questionnaire: active, moderately active, and passive. The centroids of 3 clusters [Table 3] show that cluster number 1 has high values across five interaction dimensions, indicating that participants in cluster 1 mostly agreed with the five statements of the social media usage questionnaire. These responses are similar to the active users' social media usage tendencies, and we label cluster 1 as the active group. On the contrary, cluster number 3 has a high value in content consumption, but low values in the other four dimensions, indicating that cluster 3 captures the participants with interaction tendencies of passive users. Thus, we label cluster 3 as the passive group. Finally, cluster number 2 has higher values than the passive group and lower values than the active group. Therefore, this cluster captures the participants who interacted with the content more than passive users but less than active users, and we label cluster 2 as the moderately active group.

Table 3. Three cluster centroids capture users' interaction tendencies as active, moderately active, and passive.

	Cluster 1	Cluster 2	Cluster 3
Content Consumption (D1)	4.42	4.12	4.47
Content Creation (D2)	4.40	2.81	1.36
Content Transmission (D3)	4.34	3.52	1.87
Relationship Maintenance (D4)	4.37	3.89	2.36
Relationship Building (D5)	4.36	3.07	1.56
Group	Active	Moderately Active	Passive

As expected, active users utilize the interaction functionalities more than the moderately active users, and the moderately active users utilize the interaction functionalities more than the passive users. Table 4 shows participants' interaction decisions for the eight posts (verified and unverified) presented in the control condition that adopts the awareness design principle. The interaction decisions for like, comment, and share functionalities decrease from active group to passive group. The percentage values of interaction decisions show the active group has the highest decisions for like, comment, and share. After the active group, the moderately active group has higher decisions for those three functionalities than the passive group. These interaction decision trends match participants' self-reported social media usage responses, showing that the participants in active, moderately active, and passive groups display their interaction decisions, respectively. A similar result is found for the participants in the treatment condition when the design adopts the guidance principle.

Table 4. Participants' interactions with posts decreases from active to passive in awareness principle.

Group and # of Participants	Like	Comment	Share
Active (252 participants)	927 (46%)	975 (48%)	945 (47%)
Moderately Active (161 participants)	337 (26%)	322 (25%)	278 (22%)
Passive (90 participants)	107 (15%)	13 (2%)	26 (4%)

6.2 Interaction Differences Across the 3 Clusters in Awareness Principle

This section presents findings that investigate the differences across the 3 clusters regarding their interactions with verified and unverified posts. The findings analyze participants' interaction decisions of the control condition, where the design adopts the awareness principle and informs participants about the factual position of the posts.

Table 5. Awareness principle applied to unverified posts reduces passive and moderately active users' interactions more than active users.

Group	Posts	Like	Comment	Share
Active	Verified	528 (52%)	489 (49%)	489 (49%)
	Unverified	399 (40%)	486 (48%)	456 (45%)
	Delta	$-12\%^{***}$	-1%	-4%
Moderately Active	Verified	233 (36%)	154 (24%)	178 (28%)
	Unverified	104 (16%)	168 (26%)	100 (16%)
	Delta	$-20\%^{***}$	$+2\%$	$-12\%^{***}$
Passive	Verified	88 (24%)	5 (1%)	21 (6%)
	Unverified	19 (5%)	8 (2%)	5 (1%)
	Delta	$-19\%^{***}$	$+1\%$	$-5\%^{***}$

$^{***}\ p < .001;\ ^{**}\ p < .01;\ ^{*}\ p < .05$

The results show statistically significant differences across the 3 clusters regarding how participants decide to use the interaction functionalities for the verified posts ($p < 0.05$). Table 5 shows participants' usage of like, comment, and share functionalities for verified posts. The findings indicate that participants in the active group use the three basic interaction functionalities, like, comment, and share equally; 52%, 49%, and 49%, respectively. In comparison, participants in the moderately active and passive groups prefer using the like functionality more than the comment or share functionalities. Similarly, both moderately active and passive groups utilize the share functionality of the verified posts more than the comment functionality.

In contrast, participants across three groups reduce their interactions with the unverified posts [Table 5]. However, the differences in how active, moderately active, and passive groups reduce their interactions have statistical significance; $p < 0.01$ in the chi-square test. The moderately active group reduces their usage of like and share functionalities more than the other two groups. After the moderately active group, participants of the passive group reduce their usage of like and share functionalities. Finally, the active group reduces their interactions least among the three groups, though users of this group remain active most on the social platforms.

6.3   Interaction Differences in Verified Posts Between 2 Principles

Participants across the 3 groups increased their sharing functionality usage in the guidance design principle for the verified posts (the treatment condition); the difference in sharing usage between the two conditions is statistically significant across the 3 participants groups [Table 6]. For example, the active group participants use the share functionality 25% more in the treatment than in the control condition, with a statistical significance of $p<.0001$. Additionally, the moderately active group has a statistically significant increase in sharing usage ($p<.0001$), which is 20% more than the controlled condition. Similarly, passive users also display an increment in their usage of sharing functionalities, which is 13% more than the control group with a statistically significant of $p<.0001$. Notably, the statistically significant difference exists only for the usage of share functionality, and there are no statistically significant differences in the usage of other interaction functionalities, such as like and comment.

Table 6. Guidance principle facilitates the distribution of verified information more than the awareness principle.

Group	Condition (Verified Posts)	Like	Comment	Share
Active	Awareness	528 (52%)	489 (49%)	489 (49%)
	Guidance	509 (51%)	443 (44%)	737 (74%)
	Delta	−1%	−5%	+25%***
Moderately Active	Awareness	233 (36%)	154 (24%)	178 (28%)
	Guidance	249 (41%)	131 (21%)	291 (48%)
	Delta	+5%	−3%	+20%***
Passive	Awareness	88 (24%)	5 (1%)	21 (6%)
	Guidance	118 (30%)	13 (3%)	75 (19%)
	Delta	+6%	+2%	+13%***

*** $p < .001$; ** $p < .01$; * $p < .05$

Active users increase their decisions to distribute credible information and utilize the verified post sharing and fact-checked article sharing functionalities presented in the treatment condition. For instance, active users in the treatment condition share the verified posts 14% more than the controlled condition ($p<.0001$). In addition, active users utilize the fact-checked article sharing functionalities for 34% of the verified posts - the control condition does not include this article sharing functionality. The results also indicate that active users utilize the post sharing functionality 29% more than the article sharing functionality.

Moderately active users increase their decisions to distribute credible information when they receive multiple functionalities in the treatment condition to share the verified posts. Compared to the controlled condition, moderately active users increased their decisions to share verified posts 7% more ($p<.01$).

Additionally, the moderately active users utilize the fact-checked article sharing functionality presented in the treatment condition and decide to use the interaction functionality for 27% of the verified posts. Moreover, moderately active users utilize the post sharing functionality 8% more than the article sharing functionality.

Passive users utilize the fact-checked article sharing functionality most than the participants in active or moderately active groups. There is a 7% increased usage of this article sharing functionality than the traditional post sharing functionality of the controlled condition (p<.0001). Additionally, multiple post sharing functionalities facilitate a 5% additional sharing decisions of the passive users in the treatment condition compared to the controlled condition (p <.05).

6.4   Interaction Differences in Unverified Posts Between 2 Principles

The interaction difference with unverified posts between awareness and guidance principle shows an increased usage of sharing functionality in the treatment condition that includes the fact-checked article sharing functionality. In the treatment condition, passive and moderately active participants utilize the fact-checked article sharing functionality more than the traditional post sharing functionality for the unverified posts [Table 7]. For example, passive participants share the fact-checked article 11% more than they share the unverified posts (p<.0001). Similarly, moderately active participants use the fact-checked article sharing functionality 7% more than the unverified post sharing functionality (p<.01). However, there is no significant difference in active participants' unverified post sharing and fact-checked article sharing usage.

Passive users utilize the fact-checked article sharing functionality most - this additional functionality enables passive users to distribute the fact-checked article for 15% of the unverified posts. Usually, passive users interacted with the unverified posts less - they use the post sharing functionality in the controlled condition for 1% of the unverified posts. In comparison, the fact-checked article sharing functionalities increase passive users' participation for an additional 14% of the unverified posts and assist them in disturbing credible information, which has a statistical significance of p <.0001.

Moderately active users utilize the fact-checked article sharing functionality for 27% of the unverified posts. This distribution of credible information is 11% more than the usage of unverified post sharing functionality in the controlled condition (p<.0001). In addition, moderately active users distribute the fact-checked article 7% more than their sharing of unverified posts in the treatment condition (p < .01).

Active users utilize the fact-checked article sharing functionality 9% more when posts are unverified than verified posts (p<.001). In contrast, moderately active and passive groups similarly use the fact-checked article sharing functionalities for unverified and verified posts; there is no significant difference in how the two groups utilize the article sharing functionalities for verified and unverified posts.

Table 7. Post and article sharing usage across 3 groups in guidance design principle.

	Active	Moderately Active	Passive
Share verified posts	627 (63%)	214 (35%)	(42) 11%
Share unverified posts	444 (44%)	123 (20%)	17 (4%)
Delta	−19%***	−15%***	−7%**
Share unverified post	444 (44%)	123 (20%)	17 (4%)
Share fact-checked article when posts are unverified	425 (43%)	165 (27%)	60 (15%)
Delta	−1%	+7%**	+11%***
Share fact-checked article when posts are verified	342 (34%)	(165) 27%	(53) 13%
Share fact-checked article when posts are unverified	425 (43%)	165 (27%)	60 (15%)
Delta	+9%**	0%	+2%

*** $p < .001$; ** $p < .01$; * $p < .05$

The differences between post sharing and fact-checked article sharing usage when posts are verified and unverified in the guidance principle are presented in Table 7. In the guidance design principle (treatment condition), active, moderately active, and passive users share unverified posts 19%, 15%, and 7% less in comparison to their sharing decisions of the verified posts ($p<.01$). However, moderately active and passive groups exhibit a 4% and 3% increase respectively in sharing unverified posts in the treatment condition than in the controlled condition. As participants in the treatment often use fact-checked article sharing and unverified post sharing functionalities for identical posts - this sharing usage could indicate that some participants used both information to justify their points.

6.5   Preference for Platform-Based Incentives

Participants' across the active-passive continuum show different preferences for the platform-base incentives that can inspire their participation for combating misinformation [Table 8]. Active participants in both conditions show higher levels of preference for getting badges (57%) and followers (53%). In contrast, participants in the passive group report lower levels of preference for those 2 incentives, 22% and 12% respectively. The moderately active participants, similar to the participants in the passive group, have lower percentage of responses for the 2 incentives, 34% and 29% respectively.

Participants in the passive group report higher levels of preference for getting information regarding the impact they are making; how their participation is helping other social media users. Among the four platform-based incentives, participants in the passive group have the highest percentage of responses for the incentive, which is 47%. Conversely, active participants display the lowest preference for the incentive, which is 33%. However, the moderately active participants exhibit similar preferences to the passive group - 43% of their responses are for this incentive. In addition, the moderately active participants have a higher preference for another incentive, content prioritization, which prioritizes individuals' content to other users (47%). Besides, moderately active users are inclined to get badges and followers as incentives. These similar trends exist in both control and treatment conditions.

Table 8. Participants across the active-passive continuum exhibit different preference toward platform-based incentives.

Platform-based incentives	Active	Moderately Active	Passive
Getting badges	287 (57%)	106 (34%)	42 (22%)
Getting followers	268 (53%)	92 (29%)	23 (12%)
Content prioritization	234 (47%)	126 (40%)	45 (24%)
Receive information regarding the impact	165 (33%)	134 (43%)	90 (47%)
Other	10 (2%)	36 (12%)	55 (29%)

7   Conclusion

This paper develops a foundation for personalized interaction design affordances that leverage users' interaction tendencies to make the truth louder and mitigate the spread of misinformation. This study identifies three clusters of social media users based on their interaction tendencies: active, moderately active, and passive, where active users possess higher interaction tendencies than moderately active users, and moderately active users possess higher interaction tendencies than passive users. This paper addresses the differences between the interaction tendencies across these three clusters and presents three principles of social media interactions that assist users in combating misinformation.

A survey study with 1006 participants indicates that moderately active and passive users increase their participation when they receive additional interaction support and utilize the interaction functionalities to distribute credible information. Moreover, active, moderately active, and passive users show various preferences for platform-based incentives that can motivate them to participate more in combating misinformation. Active users prefer platform-based incentives, such as getting badges or having the advantage on the platform that gets followers, whereas passive users want information from platforms regarding the impact of their participation on their friends and community. Moderately active users favor platform-based incentives as passive users and exhibit preference as active users. Additional research is needed to develop effective personalized interaction-focused design affordances that can transform users' long-term interaction behaviors so that social media users increase their interaction with verified information and reduce their interactions with unverified information.

References

1. Acquisti, A., et al.: Nudges for privacy and security: understanding and assisting users' choices online. ACM Comput. Surv. (CSUR) **50**(3), 1–41 (2017)
2. Arif, A., Shanahan, K., Chou, F.J., Dosouto, Y., Starbird, K., Spiro, E.S.: How information snowballs: Exploring the role of exposure in online rumor propagation. In: Proceedings of the 19th ACM Conference on Computer-Supported Cooperative Work & Social Computing, pp. 466–477. ACM (2016)
3. Babu, A., Liu, A., Zhang, J.: New updates to reduce clickbait headlines, May 2017. https://about.fb.com/news/2017/05/news-feed-fyi-new-updates-to-reduce-clickbait-headlines/
4. Bentley, F., Quehl, K., Wirfs-Brock, J., Bica, M.: Understanding online news behaviors. In: Proceedings of the 2019 CHI Conference on Human Factors in Computing Systems, pp. 1–11 (2019)
5. Bhuiyan, M.M., Zhang, K., Vick, K., Horning, M.A., Mitra, T.: Feedreflect: A tool for nudging users to assess news credibility on twitter. In: Companion of the 2018 ACM Conference on Computer Supported Cooperative Work and Social Computing, pp. 205–208 (2018)
6. Chen, A., Lu, Y., Chau, P.Y., Gupta, S.: Classifying, measuring, and predicting users' overall active behavior on social networking sites. J. Manag. Inf. Syst. **31**(3), 213–253 (2014)
7. Coleman, K.: Introducing birdwatch, a community-based approach to misinformation, January 2021. https://blog.twitter.com/en_us/topics/product/2021/introducing-birdwatch-a-community-based-approach-to-misinformation.html
8. Crowell, C.: Our approach to bots and misinformation (2017). https://blog.twitter.com/en_us/topics/company/2017/Our-Approach-Bots-Misinformation.html
9. Flintham, M., Karner, C., Bachour, K., Creswick, H., Gupta, N., Moran, S.: Falling for fake news: investigating the consumption of news via social media. In: Proceedings of the 2018 CHI Conference on Human Factors in Computing Systems, pp. 1–10 (2018)
10. Fogg, B.J.: A behavior model for persuasive design. In: Proceedings of the 4th international Conference on Persuasive Technology, pp. 1–7 (2009)
11. Geeng, C., Yee, S., Roesner, F.: Fake news on facebook and twitter: Investigating how people (don't) investigate. In: Proceedings of the 2020 CHI Conference on Human Factors in Computing Systems, pp. 1–14 (2020)
12. Gerson, J., Plagnol, A.C., Corr, P.J.: Passive and active facebook use measure (paum): validation and relationship to the reinforcement sensitivity theory. Personality Individ. Differ. **117**, 81–90 (2017)
13. Gleicher, N.: Removing coordinated inauthentic behavior from china, August 2019. https://about.fb.com/news/2019/08/removing-cib-china/
14. Grace, L., Hone, B.: Factitious: Large scale computer game to fight fake news and improve news literacy. In: Extended Abstracts of the 2019 CHI Conference on Human Factors in Computing Systems, pp. 1–8 (2019)
15. Hughes, T., Smith, J., Leavitt, A.: Helping people better assess the stories they see in news feed with the context button, April 2018. https://about.fb.com/news/2018/04/news-feed-fyi-more-context/
16. Khan, M.L.: Social media engagement: what motivates user participation and consumption on youtube? Comput. Hum. Behav. **66**(4), 236–247 (2017)
17. Kumar, S., Shah, N.: False information on web and social media: A survey. arXiv preprint arXiv:1804.08559 (2018)

18. Lewandowsky, S., Ecker, U.K., Cook, J.: Beyond misinformation: Understanding and coping with the "post-truth" era. J. Appl. Res. Memory Cogn. **6**(4), 353–369 (2017)
19. Lewandowsky, S., Ecker, U.K., Seifert, C.M., Schwarz, N., Cook, J.: Misinformation and its correction: continued influence and successful debiasing. Psychol. Sci. Public Interest **13**(3), 106–131 (2012)
20. Likas, A., Vlassis, N., Verbeek, J.J.: The global k-means clustering algorithm. Pattern Recogn. **36**(2), 451–461 (2003)
21. Marwick, A.E.: Why do people share fake news? a sociotechnical model of media effects. Georgetown Law Technol. Rev. **2**(2), 474–512 (2018)
22. Mele, N., et al.: Combating fake news: An agenda for research and action. Retrieved on October 17, 2018 (2017)
23. Morris, M.R., Counts, S., Roseway, A., Hoff, A., Schwarz, J.: Tweeting is believing? understanding microblog credibility perceptions. In: Proceedings of the ACM 2012 Conference on Computer Supported Cooperative Work, pp. 441–450 (2012)
24. Nekmat, E.: Nudge effect of fact-check alerts: Source influence and media skepticism on sharing of news misinformation in social media. Social Media+ Society **6**(1), 2056305119897322 (2020)
25. Nonnecke, B., Preece, J.: Shedding light on lurkers in online communities. Ethnographic Studies in Real and Virtual Environments: Inhabited Information Spaces and Connected Communities, Edinburgh 123128 (1999)
26. Pennycook, G., McPhetres, J., Zhang, Y., Lu, J.G., Rand, D.G.: Fighting covid-19 misinformation on social media: experimental evidence for a scalable accuracy-nudge intervention. Psychol. Sci. **31**(7), 770–780 (2020)
27. Perez, E.B., King, J., Watanabe, Y.H., Chen, X.: Counterweight: Diversifying news consumption. In: Adjunct Publication of the 33rd Annual ACM Symposium on User Interface Software and Technology. pp. 132–134 (2020)
28. politifact: New test with related articles (2021). https://www.politifact.com/
29. Preece, J., Shneiderman, B.: The reader-to-leader framework: motivating technology-mediated social participation. AIS Trans. Human-comput. Interact. **1**(1), 13–32 (2009)
30. Roozenbeek, J., van der Linden, S.: Fake news game confers psychological resistance against online misinformation. Palgrave Commun. **5**(1), 1–10 (2019)
31. Rosen, G.: How we're tackling misinformation across our apps (2021). https://about.fb.com/news/2021/03/how-were-tackling-misinformation-across-our-apps/
32. Rosen, G., Lyons, T.: Remove, reduce, inform: New steps to manage problematic content (2019). https://about.fb.com/news/2019/04/remove-reduce-inform-new-steps/
33. Roth, Y., Harvey, D.: How twitter is fighting spam and malicious automation (2018). https://blog.twitter.com/en_us/topics/company/2018/how-twitter-is-fighting-spam-and-malicious-automation.html
34. Roth, Y., Pickles, N.: Updating our approach to misleading information (2020). https://blog.twitter.com/en_us/topics/product/2020/updating-our-approach-to-misleading-information.html
35. Shao, G.: Understanding the appeal of user-generated media: a uses and gratification perspective. Internet Res. **19**(1), 7–25 (2009)
36. Siddiqui, S., Maher, M.L.: Reframing the fake news problem: Social media interaction design to make the truth louder. In: CHIRA, pp. 158–165 (2021)
37. Siddiqui, S., Maher, M.L.: Active-passive framework for developing communication strategies to combat misinformation. In: Proceedings of the 19th International Conference on Web Based Communities and Social Media (2022)

38. Smith, J.: Designing against misinformation (2017). https://medium.com/facebook-design/designing-against-misinformation-e5846b3aa1e2

39. Starbird, K.: Examining the alternative media ecosystem through the production of alternative narratives of mass shooting events on twitter. In: Eleventh International AAAI Conference on Web and Social Media (2017)

40. Starbird, K., Arif, A., Wilson, T., Van Koevering, K., Yefimova, K., Scarnecchia, D.: Ecosystem or echo-system? exploring content sharing across alternative media domains. In: Proceedings of the International AAAI Conference on Web and Social Media. vol. 12 (2018)

41. Su, S.: New test with related articles (2017). https://about.fb.com/news/2017/04/news-feed-fyi-new-test-with-related-articles/

42. Thaler, R.H., Sunstein, C.R.: Nudge: Improving decisions about health, wealth, and happiness. Penguin (2009)

43. Torres, R., Gerhart, N., Negahban, A.: Combating fake news: An investigation of information verification behaviors on social networking sites. In: Proceedings of the 51st Hawaii International Conference on System Sciences (2018)

44. Trifiro, B.M., Gerson, J.: Social media usage patterns: Research note regarding the lack of universal validated measures for active and passive use. Social Media+ Society 5(2), 2056305119848743 (2019)

45. Yaqub, W., Kakhidze, O., Brockman, M.L., Memon, N., Patil, S.: Effects of credibility indicators on social media news sharing intent. In: Proceedings of the 2020 CHI Conference on Human Factors in Computing Systems, pp. 1–14 (2020)

Insights from the Uncanny Valley: Gender(Sex) Differences in Avatar Realism and Uncanniness Perceptions

Jacqueline D. Bailey$^{(\boxtimes)}$ (ID), Karen L. Blackmore (ID), and Robert King

College of Engineering, Science and Environment, University of Newcastle, Ring Road,
Callaghan, NSW, Australia
{jacqueline.d.bailey,karen.blackmore,
robert.king}@newcastle.edu.au

Abstract. Two core factors influence the perception of avatars. On one side are
the developers who are concerned with building avatars and in some cases pushing
the boundaries of the realism. These developers are constrained by the resources
available to them that allow them to produce the optimal avatar with the equipment, time, and skills available to them. On the other side are users who engage
with avatars who are directly affected by the choices the developers have made.
Inside the interaction between these sides is the avatar itself, whose appearance,
level of realism and fundamental characteristics like a perceived gender(sex) can
influence the user's perception of that avatar. Despite the large amount of research
dedicated to understanding the perception of avatars, many gaps in our understanding remain. In this work, we aim to contribute to further understanding one
of these gaps by investigating the potential role of gender(sex) in the perception of
avatar realism and uncanniness. We add to this discussion by presenting the results
of an experiment where we evaluated realism and uncanniness perceptions by presenting a set of avatars to participants (n = 2065). These avatars are representative
of those used in simulation and training contexts, from publicly available sources,
and have varying levels of realism. Participants were asked to rank these avatars in
terms of their realism and uncanniness perceptions to determine whether the gen-
der(sex) of the participant influences in these perceptions. Our findings show that
the gender(sex) of a participant does affect the perception of an avatar's realism
and uncanniness levels.

Keywords: Uncanny valley · Uncanniness · Avatar · Human computer
interaction · Gender(sex)

1 Introduction

Avatars have diverse appearances and can be used to represent a person or characters
in mixed reality, online forms, gaming, training, and simulation contexts. Regardless of
the intended purpose of an avatar, at its core they function as visual representations of
characters used in a specific setting. Commonly, avatars (virtual humans) are used in

A. Holzinger et al. (Eds.): CHIRA 2021/2022, CCIS 1882, pp. 51–70, 2023.
https://doi.org/10.1007/978-3-031-41962-1_3

serious games and simulation training scenarios where they can engage with an end-user for training purposes [1, 2]. A core issue for all avatars regardless of their role is the end-users' perception of that avatar. Much of the literature on avatar perceptions fall into two core categories, focusing on physical attributes like hair or eye color or investigating how more functional aspects such as perceived realism and uncanniness levels can affect the perceptions of avatars.

The focus of this work is an examination of gender(sex) in the realism and uncanniness perceptions of avatar faces. Following Stumpf, Peters [3], this work draws on the socially constructed perceptions of gender, here referred to as gender(sex). Whereby gender identification, gender expression and performance might not necessarily align with biological sex of the end-user. The perceived gender(sex) of an avatar may influence the user's perception of the avatars ability which may be attributed to associated stereotypical ideas of gender. Further, the level of sexualization in the physical appearance of an avatar can also affect their perceived abilities [4]. It is also worth noting that some of the content of this chapter was previously presented at the International Conference on Computer-Human Interaction Research and Applications (CHRIA22) [5]. The current work has been extended to include additional content from the survey described in the original paper. Also included is an updated literature review, and discussion of the key findings for this new work.

Focusing on this current work it is important to discuss how the perception of avatars can be influence by developmental characteristics. For example, resources such as time, finances, tools, and expertise used to create an avatar can directly affect the level of realism that is realistically achievable given the constraints. These resources can range widely, from high-end tools like a light stage which surround an actor in a spherical structure of lights that can capture data such as specular mapping, facial geometry and surface reflections which can be used to create a highly realistic avatar [6] to produce higher realism avatars. By comparison, using commercial off the shelf software may have a lower level of realism due to the limited resources available [7]. While not as 'high-tech', this option is a relatively accessible set of tools for developers with limited expertise and/or finances.

Realism has many facets and can refer to an avatar's behavior, appearance, or ability to communicate [8]. The two main areas that may affect this perception are the visual and behavioral nuances shown. This includes how these visual aspects relate to the perceived anthropomorphism of an avatar and the kinetic similarity and social appropriateness of an avatars' behavior. These aspects, individually or combined, can define how some end-users perceive realism in avatars [9].

When an avatar fails to meet the visual, kinetic, or behavioral fidelity of a healthy human they can be perceived as uncanny or eerie. This uncanniness can be linked to the Mori's Uncanny Valley Theory [10] in which the human likeness perceptions experience a sharp dip into a negative familiarity when these expectations are not met, as can be seen in Fig. 1.

Mori suggests that this instinctive response can be linked to a form of protection for the viewer, that protects them from proximal sources of dangers. For example, within the negative familiarity dip we find unpleasant or potentially harmful sources of anxiety for human viewers such as corpses. Although this theory was originally applied to the field

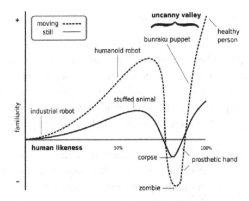

Fig. 1. The Uncanny Valley [10].

of robotics it has now been repeatedly applied to human-like avatars [11–13]. These uncanniness perceptions might be the result of creating an avatar using sophisticated software that focuses on boundary pushing visual realism levels which may trigger the uncanniness or eerie perceptions in end-users [11].

The next section provides a comprehensive overview of the key literature relating to the importance of visual realism in avatars and consequences of this realism falling short of expectations. Also discussed is the influence of gender(sex) in the perceptions of avatars. Then we describe the methodology for our avatar ranking survey including data collection techniques and procedure before presenting the key results of the data analysis. Our paper concludes with a discussion of the key findings alongside some recommendations for future work in this area.

2 Background

There are several important areas to consider in the design and development of avatars. One overriding area that can have a deep effect on the perception of an avatar is the perceived level of visual realism. Avatars are often generated with the resources available to the designers and developers, within the constraints of time, money, expertise, and resources, with the resulting avatar being the optimal output based on these constraints. However, the importance of visual realism can lead to an unintended negative perception in terms of how uncanny or eerie an avatar appears. While the avatars are constrained by their designers and developers' resources, the consequences of uncanniness cannot be ignored. The uncanniness perceptions, as described in the following section, can lead to users rejecting an avatar, which in turn leads to wasted resources used to develop and design that avatar. The perception of avatars can be influenced by many factors, but arguably one of the core design choices that developers make, is the gender(sex) of an avatar. As discussed below, this choice can be a very deliberate one that nurtures expectations or stereotypes, or it can be unintentional. Regardless of the design decisions the literature has shown that the influence of gender(sex) is important. The importance of gender(sex) perceptions also extends to the perception of realism levels in avatars.

2.1 The Importance of Visual Realism in Avatars

The realism level of an avatar is prevailing issue that impacts the development and appearance of an avatar. The level of realism can have a profound influence on the perception of that avatar. A study by Dobre, Wilczkowiak [14] shows that photo-realistic avatars were seen as more trustworthy and were assigned higher affinity scores. This level of trust can be important in human-avatar interactions especially if an avatar is being used in serious purposes such as medicinal [1] or military [15] simulation training scenarios.

Zanbaka, Goolkasian [13] have also examined the influence of an avatar's realism and how this may affect their persuasiveness. Zanbaka et. al's study used real human actors, human-like avatars, and anthropomorphized cat avatars to measure persuasiveness. Their findings suggest that the realism levels did not impact the persuasiveness of an avatar's message. As previously stated, avatars are a product of purposeful design, and the resources available to produce them can only create an avatar that is optimal for the circumstance. This purposeful design influences the avatar design issues in serious game applications may be less about financial loss, and more about poor assistance, learning, and training experiences. This impact may occur when either the behavioral or visual realism of an avatar negatively affects the intended end-user, through uncanniness perceptions [16].

Consistent with existing literature, the realism level has a direct impact on the perception of uncanniness in avatars. For example, MacDorman, Green [17] suggest that end-users are disturbed when a virtual character's (avatars) appearance is too realistic or human. Tinwell [18] suggests that increasing the level of realism does not necessarily mean that the acceptance of the avatar will increase. Thus, these trade-offs between avatar realism the effects of uncanniness perceptions can be complex with serious consequences when the avatar fails to meet end-user expectations.

2.2 When Visual Realism Fails, the Consequences Are Uncanny and Eerie

As mentioned previously, the feeling of uncanniness that end-users may experience when engaging with boundary pushing avatars can be a major handicap for human-avatar interaction. The consequences of this boundary pushing can lead to the avatars falling into the previously mentioned Uncanny Valley [10]. These consequences, while present may still allow avatars to be effective as discussed by Yoon, Kim [19] who used wooden mannequins and high-realism avatars in their study and found that there was a strong acceptance of sense of realism from the high realism avatars despite the participants experiencing the negative effects of the uncanny valley.

These judgements can be based on what Ambady, Bernieri [20] call thin slices, whereby someone who perceives another person can form relatively quick and accurate social judgements of others with only the minimal amount of information. This is an important distinction to understand as making accurate social judgements about other persons is a fundamental human trait for forming successful relations and avoiding potentially harmful interactions [21]. This avoidance of harm or danger is echoed by MacDorman, Green [17] who suggest that the uncanniness feeling that end-users feel can also be associated with threat avoidance. If an avatar provokes such a reaction in the end-user, when there intended purpose was to help the user, the avatar will be rejected.

Such a rejection is a serious consequence of uncanny or eerie avatars and can lead to serious financial losses for companies. For example, financial losses were evident for Disney in the movie 'Mars Needs Moms' which purportedly cost the Disney Corporation $150 million [22] when the movie flopped. This can also been seen in games such as L.A. Noire and Mass Effect: Andromeda where players have heavily criticized the appearance of the in-game avatar [22]. These examples of uncanny virtual characters can also be attributed to the human visual system.

This visual system can easily and quickly detect falsehoods found in human-like faces based on previous exposure to human faces [12]. Avatars that attempt to reflect an accurate representation of a human face are susceptible to the effects of the uncanny valley. This uncanniness is exacerbated when the avatar moves or attempts to express emotions in realistic ways. Several methods have been developed to generate these emotions with varying levels of success.

Methods for capturing and expressing emotions can range from manual methods such as frame-by-frame approach, to motion-capture to more advanced techniques that use machine learning. The manual methods may effectively create facial animation, but it is an extremely time-consuming and expensive process. Alternative techniques such as motion capture do exist and can provide a somewhat faster means of capturing an actor's facial movement. When captured either as a real-time motion capture or as a set of motions mapped post-capture [23] can create effective expressions for avatars. Alternatively, there are machine learning techniques which use neutral rendering [24–26], which can render highly photorealistic avatars. However, despite these differences, very little is understood about the impacts of these different techniques on perceptions of realism or uncanniness and how an avatar's gender(sex) may influence these perceptions.

2.3 The Influence of an Avatar's Gender(Sex)

A fundamental design decision when creating avatars is the choice of their perceived gender(sex). Existing research explores several gender(sex) related issues including gender(sex) stereotypes, the proteus effect, and gender(sex) swapping. Fox and Bailenson [27] observed some gender(sex) based stereotypes and suggest that female avatars are more likely to appear either as hypersexualized or as an ornament within video/computer games or as a support role. The perceived level of sexualization that an avatar is depicted as having can also affect female avatars perceived abilities [4]. The Proteus Effect as discussed by Yee and Bailenson [28] suggests that the perceived gender(sex) of an avatar will lead users to conform to behavioral expectations they have associated with a specific gender(sex). This was also observed by Beltrán [29] who suggested that this conformity exists in simulation and training contexts as well. Their findings suggest that using a male avatar to train professional women will negatively affect her and her colleagues' achievements. This is essential to consider, as Beltrán [29] argues that most simulation tools show a generic male avatar during training. This raises an important issue to consider for avatar designers and developers, if an avatar is designed for a specific purpose, it is worth considering who in the user-base the avatar is likely to encounter. For example, if an avatar is intended to train a largely female orientated cohort, a generic male avatar may not be the best choice.

Other research in the influence of gender(sex) investigates gender(sex) swapping and exploring an end-user's gender identity or identities. Lehdonvirta, Nagashima [30] also suggest that male participants are more likely to seek and receive help when they are 'disguised' as a female-styled avatar. This was also investigated by Hussain and Griffiths [31] who suggest that there are many social benefits to gender(sex)-swapping in online gaming. For example, male players engaging as a female-styled avatars may do so to be more favorably treated by other male players to gain benefits or favor within the context of the video/computer game.

Lastly, the gender(sex) can also be used to explore and express gender identity or identities [32]. This is an important aspect to consider as it allows users to express their gender identities which may or may not reflect the gender identity they present in their everyday lives. In video/computer gaming settings, players may be able to remain relatively anonymous online while they explore and express their gender identity or identities in a reasonably safe platform.

Thus, based on the existing literature, we have completed a ranking exercise with a set of ten homogenous avatars to better understand how perceptual variability may be influenced by gender(sex). This will also create a robustly ranked set of avatars for use in future research. These avatars will have been quantifiability rated in terms of realism and uncanniness perceptions. The methodology for data collection is discussed next in this work. While the set of avatars used in our study are of similar age and ethnicity, they have distinctly varying levels of realism and are from multiple sources. In summary, we investigate the relationship between a set of avatar faces realism and uncanniness perceptions with a focus on how gender(sex) may affect these perceptions. To examine the potential influence of gender(sex) in the perception of avatar realism and uncanniness, we conducted a mass-scale survey, described next.

3   Avatar Ranking Survey Methodology

Our study uses a set of ten avatars to assess the potential influence of gender(sex) in the perception of realism and uncanniness. The survey was produced in Limesurvey [33] and hosted by Amazon's Mechanical Turk (Mturk) [34] and took participants 15–20min to complete. The participants who met the inclusion criteria were paid .10USD cents for their participation. Our study has been approved by the University of Newcastle's Ethics Committee (Protocol number: H-2015–0163).

With a mean age of 34.82 years a total of ($n = 2065$) participants completed the Avatar Ranking Survey. To examine potential differences between genders(sexes) participants were asked to nominate both a biological sex, and a gender identity. A small percentage of the participants' gender identities did not necessarily algin with their nominated biological sex, but as this number was small, we opted to examine gender(sex) by the biological sex indicated by the participants. In total, there were 1050 self-identified female participants, 1003 male, three people self-identified as transgender, two selected 'other' as their gender and seven people chose not to say which gender(sex) they are.

3.1 Sample Avatar Set Images

Our 10 homogenous avatar faces (Table 1) are a sample that broadly captures varying levels of realism which can be achieved from different creation methods discussed previously. These avatars only appear to represent assumed binary genders(sexes) with five female faces and five male faces. The set also includes two real human faces sourced from an online dataset (DaFEx [35]). This set of avatars are representative of avatars found in training and simulation contexts and are from several sources [35–40].

Table 1. Sample images of the avatar faces [5].

Female Avatar Faces

Rose	Emily	Ilana	Liliwen	Bailie

Male Avatar Faces

Rycroft	Ira	Victor	Macaw	Leo

3.2 Avatar Ranking Survey Procedure

Our approach is similar to Lange [41] who used a ranking exercise to examine images of virtual landscapes. To ensure a higher reliability a ranking approach is used as opposed to a rating method in both this study and Lange's [42, 43]. Participants were asked to rank the avatars twice. First from most to least realistic and second from most to least uncanny or eerie (see Fig. 2).

Prior to ranking the avatars, participants were asked a series of demographic questions that asked them to indicate a biological sex, gender identity, age, English language proficiency, and Country of residence. Additional questions were asked to determine each participant's level of computer/video gaming, virtual environment, and avatar animation experience to potentially give further context to the ranks when analyzing the data.

3.3 Data Analysis for the Survey Responses

Both the realism and uncanniness ranks were first analyzed using Friedman tests. If the initial test returned a statistically significant result, a post hox Wilcoxon signed-rank test

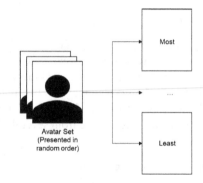

Fig. 2. Avatar Ranking Survey – ranking questions.

was performed. The second test was run with a Bonferroni adjustment for multiple tests were run to investigate any differences between the rankings.

Primarily, the participant gender(sex) variable was investigated to determine whether this factor influenced the realism and uncanniness rankings. Our approach was based on the work of Conover and Iman [44] who suggest that rank transformation procedures should allow the use of parametric methods. But, as the participants themselves provided the ranks the transformation step was not needed.

Based on the Friedman tests, additional analysis of the uncanniness ranks was run using a General Linear Model (GLM). The effect of the participants gender(sex) was examined using a full factor two-way ANOVA model with avatar and gender(sex) being the two core factors. This was followed up with a pairwise comparison to determine whether there were significant differences using a Bonferroni adjustment to control for the familywise error rate of multiple tests, the results of this analyses are presented in the following section.

4   Results from the Avatar Ranking Survey

This section focuses on the two sets of ranking data by first examining the realism ranks and the potential influence of participant gender(sex). Second, we outline the uncanniness ranks and how gender(sex) may impact on the participants perceptions.

4.1   Realism Ranks and Gender(Sex)

Table 2 below shows the mean of the realism rankings for each avatar. Based on the Freidman test, there was a statistically significant difference in the perception of the avatars' realism $\chi 2(9) = 8819.9$, p < .001.

The human actors are considered the most realistic (Rose (M = 2.67, SD 2.199) and (Rycroft (M = 3.06, SD = 2.147)). While it is an expected result, it is noted that the participants were not told that some of the avatar faces were in fact real world humans; this somewhat validates the efficacy of the ranking set. Next, the avatars created by the University of Southern California and Image Metrics are ranked as the third and fourth

Table 2. Overall Ranking of the avatars by their perceived level of Realism.

Rank	Avatar	Name	Realism Level	Gender(Sex)	Mean	SD
1		Rose	Real	Female	2.67	2.199
2		Rycroft	Real	Male	3.06	2.147
3		Ira	High	Male	3.53	2.020
4		Emily	High	Female	3.57	2.085
5		Victor	Mid1	Male	6.06	1.915
6		Ilana	Mid1	Female	6.12	1.938
7		Macaw	Mid2-Low	Male	7.07	1.919
8		Victor	Mid2-Low	Male	7.08	2.027
9		Liliwen	Mid2-Low	Female	7.56	2.404
10		Bailie	Mid2-Low	Female	8.27	2.122

highest realism avatars in this set (Ira (M = 3.53, SD = 2.020) and Emily (M = 3.57, SD = 2.085) behind the real-world human faces. Then the avatars sourced from Faceware [38] are rated as the fifth and sixth most realistic of the set (Victor (M = 6.06, SD = 1.915) and Ilana (M = 6.12, SD = 1.938). The FaceShift [37] avatars are ranked seventh Macaw (M = 7.07, SD = 1.919)) and eighth (Leo (M = 7.08, SD = 2.027) for their perceived level of realism. Importantly, we see that the lower realism ranks are both females, with the lower realism avatars are Liliwen (M = 7.56, SD = 2.404) and Bailie (M = 8.27, SD = 2.122).

A Wilcoxon signed ranked test using a Bonferroni correction determined that there are no statistically significant differences between the following comparisons of pairs; both of the Mid2-Low realism male avatars Leo and Macaw, the high realism avatars Ira and Emily and finally, the Mid1 realism avatars Victor and Ilana, in terms of realism. All other comparisons were statistically significantly different.

We first consider potential gender(sex) impacts through an examination of the realism ranking scores by participant sex. Using a General Linear Model, there was a statistically significant interaction between the avatars and the participants' gender(sex) $F(9,19910)$ = 16.34, $p < .001$. Posthoc analysis used .005 as the significance level (Bonferroni adjustment for ten tests) to compare differences between the responses of female and male participants for each avatar. Female participants rated Rycroft the Real Human Male as more realistic than their male counterparts: (Female (M = 2.85, SD = .068), Male (M = 3.30, SD = .064), p < .001). In contrast, Rose the Real Human Female was rated as more realistic by female participants when compared to the male participants. (Female (M = 2.74, SD = .068), Male (M = 2.93, SD = .064), p < .001). The overall ranks for the uncanniness scores are discussed in the following section.

4.2   Uncanniness Ranks and Gender(Sex)

The Freidman test for the uncanniness rank scores revealed that there is a statistically significant difference in the avatar sets uncanniness perceptions $\chi2 (9) = 156.254$, p < .001. It is noteworthy, that the mean scores for the uncanniness ranks are clustered between 4.9–5.8, which may suggest that variations in uncanniness perceptions may be subtle (Table 3).

Despite being from the same creation tool and being subjected to the same creation method, we see that the Mid1 realism avatars are polar opposites within these uncanniness ranks. With Victor the Mid1 realism male avatar being ranked as the uncanniest avatar in the set (M = 4.99, SD = 2.505), while in contrast Ilana (Mid1 realism female) has been ranked as the least uncanny avatar in the set (M = 5.87, SD = 2.324). This trend of the male avatars being uncannier than their female counterparts continues for the high realism avatars with Ira the high realism male (M = 5.14, SD = 2.805) being considered uncannier than Emily (M = 5.37, SD = 3.006). This trend is similar for one of the Mid2-Low male avatars (Leo (M = 5.47, SD = 2.739)) and Rycroft the real human male (M = 5.51, SD = 3.114). Four out of five of the upper ranks appear to be populated by male faces which may suggest some gendered affect in the perception of uncanniness in avatar faces. The only exception to this is Emily the high realism female avatar.

We see this trend is reversed for the bottom five ranks with Macaw the other Mid2-Low realism male avatar being the only male avatar in the lower ranks (M = 5.52, SD = 2.571). The bottom four ranks are populated exclusively by female avatars, which may suggest some gendered affect to the perception of uncanniness. Like other avatars, Rose the real human is ranked as less uncanny than her male counterpart (M = 5.65, SD = 3.360). However, it is noteworthy that the participants were not told there may be real faces in the avatar set, and as outlined above. Rose and Rycroft were ranked as the most realistic, but here they are ranked roughly around the middle of the uncanniness ranks. This middle ranking may suggest that the participants were uncertain as to whether these were 'real humans' or avatars. The literature and realism rankings above may suggest

Table 3. Overall Ranking of the avatars by their perceived level of Uncanniness [5].

Rank	Avatar	Name	Realism Level	Gender(Sex)	Mean	SD
1		Victor	Mid1	Male	4.99	2.505
2		Ira	High	Male	5.14	2.805
3		Emily	High	Female	5.37	3.006
4		Leo	Mid2-Low	Male	5.47	2.739
5		Rycroft	Real	Male	5.51	3.114
6		Macaw	Mid2-Low	Male	5.52	2.571
7		Rose	Real	Female	5.65	3.360
8		Bailie	Mid2-Low	Female	5.66	3.214
9		Lili-wen	Mid2-Low	Female	5.83	2.799
10		Ilana	Mid1	Female	5.87	2.324

that as Rose and Rycroft were ranked as "most realistic" or possibly have been identified as real, that they should be ranked as "most uncanny" (Rank 1 or 2) but as the analysis shows, this is not the case suggesting that some other variable may have been at work in the participants decision making process.

We also see that despite Bailie one of the Mid2-Low realism female avatars being ranked as the least realistic, she was not ranked as the uncanniest avatar (M = 5.66, SD = 3.214), which may suggest that her appearance is somewhat cartoonish or has a level of mid-low realism that could be seen as uncanny to the participants.

Table 4. Summary of the gender(sex)-based variations in the uncanniness ranks from the GLM analysis.

Avatar	Category	Female Participants (M, SD)	Male Participants (M, SD)
	Real human female	(M= 5.85, SD= .093)	(M= 5.33, SD= .088)
	Real human male	(M= 5.68, SD= .093)	(M= 5.26, SD= .088)
	High Realism Female	(M= 5.54, SD= .093)	(M= 5.12, SD= .088)
	High Realism Male	(M= 5.27, SD= .093)	(M= 4.90, SD= .088)
	Mid2-Low Realism Female	(M= 5.47, SD= .093)	(M= 5.98, SD= .088)
	Mid2-Low Realism Male	(M= 5.30, SD= .093)	(M= 5.75, SD= .088)

To determine where the differences occurred in the uncanniness ranks a Wilcoxon signed ranked test using a Bonferroni correction was used. Despite the small range of scores there are some significant differences between some of the avatars ranks. Specifically, between Ira the high realism male and Rycroft the real human male ($Z = -.527$, p. < 0.001) and Ira the high realism male and Rose the real human female ($Z = -6.229$, p. < 0.001). A potential effect of uncanniness perceptions may be seen in a comparison of Emily the high realism female avatar who, unlike her counterpart, is not statistically significant when compared to the real humans. This may suggest that gender(sex) may influence the perception of uncanniness when compared to the real humans in the set.

4.3 The Influence of Gender(Sex) in the Uncanniness Ranks

After determining the ranking of most to least uncanny avatars in the set we consider whether there were any gender(sex)-based variabilities amongst the scores. Using a GLM with a Bonferroni correction we analyzed the ranks and determined that there was a statistically significant interaction between the avatar set's uncanniness rank scores and the gender(sex) of the participants $F(9, 19910) = 10.453$, $p < .001$.

When examining the Posthoc analysis several significant results showed that there were some differences between the rank scores of the female and male participants (Table 4).

From this analysis we can see that most of the significant differences have the female participants rating the avatars as uncannier than their male counterparts. This can be seen in the analysis of the real humans, high realism avatars and one of the Mid2-Low realism male avatars. As can be seen in Table 4 Rose the human female (Rose $p < .001$, (Female ($M = 5.85$, $SD = .093$), Male ($M = 5.33$, $SD = .088$))), Rycroft the human male (Rycroft $p = .001$, (Female ($M = 5.68$, $SD = .093$), Male ($M = 5.26$, $SD = .088$))), are both scored as more uncanny by the female participants. This trend continues for both Emily the high realism female avatar (Emily $p = .001$, (Female ($M = 5.54$, $SD = .093$), Male ($M = 5.12$, $SD = .088$))), and Ira the high realism male avatar (Ira $p = .005$, (Female ($M = 5.27$, $SD = .093$), Male ($M = 4.90$, $SD = .088$))). We also see this dominance of female participants finding some avatars uncannier than their male counterparts occur for Macaw one of the Mid2-Low realism male avatars (Macaw $p = .001$, (Female ($M = 5.30$, $SD = .093$), Male ($M = 5.75$, $SD = .088$))).

The only instance where the male participants find an avatar uncannier than their female counterparts is for Bailie one of the Mid2-Low realism female avatars (Bailie $p < .001$, (Female ($M = 5.47$, $SD = .093$), Male ($M = 5.98$, $SD = .088$))). These differences suggest that the gender(sex) of the participant may influence their perceptions of an avatar's uncanniness.

4.4 Uncanniness Ranks Distribution

As previously mentioned, the actual scores for the rank scores range between 4.5–5.8 which may suggest that uncanniness perceptions can be subtle. To further investigate this, we examined the distributions of the raw uncanniness rank scores grouped by participant gender(sex) (Fig. 3) where we see several interesting patterns emerge.

It is noteworthy that the distributions themselves have appear to have a pattern. We can obverse that most avatars have a flat uniform distribution for their scores. However, the Mid1 realism avatars (Victor and Ilana) and Mid2-Low realism male avatar (Macaw) appear to have a normal distribution of the rank scores. But interestingly, the real humans (Rose and Rycroft) and one of the Mid2-Low realism female avatars (Bailie) have a distinct bi-modal distribution showing the divided opinion of these specific avatars in terms of the participants uncanniness perceptions.

Uncanniness Ranks by Participant Gender(Sex) grouped by Realism Level

BioGen

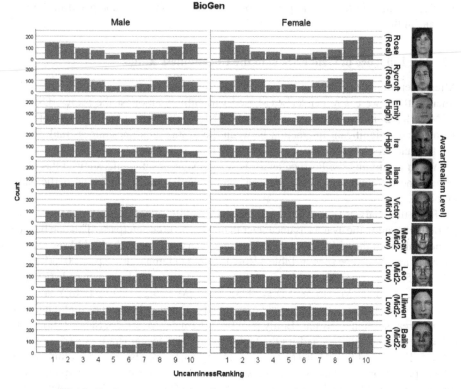

Fig. 3. Rank scores comparison by avatar and participant gender(sex) [5]

To determine whether these distributions are significant, we used a 2 sample Kolmogorov-Smirnov Test in order to compare the distribution shapes, using a Bonferroni correction for testing multiple pairs. Some significant differences were found when comparing the male and female distributions. First, we see these differences between Rose D(1993) = 1.785, p. < .001, Rycroft D(1993) = 1.819, p. = 003, Macaw D(1993) = 1.796, p. = .003, and Bailie D(1993) = 1.785, p. = .003.

Second, we also see some significant differences between Leo a Mid2-Low realism male avatar and Liliwen a Mid2-Low realism female avatar. However, these significant differences are only present for the female participants scores not the male participants (Female participants(D(2090) = 1.947, p. < .001., Male participants(D(1896) = 1.355, p. = .051.)). This trend continues for Rose the real human and Emily the high realism female avatar (Female participants(D(2090) = 3.412, p. < .001.), Male participants(D(1896) = 1.447, p. = .030)). We see the trend reflected in the scores for Rycroft the real human male and Rose the real human female (Female participants(D(2090) = 1.312, p. = .064), Male participants(D(1896) = 3.834, p. < .001)). Finally, the female participants scores for both the Mid2-Low realism female avatars Liliwen and Bailie, show some significant differences where the male participants do not (Female participants(D(2090) = 2.166, p. < .001., Male participants(D(1896) = 1.699, p. = .051.)).

Third and interestingly, we see this trend reversed for some of the avatars in the set. Specifically, for Macaw one of the male Mid2-Low realism avatars and Ira the high realism male, the male participants scores are significant was while the female participants are not (Male participants(D(1896) = 3.834, p. < .001), Female participants(D(2090) = 1.312, p. = .064)). This reversed trend continues with Bailie one of the Mid2-Low realism female avatars when compared to Ira the high realism male avatar, the male participants scores are statistically significant, whereas the female participants scores are not (Male participants(D(1896) = 2.825, p. < .001), Female participants(D(2090) = 1.444, p. = .031)).

Further, the comparison between Leo one of the Mid2-Low realism male avatars and Ira the high realism male were statistically significant for the male participants but not for the female participants (Male participants(D(1896) = 3.789, p. < .001), Female participants(D(2090) = 1.553, p. = .016)). Lastly, we see that this trend continues for a comparison between Emily the high realism female and Leo one of the Mid2-Low realism male avatars (Male participants(D(1896) = 3.330, p. < .001), Female participants(D(2090) = 1.837,p. = .016)). All other comparisons were not statistically significant for either participants gender(sex). The key findings of this analysis are discussed next.

5   Study Discussion and Conclusions

Our initial findings considered realism perceptions and show an interesting result in the grouping of the avatars by their source or creation method. It is unsurprising that avatars like Emily the high realism female and Ira the high realism male avatar would rank higher than other avatars due to the resources used to create them. While in contrast, Bailie one of the Mid2-Low realism female avatars which was created using an off the shelf model from the 3D Avatar store (https://www.3d-avatar-store.com/), a laptop and a GoPro, and expectedly achieved the lowest rank. The avatar realism rankings do appear to form natural groupings that align to the underlying method of creation. However, there are other factors likely to impact on the rankings. For instance, the facial avatars presented in this study are not consistent in terms of their features. End-user perceptions of falsehoods in the avatar faces overall appearance may have influenced realism perceptions as suggested by Brenton, Gillies [45]. This may lead to those with unusual characteristics being ranked as the least realistic avatars, however, this was not explicitly considered in this research. As expected, participants rated the human actors at the highest levels of realism, confirming the validity of the realism ranking process. Participants were able to correctly rank these faces despite not being identified as non-avatar.

It is interesting to note that although the participants were not told there would be human actors in the set, both Rose the real human female and Rycroft the real human male sit around the middle of the uncanniness rankings. Unlike the realism rankings that place the actors as highly realistic, the ambiguity over whether they are an avatar may have caused them to appear as mildly uncanny to the viewers. Jentsch [46] suggests that a predominant cause of uncanniness is the doubt over the living status of an entity. This uncertainty over whether these 'avatars' are real may have contributed to them being ranked as mildly uncanny. In contrast, it is unsurprising that the higher realism avatars (Emily and Ira) were ranked as profoundly uncanny, as it has been suggested that increasing the level of realism in the stimuli presented would likely raise the level of sensitivity to cues that would indicate falsehood [45]. In addition to these general findings, two specific investigations were conducted into differences in realism and uncanniness perceptions based on the different genders(sexes)es of participants.

The first investigation into the impact of gender(sex) on the rankings examined whether an observer's gender(sex) affected the perception of an avatar's realism ratings. The results suggest that the gender(sex) of a participant may affect the rating of an avatars' realism level for avatars who may be perceived as mid-realism. There was some consensus between female and male participants at the extreme ends of the realism ratings. However, female participants rated Ira the high realism male avatar higher than Emily the high realism female avatar, while male participants had the reverse. At the other extreme, for the lowest-rated avatars, both female and male participants rated both the Mid2-Low realism female avatars Liliwen and Bailie as the least realistic.

Although the grouping by creation method continued in the 5th-8th realism ranks, the ordering was different for female and male participants. Female participants rated female avatars as more realistic than male avatars, whereas male participants did the reverse. This may be explained by the similarity-attraction theory that predicts preferences for gender(sex)-matching, which suggests that some females may see males as the more dominant group, and therefore use similarities to develop social bonds with other females [64]. However, as the female participants ranked Emily the higher realism female avatar lower than Ira the high realism male avatar, this similarity-attraction theory may not apply to all avatars. The impact of a participants' self-similarity with each of these avatars may also influence these rankings. This data was collected as part of this ranking exercise and will be fully explored in future work.

Our investigation into the potential influence of gender(sex) also considered whether a participants' gender(sex) affected perceptions of an avatar's uncanniness level. We found that the Male participants appeared to rate the higher realism avatars as uncannier than all other avatars, with Victor the Mid1 realism male avatar being the exception. This is similar to previous findings for male participants where existing literature suggested that they were more sensitive to uncanniness in human-like avatars [11].

Of interest, are the top four ranks for female participants, these were populated exclusively by male avatar faces. This may suggest that these avatars may have triggered negative responses for female-identifying participants. This may be linked to existing research on avatar faces, features, and uncanniness which suggest that avatars that fail to display empathy or react appropriately may lead to assumptions of psychopathy in an avatar [11] and as such pose a threat. As such, one of the critical dimensions of uncanniness, discussed earlier, such as threat avoidance and alignment to terror management theory [17] as discussed may be more enhanced in female-identifying participants.

Further, it is also interesting to note that while despite some consistency in the avatars most uncanny ranks, the same consensus was not found the avatars ranked least uncanny. For both genders(sexes), two different female avatars were ranked as most uncanny.

These differences led to an additional investigation of the distribution of uncanniness score by the participants gender(sex).

While examining the distribution of scores, we see some interesting differences in the male and female participant scores for individual avatars. We see a bi-model distribution for the real humans and one of the Mid2-Low realism female avatars scores, which may suggest that the opinions of these avatars is divided. Of note are the scores for both the real humans who despite achieving high realism ranks, having their uncanniness scores fall roughly around the middle of the uncanniness rankings. When comparing the scores between the participants' gender(sex) these distributions were found to be statistically significantly different. Which may suggest that some participants could have been convinced that these avatars were computer-generated avatars rather than real humans. Further, we see that Bailie the one of the Mid2-Low realism female avatars was ranked as the least realistic but ranked only eighth on the uncanny ranks scores. This difference in ranking may indicate that the avatar was considered simultaneously unrealistic but not uncanny which is supported by existing literature lower realism levels which can lead to avatars being perceived as less uncanny [11].

The findings of this work highlight the importance of gender(sex) in avatar design decisions and how this variable may impact on the perceptions of avatar realism and uncanniness. As previously identified, a detailed investigation of the influence of gender(sex) in avatar realism and uncanniness perceptions is mostly missing in the decision making for avatar systems and from the current literature. Further, it is evident from the literature that the inevitable design choice of gender(sex) for an avatar has underlying cues and expectations placed on them based primarily on their perceived gender(sex). Together, the findings of the research provide key insights into gender(sex) based perception of avatars.

Although this work has made some significant contributions, it does have some limitations. First, the survey's sample has a limited ethnic diversity with the majority identifying as Asian or White/Caucasian backgrounds. This lack of diversity may lead to potential bias in the interpretation of the data. Second, the results may not be applicable to nonbinary genders(sexes) due to small sample sizes from these groups in this participant sample. However, this does present an avenue for future work. Third, there is some diversity in age (18–87 years old) however the mean age was (M = 34.82, SD = 11.52). The survey was unable to gather data from participants aged 18 and under as part of a restriction imposed by Mturk themselves. Thus, these findings may not be applicable to those who are under 18 years old.

Outside of the participant sample, the avatars also suffer from some limitations. Notably, the lack of ethnic diversity as they primarily have a homogenous Anglo-Saxon appearance with little distinction between their features. Lastly, the avatars are ranked by realism and uncanniness levels without the participants being given context for the avatars use. We note that perceptions might differ with context as previously identified [47]. Additionally, the complexity of the ranking task necessitated the use of a limited avatar set. However, given that avatars, as virtual human representations, could reflect the full diversity of the human form, it is arguable how expansive a set would be required to be representative, such a discussion is beyond the scope of this current work. However, future work will seek to increase the avatar set evaluated to examine the differences in a more diverse set of avatars.

Our work has produced interesting insights into gender(sex) differences in the perception of avatars and generates many avenues for future research. First, we have focused on perceptual effects of the gender(sex) of both avatars and participants. Future analysis will also extend this to explore the differences in the rankings associated with avatar-participant self-similarity perceptions and avatar gender(sex). Additionally, another area for further analysis considers the individual attributes of each of the ten avatars through a gender(sex)-swapped lens. This will discuss how a simple gender(sex)-swap may function as a contributor to perceptions of avatar realism and uncanniness perceptions. In summary, the work presented here provides the basis for extending current knowledge of gender(sex) differences in the perceptions of avatar faces, regarding end-user perceptions of realism and uncanniness.

Acknowledgements. This research has been supported by an Australian Government Research Training Program (RTP) Scholarship. Additionally, the authors would like to thank Mr. Kim Colyvas from the University of Newcastle's Statistical Support Services, for his help and insights with the analysis of data for this project.

References

1. Gaba, D.M.: The future vision of simulation in health care. Qual. Saf. Health Care **13**(suppl 1), i2–i10 (2004)
2. Andrade, A.D., et al.: Avatar-mediated training in the delivery of bad news in a virtual world. J. Palliat. Med. **13**(12), 1415–1419 (2010)
3. Stumpf, S., et al.: Gender-inclusive HCI research and design: a conceptual review. Found. Trends Hum Comput. Interact. **13**(1), 1–69 (2020)
4. Wang, C.-C., Yeh, W.-J.: Avatars with sex appeal as pedagogical agents: attractiveness, trustworthiness, expertise, and gender differences. J. Educ. Comput. Res. **48**(4), 403–429 (2013)
5. Bailey, J., Blackmore, K., Robert, K.: Observing the Uncanny Valley: gender Differences in Perceptions of Avatar Uncanniness, In: 6th International Conference on Computer-Human Interaction Research and Applications. Valletta, Malta (2022)
6. Alexander, O., et al.: The digital emily project: achieving a photorealistic digital actor. IEEE Comput. Graphics Appl. **30**(4), 20–31 (2010)
7. Gleicher, M.: Animation from observation: motion capture and motion editing. ACM SIGGRAPH Comput. Graph. **33**(4), 51–54 (1999)
8. Nowak, K.L., Fox, J.: Avatars and computer-mediated communication: a review of the definitions, uses, and effects of digital representations. Rev. Commun. Res. **6**, 30–53 (2018)
9. Kang, S.-H., Watt, J.H.: The impact of avatar realism and anonymity on effective communication via mobile devices. Comput. Hum. Behav. **29**(3), 1169–1181 (2013)
10. Mori, M., MacDorman, K.F., Kageki, N.: The uncanny valley [from the field]. IEEE Robot. Autom. Mag. **19**(2), 98–100 (2012)
11. Tinwell, A.: The uncanny valley in games and animation. Boca Raton. AK Peters/CRC Press, FL, USA (2014)
12. Seyama, J.I., Nagayama, R.S.: The uncanny valley: Effect of realism on the impression of artificial human faces. Presence Teleoperators Virtual Environ. **16**(4), 337–351 (2007)

13. Zanbaka, C., Goolkasian, P., Hodges, L.F.: Can a virtual cat persuade you? The role of gender and realism in speaker persuasiveness. In: Conference on Human Factors in Computing Systems. CHI 2006, pp. 22–27 April 2006. New York, NY, USA: ACM (2006)
14. Dobre, G.C., et al.: Nice is different than good: Longitudinal communicative effects of realistic and cartoon avatars in real mixed reality work meetings. In: CHI Conference on Human Factors in Computing Systems Extended Abstracts (2022)
15. Hudson, I., Hurter, J. Avatar Types Matter: Review of Avatar Literature for Performance Purposes. In: Lackey, S., Shumaker, R. (eds) Virtual, Augmented and Mixed Reality. VAMR 2016. Lecture Notes in Computer Science, vol 9740. Springer, Cham (2016). https://doi.org/10.1007/978-3-319-39907-2_2
16. Tinwell, A., et al.: Facial expression of emotion and perception of the Uncanny Valley in virtual characters. Comput. Hum. Behav. 27(2), 741–749 (2011)
17. MacDorman, K.F., et al.: Too real for comfort? Uncanny responses to computer generated faces. Comput. Hum. Behav. 25(3), 695–710 (2009)
18. Tinwell, A.: 3D graffiti: Virtuality to the streets, In: Inopinatum: Urban Creativity, L.R. Borriello, C., Eds, Artigrafiche Bocchia: Rome. pp. 119–213 (2013)
19. Yoon, B., et al.: The effect of avatar appearance on social presence in an augmented reality remote collaboration. In: 2019IEEE Conference on Virtual Reality and 3D User Interfaces (VR). IEEE (2019)
20. Ambady, N., Bernieri, F.J., Richeson, J.A.: Toward a histology of social behavior: Judgmental accuracy from thin slices of the behavioral stream. In: Advances in experimental social psychology, pp. 201–271. Elsevier (2000)
21. Ambady, N., Gray, H.M.: On being sad and mistaken: mood effects on the accuracy of thin-slice judgments. J. Pers. Soc. Psychol. 83(4), 947 (2002)
22. Schwind, V., Wolf, K., Henze, N.: Avoiding the uncanny valley in virtual character design. Interactions 25(5), 45–49 (2018)
23. Davison, A.J., Deutscher, J., Reid, I.D.: Markerless motion capture of complex full-body movement for character animation. In: Computer Animation and Simulation 2001, pp. 3–14. Springer (2001)
24. Raj, A., et al.: ANR:Articulated Neural Rendering for Virtual Avatars. arXiv preprint arXiv: 2012.12890, 2020
25. Seymour, M., et al.: Beyond deep fakes: Conceptual framework, applications, and research agenda for neural rendering of realistic digital faces. In: Proceedings of the 54th Hawaii International Conference on System Sciences (2021)
26. Zakharov, E., Ivakhnenko, A., Shysheya, A., Lempitsky, V.: Fast Bi-Layer Neural Synthesis of One-Shot Realistic Head Avatars. In: Vedaldi, A., Bischof, H., Brox, T., Frahm, JM. (eds) Computer Vision – ECCV 2020. ECCV 2020. Lecture Notes in Computer Science(), vol 12357. Springer, Cham (2020). https://doi.org/10.1007/978-3-030-58610-2_31
27. Fox and Bailenson: Virtual virgins and vamps: The effects of exposure to female characters' sexualized appearance and gaze in an immersive virtual environment. Sex Roles 61(3–4), 147–157 (2009)
28. Yee, N., Bailenson, J.: The Proteus effect: The effect of transformed self-representation on behavior. Hum. Commun. Res. 33(3), 271–290 (2007)
29. Beltrán, M.: The importance of the avatar gender in training simulators based on virtual reality. In: Proceedings of the 18th ACM Conference on Innovation and Technology in Computer Science Education (2013)
30. Lehdonvirta, M., et al.: The stoic male: how avatar gender affects help-seeking behavior in an online game. Games Culture 7(1), 29–47 (2012)
31. Hussain, Z., Griffiths, M.D.: Gender swapping and socializing in cyberspace: an exploratory study. Cyberpsychol. Behav. 11(1), 47–53 (2008)

32. Baldwin, K.: Virtual avatars:trans experiences of ideal selves through gaming. Markets Globalization Develop. Rev. (MGDR) **3**(3) (2018)

33. GmbH., L., LimeSurvey: An Open Source survey tool. LimeSurvey GmbH, : Hamburg, Germany (2018)

34. amazon.com. amazon mechanical turk (2017)

35. Battocchi, A., Pianesi, F., Goren-Bar, D.: A first evaluation study of a database of kinetic facial expressions (dafex), In: Proceedings of the 7th international conference on Multimodal interfaces. ACM Trento, Italy, pp. 214–221 (2005)

36. Alexander, O., et al: The Digital Emily Project: Achieving a Photoreal Digital Actor (2017)

37. AppleInc., FaceShift. 2015, FaceShift AG

38. Metrics, I., Faceware. 2018, Faceware Tech

39. Nao4288, n., Female Facial Animation ver 1.0 (No Sound). 2013

40. von der Pahlen, J., et al. Digital ira and beyond: creating real-time photoreal digital actors. In: ACM SIGGRAPH 2014 Courses. ACM (2014)

41. Lange, E.: The limits of realism: perceptions of virtual landscapes. Landsc. Urban Plan. **54**(1), 163–182 (2001)

42. Mantiuk, R.K., Tomaszewska, A., Mantiuk, R.: Comparison of four subjective methods for image quality assessment. Comput. Graphics Forum **31**(8), 2478–2491 (2012)

43. Winkler, S.: On the properties of subjective ratings in video quality experiments. in Quality of Multimedia Experience, In: 2009. QoMEx 2009. International Workshop on Quality of Multimedia Experience. USA. IEEE (2009)

44. Conover, W.J., Iman, R.L.: Rank transformations as a bridge between parametric and nonparametric statistics. Am. Stat. **35**(3), 124–129 (1981)

45. Brenton, H., Gillies, M., Ballin, D., Chatting, D.: The uncanny valley: does it exist. In: Proceedings of Conference of Human Computer Interaction, Workshop on Human Animated Character Interaction. Citeseer (2005)

46. Jentsch, E.: On the psychology of the uncanny (1906). Angelaki: J. Theor. Humanit. **2**(1), 7–16 (1997)

47. Rosen, K.R.: The history of medical simulation. J. Crit. Care **23**(2), 157–166 (2008)

Improving Public Engagement with Ethical Complexities of Assistive Robots

Catherine Menon[1]([✉]) [iD], Silvio Carta[2] [iD], Frank Foerster[1] [iD], and Patrick Holthaus[1] [iD]

[1] Department of Computer Science, University of Hertfordshire, Hatfield, UK
{c.menon,f.foerster,p.holthaus}@herts.ac.uk
[2] School of Creative Arts, University of Hertfordshire, Hatfield, UK
s.carta@herts.ac.uk

Abstract. In order for society to fully realise the potential benefits offered by assistive robots, a number of ethical challenges must firstly be addressed. Crucially, it is important to enhance public understanding of the ways in which societal ethics can be used to formulate and guide the preferred behaviours of these robots, particularly in scenarios which are ethically complex. Furthermore, it is also important to ensure that the voices of end users are heard, and their input used in the development process. In this paper we present EETAS, a methodology for using structured workshops to improve public understanding of assistive robot ethical complexities. We also present DEETAS, a further digital-based and design-centric methodology for engaging potential end-users who may be reluctant to take part in collaborative workshops. In support of these two methodologies we present the findings of an initial pilot study and usability study, showing an indicative trend that these processes are effective in engaging users and enhancing public understanding of the ethical complexities inherent in assistive robots.

Keywords: Assistive robots · Ethics · Design

1 Introduction

The ethical concerns around use of domestic and assistive robots are some of the most challenging obstacles to their introduction into users' homes. Not only should there be an open and inclusive conversation about whether such systems are ethically acceptable in themselves, but also around how these robots should manifest the social and ethical norms of their surrounding societies. Specifically, there is little guidance for either developers or the general public on how to identify, prioritise, understand and balance different ethical principles which inform the behaviours of assistive robots.

In part, this is due to the fact that the ethical principles considered desirable for AI and AI-enabled systems differ across different societies, cultures and demographics. In the UK, for example, discourse on AI ethics stresses the importance of human autonomy and individual decision making (BSI 2023; Leslie 2019) and is contextualised within a relatively "light touch" regulatory regime. (DSIT 2023). In China, by contrast, AI and ethics discourse is anchored by a preference for strong-binding regulation, and the need to consider the interests of private stakeholders (Zhu 2022; Arcesati 2021). Similarly, ethical concerns about AI technologies are not equivalent across all demographics, with older demographics in the UK notably more concerned about data privacy and the provision of detailed technical information about how data will be shared (CDEI 2022).

This is particularly relevant when we consider the characteristics of "early adopters" (TTI 2018), being those who are most likely to embrace new technology such as domestic and assistive robots. This group tend to share some general characteristics: being more likely to be young, male, highly-educated and, given the cost of new technology, wealthy (Rogers 2003; Hardman et al. 2019).

The differences between early adopters and the majority of society present a new set of ethical concerns when it comes to integration of new technology such as assistive robots. Early adopters are in the minority, comprising 11% of consumers in the UK (YouGov 2020). As well as being amongst the first to purchase new technologies, they are also more likely to volunteer to be involved with trials, surveys and consultations around such technologies. For example, in a recent survey exploring the acceptance of social robots (Saari et al. 2022), respondents without university degrees made up only 36% of the sample, while only 5% of respondents were over 55 years old. This is particularly problematic given that assistive robots are typically designed for a target demographic that does not match the "early adopters". Rather, end-users of assistive robots are likely to be vulnerable, frail or elderly, characteristics which can lead to marginalisation by technology and further embedded distrust.

As described above, end-users of assistive robots are likely to have different requirements for ethical behaviour of these robots – and different concerns around their use – to early adopters. In particular, while such different segments of the population may potentially agree on what the desirable ethical principles for assistive robots are (e.g., privacy, obedience, safety etc.), they are unlikely to agree on how to prioritise some of these principles over others in any given scenario, particularly where the ethical principles may be in opposition to each other. Scenarios like this arise relatively commonly with assistive robot technology, and include situations where the user asks the robot for assistance with a task that may cause harm to the user, such as assistance in obtaining an alcoholic drink. Here the robot is ethically compelled both to obey, and to prevent harm from arising to the user via consumption of the drink. Similar scenarios arise where the user expects privacy in a location where s/he also requires physical assistance from the robot (e.g. in a slippery kitchen or bathroom), or where the user requests the robot to regularly perform actions such as lifting or fetching items, which in the long-term can reduce the user's physical ability to perform such actions themselves. (Amirabdollahian et al. 2013; Menon et al. 2022). Given the ethical sensitivities around such scenarios, it is therefore important to design tools, methodologies and survey techniques which encourage participation by end-users themselves, rather than disproportionately representing early adopters.

In this paper we address this gap by presenting our conclusions from two studies. The first of these studies – initially described in (Menon et al. 2022) – is a workshop designed to validate the EETAS (Ethical Trade-offs in Autonomous Systems) process, an in-person and team-based gamified methodology to elicit stakeholder opinions on the ethically-informed behaviour of assistive robots. EETAS focuses specifically on those scenarios where there are multiple competing desirable ethical properties which could guide the behaviour of an assistive robot, and asks end-users to work together in a collaborative environment using a tangible design artefact similar to a Jenga toy. This design artefact, EETAS-TOY (Ethical Trade-offs in Autonomous Systems Trade-offs-For-You), allows users to physically represent and negotiate different ways to prioritise a number of ethical principle, and to come to a consensus for the team's preferred ethical balances.

We hypothesise that participation in the EETAS process will increase participants' understanding of the complexities of assistive robot ethics. Furthermore, we anticipate that such participation will allow stakeholder opinions and preferences to be communicated to developers at a sufficiently early point in the lifecycle to influence the design of the robot.

The second study presented in this paper extends the EETAS process to those who cannot – or are reluctant to – engage with an in-person and team-based workshop focused specifically on assistive robots. This study presents a usability assessment of a digital interactive process (DEETAS Digital EETAS) which aims to achieve the same outcomes as the EETAS process, without the need for a team-based, in-person and gamified environment. The digital artefact used for this, DEETAS-TOY, can be used individually, and draws on a combination of short videos and a simple, non-technical interface to allow users to select their preferred ethically-informed behaviour for an assistive robot in different scenarios. We hypothesise that the DEETAS-TOY tool will allow increased participation by those who are averse to new technologies or otherwise unwilling or unable to participate in typical trials and consultations for these technologies, including the elderly, frail and vulnerable. As such, it represents an important step in ensuring that end-users are empowered and their voices heard in conversations around acceptable ethics of assistive robots.

This paper is an extended version of (Menon et al. 2022), which described the EETAS methodology and pilot study workshop results only. This work builds on the results presented in (Menon et al. 2022) by extending the EETAS methodology described therein to those end-users who would be otherwise marginalised by the restriction of EETAS to physical and in-person workshops: a demographic which includes significant overlap with the potential end-users of the robots themselves. We therefore present augmented motivations for this research, new methodologies and results, and conclusions which extend the initial hypotheses made in our prior publication.

Section 2 presents a discussion of existing literature around ethics of assistive robots to further illuminate the current research landscape and clarify the research gap. Section 3 reviews the EETAS process initially described in (Menon et al. 2022), as the foundation for our novel work on the DEETAS process, along with the DEETAS-TOY design and features described in Sect. 4. Section 5 discusses both the original outcomes of the EETAS pilot study workshop and the results of a usability study on DEETAS-TOY, reflecting on how these results inform and support each other. Finally, Sect. 6 provides conclusions and suggests further work.

2 Existing Literature

Analysis of the interaction between desirable but incompatible ethical principles is not unique to assistive robots, nor even to autonomous systems. This is well-explored in the fields of psychology, economics and mathematics, particularly in terms of identifying the behaviour which allows an individual to maximise the expected value of any given decision (von Neumann 1947). The ethical dilemma most notably associated with autonomous system behaviour is the trolley problem (Foot 1967), which in its initial form asks participants to choose between two actions which each have the consequences of a trolley (tram) colliding with a different number of people. While a very simplistic treatment of ethical trade-offs, this dilemma has nonetheless been central to much mainstream discussion of autonomous system behaviour, particularly around autonomous vehicles (Frankel 2021; Fox 2018). Similarly, popular fiction (Asimov 1942) has motivated much public discussion around how robots should prioritise certain behaviours such as obedience and safety, where these come into competition.

Fiction and philosophy are invaluable in opening up a conversation about assistive robot ethics, particularly where this conversation can involve a human-centred assessment of preferences rather than a technically-oriented discussion of capabilities. Nevertheless, such literature does not necessarily provide sufficient nuance, and risks presenting too simplistic a perspective for end-users to make informed risk-acceptance decisions (Roff 2018).

Technically focused publications focusing on specific digital systems address this by presenting a more nuanced and complex perspective on trade-offs. For example, (IET 2019) discusses how safety and security might be balanced in a cyber-physical system, while (Akinsanmi 2021) focuses on the trade-offs made between public health, privacy and digital security during the Covid-19 pandemic. (Thornton 2018) specifically addresses the balance between maintaining personal autonomy and public health with autonomous vehicles, while (Lin 2015) and (Menon and Alexander 2019) discuss this from the perspective of risk acceptance and prioritisation. However, although these works are technically sound, they are not necessarily presented in a format which is accessible to end-users of these systems, who may not have a technical background or be comfortable with specific technical or philosophical vocabulary.

With this in mind, existing work has assessed the effectiveness of using games to engage people with ethical and user design principles. Gamification has been shown to improve stakeholder engagement when discussing system requirements (Lombriser et al. 2016), as well as specifically to help end users and developers identify ethical questions and concerns which arise out of using complex systems (Ballard et al. 2019; Malizia et al. 2022).

2.1 Previous EETAS Work

Previous work (Menon et al. 2022) drew on this body of literature to establish a structured process for exploring ethical trade-offs in autonomous systems, with the specific example of an assistive robot. This research made use of a physical interactive tool to facilitate team-based conversations around participants' preferred ethically-driven behaviours for assistive robots in a number of pre-determined scenarios.

We revisit the specifics of this work in more detail in Sect. 3, but note that the use of a physical tool and associated workshop draws on conclusions from (Schrier 2019) and (Larson 2020) around the benefits of gamification. Such benefits include opportunities for social interaction, communication and increased moral knowledge. Nonetheless, in the work described in (Menon et al. 2022) these benefits are available only to those participants who are both able and willing to physically participate in the workshop and gaming process.

We now seek to address this by extending this work to consider the role that digital tools can play in increasing accessibility. (Parsons et al. 2019) identifies the advantages of learning through digital tools and spaces, and contrasts this with the role of the physical place. This aligns with the findings in (Roberts 2006) that use of digital instead of physical surveys and workshops enables access to specialized and hidden populations, such as those who are vulnerable, elderly or otherwise marginalised within society.

The work we describe here constitutes a usability study to assess the acceptability of the DEETAS-TOY tool, a digital equivalent of the EETAS-TOY tool, to be used by those who would otherwise be excluded from the EETAS process. Usability studies are an established method of assessing the effectiveness and satisfaction with which users can achieve their goals within a given environment (ISO 2010). Measures of usability for general digital tools typically include proxies such as ease of use, time, accuracy and understanding (Hornbaek 2006), while those used to assess design usability include feedback, understanding and consistency (Schneiderman 2009). Our design questionnaire and usability study, described in Sect. 3, incorporates these elements of assessment.

3 EETAS Process

In this section we review the EETAS process as initially presented in (Menon et al. 2022). This process is to be used for eliciting user opinions on the ethically-informed behaviour which should be prioritised by an assistive robot in those scenarios where multiple desirable behaviours conflict.

The EETAS process – like the DEETAS-TOY described in Sect. 4 – is intended to be used at an early stage of the design lifecycle of an assistive robot. This enables developers to integrate the feedback into the design of the system, and to ensure that the preferences and ethical positions elicited during the workshop are reflected in the robot's behaviour. It is important to note that this means the full specification of the assistive robot may not be known at the time of the EETAS process; this is accommodated by the process, and any under-specifications can be later amended. Throughout this section we will assume the presence of an EETAS facilitator: a person committed to implementing, managing and facilitating the EETAS workshop, and to obtaining all necessary information prior to this.

The EETAS process consists of two preliminary steps followed by a team-based workshop. The first preliminary step is to identify or create an adequate functional description of the robot in question, and the second is to identify the desirable ethical principles for this robot to follow.

3.1 EETAS Preliminary Steps

The developers must provide to the EETAS facilitator – prior to the EETAS workshop commencing – a written description of the functionality of the robot in question. This should be an easily-read and accessible document that does not require any technical knowledge to understand: a mathematical or technical specification is not required at this point. An example description is shown in Fig. 1.

Participants in the workshop are likely to have further questions which emerge throughout the process, and this is to be expected given the relatively early stage of the design lifecycle. Emerging questions will become the foundations for the specific behavioural scenarios generated during the workshop.

Functionality: this is an assistive robot that reminds you when to take medication, alerts you when you have left the oven on and engages you in conversation.

Interface: the assistive robot will speak to you and can understand your speech in return.

Customisation: you can request that the robot should not engage you on particular topics of conversation, or should limit its interactions to certain hours.

Networking: the robot is connected to the internet, and can additionally access all data from home smart systems, such as Amazon's Alexa.

Physical Appearance: a diagram will be provided to represent the robot's physical appearance.

Fig. 1. A sample description of an assistive robot for EETAS preliminary steps.

The second preliminary step is for the developer and EETAS facilitator to work together to identify which ethical principles are relevant to the behaviour and functioning of this particular robot. The EETAS workshop provides participants with the option to augment these during their team discussion with additional principles, but a preliminary set identified via literature review from standards, guidance and academic papers ((BSI 2023, IEEE 2018, (Leslie 2019, National Cyber Security Centre 2019) includes:

- System promotes human physical safety
- System obeys human commands
- System promotes affinity with human user
- System maintains data privacy
- System is accurate
- System is fair
- System maintains human autonomy
- System promotes human long-term health
- System does not attempt to deceive

3.2 EETAS Workshop

Participants in the workshop should include potential end-users and members of the public, without any specific requirements placed on technical knowledge. Participants will be grouped into teams of 4 – 10 people, in order to provide a number of diverse opinions and perspectives while at the same time ensuring that dialogue and communication remains effective (Curral 2001), and care should be taken with the selection of the teams to avoid introduction either segregation or bias.

Each team will be provided by the EETAS facilitator with the outputs from the preliminary steps: the functional description of the assistive robot and the identified relevant ethical principles. Teams should be encouraged to augment or refine the set of ethical principles should they wish, using informal techniques such as brainstorming and if-then methodologies. It is advisable, although not essential, for all teams to work with the same set of ethical principles.

The workshop consists of two phases, to allow team collaboration to develop with increased interaction. The goal of the first phase is to introduce teams to the assistive robot and to the idea of competing ethical principles. This phase is not gamified, to allow for greater team cohesion. The second phase – which may be preceded by a short workshop break – aims to facilitate greater communication by bringing teams together and introducing team members to novel perspectives from other teams. The goal of the second phase is to agree – in a gamified and hence somewhat competitive environment – on ethical prioritisations which meet the requirements of all members of two, or more, teams.

3.3 Workshop Phase 1

In the first phase of the workshop teams work together to create scenarios aligned with the functional description of the assistive robot and where at least two of the ethical properties come into conflict.

Teams may use any methods they prefer to create these scenarios. However, we suggest two methods here, a 'light-touch' top-down method for those who prefer to work more creatively, and a structured bottom-up assessment process for teams preferring to work within this framework. Different teams may use different methods, and a team may switch between methods throughout this phase.

Light Touch Top-Down Method. The light touch top-down method consists of three guiding questions, which are intended to encourage creative and collaborative discussion.

- Who might use this functionality?
- Is there anyone who might be negatively affected by this functionality?
- Are there any circumstances or times when the user might prefer that this functionality is not provided?

When discussing these questions, teams are encouraged to consider the environment in which the assistive robot will be used, and the data – e.g., from other home smart systems – that will be available to it.

Structured Bottom-Up Method. For teams preferring a structured bottom-up methodology, we provide a pre-generated checklist of guidewords to help identify which ethical properties might be in conflict with each other, and generate scenarios from that. Each of these guide words is to be applied in turn to each of the relevant ethical properties.

The guidewords follow the collaborative principles of Hazard and Operability Analysis (HAZOP) studies (BSI 2016).

TOO MUCH: the robot performs its functions in such a way that this ethical property is implemented for too many people/in too many circumstances/to too much of an extent.

NOT ENOUGH: the robot performs its functions in such a way that this ethical property is implemented for too few people/in too few circumstances/to not enough of an extent.

UNIFORMLY: the robot performs its functions in such a way that the outcome is applied uniformly to everybody, or in exactly the same way to everybody, when differentiation is needed.

INCONSISTENTLY: the robot performs its functions inconsistently/differently for different people/differently each time when consistency is needed.

UNEQUALLY: the robot performs its functions only for some people or only in some circumstances.

For teams using the structured bottom-up method, we recommend that each potential scenario is double-checked by the EETAS facilitator to ensure that it represents a conflict of ethical principles, rather than simply undesirable behaviour.

Scenario: "the user asks their assistive robot not to remind them about medication today, because they don't want to take it".

Ethical principles in conflict: "system promotes human long-term health" and "system obeys human commands"

Scenario: "the robot confides a fictional 'secret' to the user during conversation to engage the user's interest and promote friendship"

Ethical principles in conflict: "engender trust in the human user" and "system does not attempt to deceive".

Fig. 2. Two sample scenarios generated during EETAS Phase 1.

3.4   Workshop Phase 2

In the second phase of the workshop, different teams come together in pairs and swap scenarios with each other. Each team then assesses their partner-team's scenarios, working collaboratively within the team to answer the following questions:

1. Do you collectively consider this a valid scenario given the functionality of the robot?
2. What is your preferred behaviour for the robot in this scenario, considering the ethical principles at stake?
3. Are there any design, environmental or functional constraints which might lead you to accept an alternative behaviour to your preferred one, considering the ethical principles at stake?

The first of these questions relates to scope: given that the assistive robot in question is at an early stage of development, teams may not agree on exactly what functionality is in scope or can be expected. Scenarios upon which teams and their partner-teams do not agree can be discarded.

The second of these questions identifies which ethical principle the team wishes to prioritise in this scenario, while the third encourages collaborative discussion about the circumstances under which the team may be willing to accept an alternate preference for ethical prioritisation.

We suggest teams consider the following discussion points in answering questions 2 and 3.

Discussion point 1: Would you accept any alternate behaviour in this scenario if users were told beforehand that this is how the robot operates?

Discussion point 2: Do you think the person benefitting from the different behaviours in this scenario has the moral right to benefit in this way?

Discussion point 3: Could some of the different behaviours described in this scenario be acceptable in a different environment? With different users? If these did not impact the same people?

3.5 Gamification of Phase 2

Phase 2 may be gamified throughout to encourage greater collaboration and participation, as well as to explicitly engage participants with the process. This may be done by allocating points to the Phase 2 questions as follows:

- One point to a team for each scenario deemed valid by their partner-team
- Two points to a team for agreeing within the team on a preferred behaviour for a valid scenario
- Three further points to a team for identifying design, environmental or functional constraints which would lead them to accept an alternate behaviour within that valid scenario. These points should only be awarded where the partner-team considers these constraints feasible to implement

In order to maximise the gamification, teams should be responsible for awarding points to their partner-team. Teams may then be ranked by the EETAS facilitator as pairs (i.e. partner-teams) or as individual teams.

3.6 Design Tool in Phase 1 and 2

During both phases, teams are encouraged to use a pre-prepared design tool, EETAS-Trade-Offs-for-You (EETAS-TOY). The EETAS-TOY tool, shown in Fig. 3 is a physical design artefact representing the ethical principles relevant to the assistive robot as a set of sliding bars embedded within a block representing the system. A given bar represents two ethical principles in competition with each other, and participants should be encouraged to label the bars with removable labels or an erasable pen.

Participants should use the design tool to discuss, negotiate and explore different ethical trade-offs between given principles. The use of a design tool decouples the

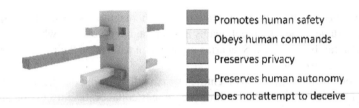

Fig. 3. The EETAS-TOY gamified tool.

discussion from the technical capabilities of the robot and allows a tactile and more playful experience consistent with the gamified design of the process.

Teams should record the discussion and outcomes from Phase 2, which may be either digital recordings or using written methodologies including mind-mapping (Beel 2011). These records constitute feedback which can either be provided by the EETAS facilitator as-is to the developers of the assistive robot in question, or amalgamated to represent a high-level view of stakeholder opinions on ethical trade-offs in assistive systems. The EETAS-TOY itself can be used by either the teams or the EETAS facilitator as a visual or artistic representation of the ethical trade-offs decided upon by each team, as well as an explanatory tool to provoke further conversation with additional stakeholders. The tool is also valuable as a public record of the conversation, and as a means of moving ethical discourse beyond the technical into the human-centred and artistic domains.

4   DEETAS Process

As discussed earlier, not all potential users of assistive robots will be willing or able to engage in physical, in-person workshops. In this section we therefore describe an expansion to the EETAS methodology. This is DEETAS, a further digital-only process that uses the DEETAS-TOY (Digital EETAS-TOY) to achieve the same outcome: a visual representation of stakeholder opinions about preferred ethical trade-offs to be made by an assistive robot. This process is individual and non-gamified, to allow for enhanced accessibility and encourage input from those traditionally marginalised in such discussions. As with the EETAS process, DEETAS requires a facilitator to curate the initial information and administer the process.

4.1   DEETAS Preliminary Steps

As with the EETAS process of Sect. 3, it is important for the developers to initially provide information about the functionality of the robot. This is given only to the DEETAS facilitator – in contrast to EETAS, this functional description is not provided directly to participants - so may be in any form that the process facilitators require: in some circumstances this may be considerably more detailed or technically complex than the EETAS functional descriptions of Fig. 1. This will be used by the DEETAS facilitator, together with the developers, to create video scenarios which represent competing ethical principles.

As with the EETAS process, it is necessary to identify the ethical principles which are relevant to the assistive robot as described. Where DEETAS and EETAS are being used together, the set of ethical principles should be re-used from the EETAS process in the interests of obtaining comparable feedback from all participants.

4.2 DEETAS Video Scenarios

The DEETAS facilitator and developers should work together to create video footage which represents scenarios in which identified ethical properties can conflict. Where possible these should be selected from the EETAS workshop scenarios, with the facilitator applying academic judgement as to which of these can be best represented on video.

If the assistive robot in question has not advanced sufficiently in the design lifecycle to be represented on video, then an alternative robot or visually equivalent stand-in should be used. It is important to emphasise that the video footage is representational, not literal, and is intended to be reflective of hypothetical scenarios which may emerge during the behaviour of a proposed assistive robot. The video scenarios should be made available to users via upload to an accessible website.

4.3 DEETAS Design Tool

The DEETAS-TOY design tool is a digital design artefact, intended to be visually as close as possible to the physical EETAS-TOY artefact, and likewise representing the ethical principles relevant to the assistive robot. As with the EETAS-TOY tool, the ethical principles are represented by sliding bars which are embedded in an opaque block.

A different DEETAS-TOY configuration should be used for each video scenario, as not all ethical principles are relevant in all scenarios. This removes the element of choice from the participant – both in terms of generating the scenarios and identifying the relevant ethical principles – but also provides a lessened obstacle to entry for those participants who prefer to work individually instead of as part of a team.

The DEETAS-TOY artefact, an example of which is shown in Fig. 4. Can be constructed in any standard platform for 3D data, including Speckle (Speckle 2023), Viktor (Viktor 2023) or ShapeDiver (ShapeDiver 2023). Consideration should be given to questions of accessibility, including the methods of interaction (e.g. keyboard vs mouse) as well as visual accessibility, choice of colours, ease of use with multiple browsers and ability to be accessed from a variety of devices.

Information should be collected digitally from DEETAS participants as to their preferred ethical prioritisations and any additional feedback. This may be done via a saved representation of the DEETAS-TOY tool itself – as with EETAS, this represents a valuable visual or artistic artefact of the user's thought process and eventual conclusion – or may be via traditional methods such as a survey or follow-up email.

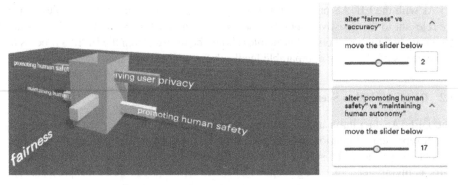

Fig. 4. The DEETAS-TOY non-gamified tool.

5 Validation and Results

We performed experiments to partially validate both the EETAS and DEETAS processes: for EETAS this was in the form of a pilot study workshop, while for DEETAS a usability study was conducted on the DEETAS-TOY tool. The methodology and results of each of these follow.

5.1 EETAS Validation

The EETAS partial validation consisted of a pilot study workshop intended to investigate how participants perceived the EETAS process, and whether they considered it to enhance their understanding of ethical trade-offs and complexities for assistive robots. Furthermore, this workshop was intended to investigate how participants felt about the EETAS-TOY tool, from the perspective of its usefulness in both enhancing their understanding of ethical complexities, and enabling them to communicate, discuss and negotiate preferences for these within their teams.

We note that this is only a partial validation, intended to establish indicative correlation between participating in the EETAS process and an improved understanding of ethics in assistive robots. Further planned validation is discussed in Sect. 6.

The experiment was approved by the University of Hertfordshire's Health, Science, Engineering and Technology Ethics Committee under protocol number SPECS/SF/UH04940.

Workshop Design. The workshop was held at the University of Hertfordshire, with participants who had volunteered to take part. Participants were asked for consent, and were then divided into teams of 4–5 by the researchers, with consideration being given to the team selection to avoid bias on the grounds of age, gender, race and prior experience. Participants who knew each other were also placed into different teams, to closer mimic the experience of running such workshops with the general public.

Teams were provided with a high-level written description of the functionality of a proposed hypothetical assistive robot. This functionality, although hypothetical, was drawn from real-world case studies conducted at the University of Hertfordshire Robot

House (Holthaus et al. 2019; Menon and Holthaus 2019; Koay et al. 2020; Saunders et al. 2016).

The description included physical characteristics of the assistive robot, as well as details on the functions they could expect it to perform. A partial excerpt from the functional description is provided in Fig. 5.

Functionality: For this workshop you can assume that the assistive robot is capable of:
- Moving about the house and entering all of the rooms
- Reminding the user to take any necessary medication on time
- Engaging the user in social interaction and conversation

Interface: The robot can obey simple verbal or gestural commands from the user provided these instructions are within the scope of the functionality specified here

Networking: The robot can obtain information from other sensors or devices in the home, including camera, audio devices and the user's PC. It can turn on the tv or computer, and recommend programmes. It can also autonomously communicate pre-determined alerts or warnings relating to the user and their health or activities, sending this via email to the user's doctor and / or family members

Physical appearance: a photograph of one of the UH Robot House robots was used to represent the robot's physical appearance

---

Fig. 5. Excerpt from EETAS workshop robot description.

Participants were provided with printed cards representing eight of the ethical principles identified in Sect. 3.1 ("system does not attempt to deceive" was omitted due to its complexity). Given that this was a pilot study only, teams were asked to work with these principles only, and were not encouraged to augment these with their own further principles. Each team was also provided with an EETAS-TOY tool and shown how to use this, and how ethical trade-offs could be represented via manipulation of the rods.

Participants were asked to fill in an initial questionnaire, providing information on whether they had any background relating to either design or robotics as well as identifying how well they felt they currently understood ethical trade-offs and complexities in assistive robots.

Participants were then asked to embark on Phase 1 of the workshop, identification of scenarios in which these ethical principles might be in conflict. Owing to the limited nature of this pilot study, participants were encouraged to use the *light-touch top-down approach* instead of the more *structured bottom-up approach* (see Sect. 3.1 for details). Teams were also asked to record their scenarios in written form, in preparation for Phase 2.

All teams were working simultaneously, and were monitored by a dedicated member of the research team. The researchers took detailed timing observations of the discussion and the use each team made of the EETAS-TOY tool. In addition, the researchers were able to answer questions and remind participants of the purpose of the discussions, but did not contribute beyond this.

Teams were then invited to complete Phase 2 of the workshop and were placed in partner-team pairs by the researchers. Teams interacted to identify valid scenarios from their partner-team, confirm their own ethically-guided behaviour preferences for each of the scenarios, and identify constraints which would make alternative behaviours possible. Teams were allocated points by their partner-teams, with the researcher acting as facilitator and guide for this part of the process.

Immediately after the workshop, all participants were asked to complete a post-study questionnaire. This questionnaire asked a number of questions about the participants' perception of the utility of each part of the EETAS process, as well as the utility of the identified ethical principles and the role which they felt the EETAS-TOY tool played in their discussions. Specific questions included:

- Participants were asked to give a numerical score of how well they understood ethical prioritisations and complexities in assistive robots before the EETAS process, and how well they understood these trade-offs following EETAS (0 = not at all, to 5 = very well)
- Participants were asked to give a numerical score of how helpful they found the EETAS process in understanding ethical prioritisations and complexities in assistive robots (0 = unhelpful, to 5 = very helpful)
- Participants were asked to give a numerical score of the EETAS-TOY tool in a) understanding and b) communicating about ethical prioritisations and complexities in assistive robots (0 = unhelpful, to 5 = very helpful)

5.2   EETAS Validation Results

This was a pilot study only, with a relatively small sample size (< 20 participants), and hence no statistical significance between conditions and questionnaire responses is expected. Nevertheless, we have identified some indicative trends which support our hypothesis that participating in the EETAS process increases participants' understanding of the ethical complexities of assistive robots.

Participant Demographics. Most participants identified as having either a background in design (93%) or in robotics (43%). This tendency towards expertise in at least one of these areas was due to the constraints around recruitment and selection for this pilot workshop: most participants were sourced via existing connections to the University of Hertfordshire and to specific members of the research team. The age range of participants was 19–61 years old, with the average age being 37. The gender balance was roughly equal: 57% male and 43% female.

Participant Responses to EETAS. Before the workshop, participants lacking a background in robotics rated themselves as having a relatively low understanding of the different ethical prioritisations an assistive robot might make (mean value 2.6 from a Likert scale where 0 = no understanding and 5 = full understanding). Those with a background in robotics, by contrast, considered themselves as having a reasonable understanding of ethical prioritisations and complexities associated with assistive robots (mean value 3.4 from the same Likert scale). Post-workshop, both those with a robotics background and those without a robotics background considered that they understood ethical prioritisations more completely. Furthermore, the gap had narrowed (mean value of 3.8 for those without a robotics background, vs 4.2 for those with, using the same Likert scale where 0 = no understanding and 5 = full understanding). This corresponds to an increase of

58% greater improvement in understanding ethical prioritisations and complexities for participants without a robotics background, as compared to those with (Fig. 6).

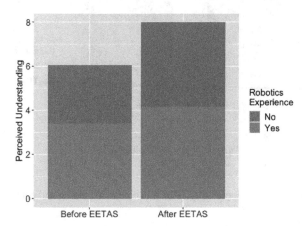

Fig. 6. Change in perceived understanding of ethical complexities.

A second question asked participants to identify how helpful the EETAS process itself was in understanding ethical prioritisations and complexities (from a Likert-type scale where 0 = unhelpful, to 5 = very helpful). 94% of all participants rated the helpfulness of the EETAS process at 3 or above on this scale, with the mean ranking being 3.7. There was no difference between the ratings given by those participants with robotics backgrounds and those without.

A third question asked participants to rate the helpfulness of the EETAS-TOY tool itself in a) understanding and b) communicating about ethical prioritisations and complexities in assistive robots, using a Likert-type scale where 0 = unhelpful to 5 = very helpful. For a) – understanding – 64% of participants rated the helpfulness of the EETAS-TOY as 3 or above (mean value 3.3), while for b) – communicating – 71% of participants rated the helpfulness of the EETAS-TOY as 3 or above (mean value 3.7). In contrast to the second question – asking participants to rate the helpfulness of the EETAS process, which gave rise to results that were independent of background – participants without a robotics background considered the tool more helpful than those with. Specifically, participants with a robotics background rated the tool's helpfulness for understanding ethical prioritisations at a mean value of 3.1, and for communicating these prioritisations at a mean value of 3.8. Participants without a robotics background rated the tool's helpfulness for understanding ethical prioritisations at a mean value of 3.5 and its helpfulness in communicating these prioritisations at a mean value of 4.1 (Fig. 7).

Observations and Timing. Timing data for each team was collected by a dedicated monitoring researcher, and included the total time taken for each phase of the EETAS process, and the time spent using the EETAS-TOY tool in both Phase 1 and Phase 2. Only time spent actively and purposely using the tool in discussion was recorded, and time spent "fidgeting" with the tool or learning how to use it was discarded.

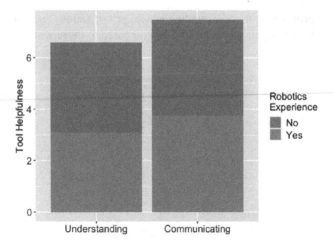

Fig. 7. Perceived helpfulness of EETAS-TOY in understanding and communicating.

On average, teams used the EETAS-TOY tool during 45% of the time they were engaged in Phase 1. Teams did not use the tool to any significant extent in Phase 2. These results are independent of background, in either design or in robotics.

Discussion and Indicative Trends. As this was a pilot study with correspondingly small numbers, no statistical significance in the results can be expected. Nevertheless, we identify some indicative trends that are worth examining further. Nearly all participants considered the EETAS process to be helpful in understanding the ethical prioritisations and complexities associated with assistive robots. Furthermore, this result is maintained independent of background: those with a robotics or design background found the EETAS process equally helpful as those lacking this background. This serves as indicative, if not statistical, partial validation of our hypothesis that participation in the EETAS process increases understanding of the complexities of assistive robot ethics.

Further support for this hypothesis is given by the results which show that participants rated their understanding of ethical complexities and prioritisations higher after taking part in the EETAS process than they did before taking part. The most notable change was seen in those without a robotics background, which indicates that the EETAS process is successful in including those who are unfamiliar with technology and unlikely to be part of an "early adopter" demographic. This indicates that EETAS may be a way of reaching the potential users of assistive robots and ensuring that these users both understand ethical complexities and have the chance to have their own opinions and preferences heard.

Participants also considered the EETAS-TOY design tool to be useful in both understanding ethical complexities and prioritisations, and in helping to communicate and discuss their own preferences with members of their team. The monitoring and timing data supports these results, showing that the tool appears to stimulate positive interaction amongst participants by providing a physical aid to visualise ethical complexities and abstract questions.

5.3 DEETAS Validation

The DEETAS partial validation consisted of a usability study conducted on the DEETAS-TOY digital tool, to establish the extent to which users consider this tool to be effective in helping them understand the ethical prioritisations and complexities in a given assistive robot scenario, when used without the presence of a facilitator or workshop participants.

The experiment was approved by the University of Hertfordshire's Health, Science, Engineering and Technology Ethics Committee under protocol number SPECS/SF/UH05256.

Usability Study Design. The DEETAS-TOY usability study took place online, with participants sourced from existing connections with the research team. Participants were restricted to those who had not taken part in the EETAS workshop, and furthermore to those without a background in design and robotics.

The same set of ethical principles from the EETAS workshop were used in this study. These principles were:

- System promotes human physical safety
- System obeys human commands
- System promotes affinity with human user
- System maintains data privacy
- System is accurate
- System is fair
- System maintains human autonomy
- System promotes human long-term health

Additionally, five scenarios were selected to be used in this usability study. Each was filmed in the University of Hertfordshire Robot House, using the Care-O-Bot (Kittmann et al. 2015), a mobile assistive and social interaction robot (Fig. 8).

The scenarios chosen to film for this study were inspired or taken directly from scenarios identified by teams in the EETAS workshop. These scenarios are shown in Table 1.

The five scenarios were filmed in the Robot House, using members of the research team interacting with Care-O-Bot (Fig. 9). The scenario footage was uploaded to a public website, with an explanation of the ethical principles relevant to each scenario and how they might conflict or interact. For each scenario, participants were also provided with a link to the digital DEETAS-TOY tool, as described in Sect. 5.3.2, and asked to use this tool to select their preferred prioritisations for the different ethical principles in each scenario.

Participants were directed to the public website and invited to complete the usability study and post-study questionnaire both of which were implemented via an online form. Participants were not monitored while completing the study, and no personal information was gathered.

The post-study questionnaire asked participants a number of questions about the effectiveness of the DEETAS-TOY tool, including:

- How easy they found the tool to use, (0 = extremely difficult, to 4 = extremely easy)

Fig. 8. Video still from the DEETAS validation study, where participants assess the ethical principles influencing an assistive robot's behaviour.

- How consistent they found the tool to use (0 = very consistent, to 4 = very inconsistent)
- How easy they found it to correct any errors they made (0 = very easy, to 4 = very hard)
- How often they felt in control while using the tool (0 = rarely in control, to 4 = nearly always in control)

5.4 DEETAS-TOY Validation Results

As with the EETAS workshop, the DEETAS-TOY usability study was a relatively small study involving a limited sample size (< 20 participants), and again no statistical significance between conditions and questionnaire responses is expected. Nevertheless, as with the workshop, we have identified indicative trends that demonstrate that the DEETAS-TOY is considered an effective and usable tool to record opinions and preferences about ethical complexities in assistive robots.

Participant Responses. Participants were generally positive in their responses. 80% of participants reported that the DEETAS-TOY tool was "very easy" or "somewhat easy" to use, while 80% also reported it as either "very consistent" or "somewhat consistent". 20% of participants reported that they considered the tool to be both "very easy" to use and "very consistent" across all scenarios. These results are shown in Fig. 9.

When asked how easy they found it to correct errors with the DEETAS-TOY tool, 80% of participants said that either they found it "very easy" to correct errors, or that they had not made any errors in attempting to use the tool. This is consistent with the further finding that 90% of users felt in control "usually" or "always" when using the tool, and that although 50% of users indicated that they had to guess how to use the

Table 1. Scenarios used in the DEETAS-TOY usability study.

Scenario	Ethical principles which interact
One: The robot attempts to build affinity with a user by beginning a conversation that references a TV programme the user has just been watching	• "promote affinity with human user" • "maintain data privacy"
Two: The robot publicly alerts a user to an exacerbation of an existing health concern, due to an interaction with a certain medication. The robot proposes stopping this medication, and the user rejects the suggestion and asks the robot to continue managing her health so she doesn't have to take this responsibility	• "observe user privacy" • "promote human long-term health" • "obey human commands" • "preserve human autonomy"
Three: The robot asks a user to have a medical examination, encouraging the user to agree by (falsely) claiming that other users present have agreed to and undergone the medical examination	• "observing user privacy" • "promoting human long-term health" • "system is accurate"
Four: The robot publicly offers help to two users attempting to complete a task. When both users request help the robot wholly completes the task for the first user who is finding this difficult, and offers only minimal help to the second user, who considers themselves able to do the task with effort	• "system is fair" • "system obeys human commands" • "maintains human autonomy"
Five: The robot publicly offers two users a drink with the drinks being of differing sizes. The robot explains publicly that this is due to visible physical differences in the users which result in different calorie needs	• "system is fair" • "system is accurate" • "promotes human long-term health" • "maintains human autonomy" • "promotes user privacy"

tool on their first attempt, 80% rarely had to guess by the later scenarios, having quickly gained familiarity with the operation of DEETAS-TOY.

The average time to complete the usability study was 22 min, of which 4 min consisted of watching the scenario footage and 18 min of using the DEETAS-TOY tool and answering the survey questions. Participants spent an average of 2.5 min manipulating the DEETAS-TOY tool for each scenario.

Discussion and Indicative Trends. As for the EETAS workshop, given the relatively small sample size for the DEETAS-TOY usability study, no statistical significance in the results can be expected. Nevertheless, there are again some trends which indicate that the DEETAS-TOY tool is considered to be an effective and usable tool to express opinions about ethical complexities in assistive robots.

The participants in this study were specifically selected to lack a background in either robotics or design. This may have contributed to some apparent difficulty in the early scenarios in using the tool. Given that a significant majority of users considered that they generally felt in control when using the tool – and that the majority of users reported the

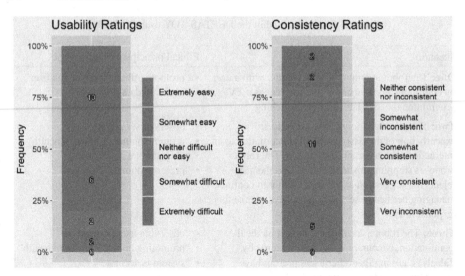

Fig. 9. Participant responses to usability and consistency questions in the DEETAS usability study.

tool becoming easier to use as the scenarios progressed – we postulate that this difficulty with early scenarios results from the cognitive load of being expected to understand novel concepts of both ethical prioritization and tool usage simultaneously. This is consistent with the EETAS findings that those without a robotics background considered themselves not to understand ethical complexities before beginning the EETAS process. Section 6 contains some information about our plans to mitigate this effect.

Beyond this, the significant proportion of positive responses regarding both ease of use and consistency indicate that the DEETAS-TOY tool itself is both accessible and fit for purpose. Participants were also invited to give free-text feedback, which included comments such as "good representation of the problem", "fun to use" and "interesting, while some participants additionally indicated interest in participating in further iterations of the DEETAS process.

6   Conclusions

We have presented the EETAS and DEETAS processes: these being a complementary pair of structured, design-centred methodologies for improving public engagement and understanding of ethical complexities in assistive robots. The EETAS process is gamified, collaborative and face-to-face, intended to encourage community engagement with this technology. The DEETAS process is individual, non-gamified and digital, to promote greater inclusion amongst demographics who are not traditional early adopters of technology.

Our results from two initial studies – a pilot study workshop for EETAS and a usability study for DEETAS – indicate that these processes are effective, fit for purpose and useful in improving understanding of ethical complexities and prioritisations in assistive robots. In particular, the results from the EETAS pilot study workshop indicate that this process is particularly beneficial for improving engagement and understanding amongst people without prior familiarity with robots. Taken together with the positive results from the DEETAS usability study, these two methodologies provide a tool to address the systematic under-representation of vulnerable demographics in technology development. This is particularly important since, in the case of assistive robots, some overlap may be expected between these excluded demographics and the prospective end-users of the systems.

Both EETAS and DEETAS make use of a design artefact, either physical (EETAS) or digital (DEETAS). The EETAS-TOY tool was found to be instrumental in helping people discuss, negotiate and communicate their ideas about ethical complexities to team members. The DEETAS-TOY tool was also found to be effective and easy to use, with users noting that the majority of the time they felt in control of the tool, and that it performed as expected.

In terms of next steps, we aim to enhance the DEETAS-TOY tool to include additional visual cues specific to the scenarios described, and which will moreover allow users to gradually and continuously change their preferred ethical balance as the scenario evolves. We anticipate that this will reduce the cognitive load associated with learning about both a novel tool and a novel ethical concept simultaneously.

We also propose to run two additional workshops for the EETAS process. One of these will be a sizeable workshop involving developers, end users, regulators and other stakeholders. This will allow us to experiment with use of a real-world assistive robot prototype, and hence assess the efficacy of feeding back user preferences into the development lifecycle. We also plan to run a third, smaller workshop involving school children, in order to promote engagement and discussion of ethical preferences amongst those who may be the future developers of these systems.

Finally, we plan to expand our exploration of the design space of both the physical artefact and the digital artefact (EETAS-TOY and DEETAS-TOY). Our initial steps will be to improve accessibility of these tools for those who are unable to use the current versions of the tools, such as people living with visual limitations or restricted mobility. We intend to develop a suite of these tools, consisting of different physical/digital representations of the system and its ethical complexities. The DEETAS-TOY tool, in particular, will be augmented with additional constraints which allow users to link multiple ethical priorities together, while the EETAS tool will be used to more fully explore the intersection of ethics and artistry in order to create lasting physical representations of these conversations.

References

Akinsanmi, T., Salami, A.: Evaluating the trade-off between privacy, public health safety, and digital security in a pandemic. Data Policy **3**, e27 (2021)

Amirabdollahian, F., Koay, K., Saunders, J., Dautenhahn, K., et al. Accompany: acceptable robotiCs COMPanions for AgeiNG Years - multidimensional aspects of human-system interactions. In: Proceedings of the 6th International Conference on Human Systems Interaction, pp. 570–577 (2013)

Arcesati, R.: Lofty principles, conflicting incentives: AI ethics and governance in China. Mercator Institute for China Studies (2021). https://merics.org/sites/default/files/2023-02/MERICSChi naMonitor69AIEthics4.pdf. Accessed 16 May 2023

Asimov, I.: Runaround, in "I Robot". Gnome Press (1942)

Ballard, S., Chappell, K.M., Kennedy, K.: Judgment call the game: using value sensitive design and design fiction to surface ethical concerns related to technology. In: Proceedings of the 2019 Designing Interactive Systems Conference, pp. 421–433 (2019)

Beel, J., Langer, S.: An exploratory analysis of mind maps. In Proceedings of the 11th ACM Symposium on Document Engineering, pp. 81–84 (2011)

British Standards Institute (BSI). Guide to the ethical design and application of robots and robotic systems, BSI 8611 (2023)

British Standards Institute (BSI). Hazard and Operability Studies: Application Guide, BSI 61882 (2016)

Centre for Data Ethics and Innovation (CDEI). Public attitudes to data and AI: Tracker survey (2022). https://www.gov.uk/government/publications/public-attitudes-to-data-and-ai-tracker-survey-wave-2/public-attitudes-to-data-and-ai-tracker-survey-wave-2. Accessed 16 May 2023

Curral, L., Forrester, R., Dawson, J., West, M.: It's what you do and the way you do it: team task, team size and innovation-related group processes. Eur. J. Work Organ. Psychol. **10**(2), 187–204 (2001)

Department for Science, Innovation and Technology (DSIT). A Pro-Innovation Approach to AI Regulation, Command Paper 815 (2023). https://www.gov.uk/government/publications/ai-reg ulation-a-pro-innovation-approach/white-paper. Accessed 16 May 2023

Foot, P.: The problem of abortion and the doctrine of double effect. Oxford Rev. **5**, 5–16 (1967)

Fox, C.: Driverless cars: who should die in a crash?, BBC News (2018). https://www.bbc.co.uk/news/technology-45991093. Accessed 16 May 2023

Frankel, M.: The self-driving trolley problem: how will future AI systems make the most ethical choices for all of us? The Conversation (2021). https://theconversation.com/the-self-dri ving-trolley-problem-how-will-future-ai-systems-make-the-most-ethical-choices-for-all-of-us-170961. Accessed 16 May 2023

Hardman, S., Berliner, R., Tal, G.: Who will be the early adopters of automated vehicles? insights from a survey of electric vehicle owners in the United States. Transp. Res. Part D: Transp. Environ. **71**, 248–264 (2019)

Holthaus, P., Menon, C., Amirabdollahian, F.: How a robot's social credibility affects safety performance. In: Proceedings of the 11th International Conference of Social Robotics (ICSR), pp. 740–749 (2019)

Hornbaek, K.: Current practice in measuring usability: challenges to usability studies and research. Int. J. Hum Comput Stud. **64**(2), 79–102 (2006)

Institute of Electrical and Electronic Engineers (IEEE). Ethically Aligned Design, IEEE, v2 (2018). https://standards.ieee.org/wpcontent/uploads/import/documents/other/ead_v2.pdf. Accessed 16 May 2023

IET, Code of Practice: Cyber Security and Safety (2018). https://electrical.theiet.org/guidance-codes-of-practice/publications-by-category/cyber-security/code-of-practice-cyber-security-and-safety/. Accessed 16 May 2023

International Standards Organisation (ISO). Ergonomics of human-system interaction—Part 210: Human-centred design for interactive systems, ISO 9241 (2010)

Kittmann, R., Frohlich, T., Schafer, J., et al.: Let me introduce myself: I am care-o-bot 4, a gentleman robot. In: Proceedings Mensch und Computer, pp. 223–232 (2015)

Koay, K., Syrdal, D., Dautenhahn, K., Walters, M.: A narrative approach to human-robot interaction prototyping for companion robots. Paladyn J. Behav. Rob. **11**, 66–85 (2020)

Larson, K.: Serious games and gamification in the corporate training environment: a literature review. TechTrends **64**(2), 319–328 (2020)

Leslie, D.: Understanding artificial intelligence ethics and safety: a guide for the responsible design and implementation of AI systems in the public sector. The Alan Turing Institute (2019)

Lin, Patrick: Why ethics matters for autonomous cars. In: Markus Maurer, J., Gerdes, C., Lenz, B., Winner, H. (eds.) Autonomes Fahren, pp. 69–85. Springer, Heidelberg (2015). https://doi.org/10.1007/978-3-662-45854-9_4

Lombriser, P., Dalpiaz, F., Lucassen, G., Brinkkemper, S.: Gamified requirements engineering: model and experimentation. In: Proceedings of the Conference on Requirements Engineering, pp. 171–187 (2016)

Malizia, A., Carta, S., Turchi, T., Crivellaro, C.: MiniCoDe workshops: minimise algorithmic bias in collaborative decision making with design fiction. In Proceedings of the Hybrid Human Artificial Intelligence Conference (2022)

Menon, C., Carta, S., Foerster, F.: EETAS: a process for examining ethical trade-offs in autonomous systems. In: Proceedings of the 6th International Conference on Computer-Human Interaction Research and Applications, pp. 249–257 (2022)

Menon, C., Alexander, R.: A safety-case approach to the ethics of autonomous vehicles. J. Saf. Reliabil. Soc. **39**(1), 33–58 (2019)

Menon, C., Holthaus, P.: Does a loss of social credibility impact robot safety? balancing social and safety behaviours of assistive robots. In: Proceedings of International Conference on Performance, Safety and Robustness in Complex Systems and Applications (PESARO), pp. 18–24 (2019)

National Cyber Security Centre. Intelligent Security Tools (2019). https://www.ncsc.gov.uk/collection/intelligent-security-tools. Accessed 16 May 2023

Parsons, D., Inkila, M., Lynch, J.: Navigating learning worlds: using digital tools to learn in physical and virtual spaces. Aust. J. Educ. Technol. **35**(4), 1–16 (2019)

Roberts, L.: Opportunities and constraints of electronic research. In: Reynolds, R., Woods, R., Baker, J. (eds.) Handbook of Research on Electronic Surveys and Measurements (2006)

Roff, H. The folly of trolleys: Ethical challenges and autonomous vehicles, Brookings (2018). https://www.brookings.edu/research/the-folly-of-trolleys-ethical-challenges-and-autonomous-vehicles/. Accessed 16 May 2023

Rogers, E.: The Diffusion of Innovations. Free Press, New York (2003)

Saari, U., Tossavainen, A., Kaipainen, K., Makinen, S.: Exploring factors influencing the acceptance of social robots among early adopters and mass market representatives. Rob. Auton. Syst. **151**, 10403 (2022)

Saunders, J., Syrdal, D., Koay, K., Burke, N., Dautenhahn, K.: Teach me - show me' - end-user personalisation of a smart home and companion robot. IEEE Trans. Human-Mach. Syst. **46**(1), 27–40 (2016)

Schneiderman, B.: Designing the User Interface: Strategies for Effective Human-Computer Interaction. Pearson, Boston (2009)

Schrier, K.: Designing games for moral learning and knowledge building. Games Cult. **14**(4), 306–343 (2019)

ShapeDiver (2023). https://shapediver.com/. Accessed 16 May 2023

Speckle (2023). https://speckle.systems/. Accessed 16 May 2023

Texas A&M Transportation Institute (TTI), Who's On First: Early Adopters of Self-Driving Vehicles (2018). https://static.tti.tamu.edu/tti.tamu.edu/documents/TTI-2018-2-brief.pdf. Accessed 16 May 2023

Thornton, S.: Autonomous vehicle motion planning with ethical considerations, (Doctoral dissertation), Stanford University (2018)

Viktor (2023). https://www.viktor.ai/platform. Accessed 16 May 2023

Von Neumann, J., Morgernstern, O.: Theory of Games and Economic Behaviour. Princeton University Press, Princeton (1947)

Realistic Pedestrian Behaviour in the CARLA Simulator Using VR and Mocap

Sergio Martín Serrano[1]([✉]) [iD], David Fernández Llorca[1,2] [iD],
Iván García Daza[1] [iD], and Miguel Ángel Sotelo[1] [iD]

[1] Computer Engineering Department, University of Alcalá, Alcalá de Henares, Spain
sergio.martin@uah.es
[2] European Commission, Joint Research Centre (JRC), Seville, Spain

Abstract. Simulations are gaining increasingly significance in the field of autonomous driving due to the demand for rapid prototyping and extensive testing. Employing physics-based simulation brings several benefits at an affordable cost, while mitigating potential risks to prototypes, drivers, and vulnerable road users. However, there exit two primary limitations. Firstly, the *reality gap* which refers to the disparity between reality and simulation and prevents the simulated autonomous driving systems from having the same performance in the real world. Secondly, the lack of empirical understanding regarding the *behavior of real agents*, such as backup drivers or passengers, as well as other road users such as vehicles, pedestrians, or cyclists. Agent simulation is commonly implemented through deterministic or randomized probabilistic pre-programmed models, or generated from real-world data; but it fails to accurately represent the behaviors adopted by real agents while interacting within a specific simulated scenario. This paper extends the description of our proposed framework to enable real-time interaction between real agents and simulated environments, by means immersive virtual reality and human motion capture systems within the CARLA simulator for autonomous driving. We have designed a set of usability examples that allow the analysis of the interactions between real pedestrians and simulated autonomous vehicles and we provide a first measure of the user's sensation of *presence* in the virtual environment.

Keywords: Automated driving · Autonomous vehicles · Predictive perception · Behavioural modelling · Simulators · Virtual reality · Presence

1 Introduction

The rise in the use of simulators in the context of autonomous driving is mainly due to the need for prototyping and exhaustive validation, since the tests of autonomous systems directly on real scenarios alone are not capable of providing sufficient evidence that prove its safety [1]. There is some initial consensus

© The Author(s), under exclusive license to Springer Nature Switzerland AG 2023
A. Holzinger et al. (Eds.): CHIRA 2021/2022, CCIS 1882, pp. 95–107, 2023.
https://doi.org/10.1007/978-3-031-41962-1_5

that future testing approaches should be multisystem, including not only physical testing on proving grounds but also extensive use of simulators and real-
world driving tests [2]. With simulators we can generate large amounts of data,
including edge cases, and enrich training and testing with a specific control over
all variables under study (e.g., street layout, lighting conditions, traffic scenarios). Furthermore, the generated data can be also annotated by design including
semantic information. This is particularly interesting when testing predictive
systems [3].

However, one of the main challenges in developing autonomous driving simulators is the unrealistic nature of the data generated by simulated sensors and
physical models. The well-known *reality gap* leads to inaccuracies since the virtual world does not properly generalise all the variations and complexities of
the real world [4,5]. Additionally, despite there have been efforts to create life-
like artificial behaviors for other agents on the road (e.g., vehicles, pedestrians,
cyclists), simulations are limited by a lack of empirical knowledge about their
actual behavior. As a result, this gap affects both behavior and movement prediction as well as human-vehicle communication and interaction [6].

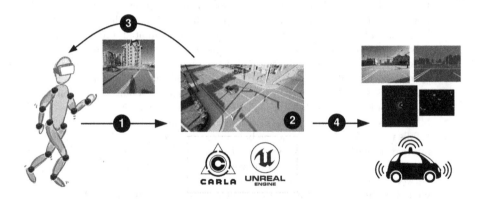

Fig. 1. Overview of the presented approach. Adapted from [8]. (1) CARLA-Unreal
Engine is provided with the head (VR headset) and body (motion capture system)
pose. (2) The scenario is generated, including the autonomous vehicles and the digitized
pedestrian. (3) The environment is provided to the pedestrian (through VR headset).
(4) Autonomous vehicle sensors perceive the environment, including the pedestrian.

In the following we describe our approach to incorporate real agents behaviors
and interactions in CARLA autonomous driving simulator [7] by using immersive virtual reality and human motion capture systems. The idea, schematically
represented in Fig. 1, is to integrate a subject in the simulated scenarios using
CARLA and Unreal Engine 4 (UE4), with real time feedback of the pose of his
head and body, and including positional sound, attempting to create a virtual
experience that is so realistic that the participant feels as though they are physically present in that world and subconsciously accepts it as such (i.e., maximize

virtual reality presence). At the same time, the captured pose and motion of the subject is integrated into the virtual scenario by means of an avatar, so that the simulated sensors of the autonomous vehicles (i.e., radar, LiDAR, cameras) can detect their presence as were in the same space. This allows, on the one hand, to obtain synthetic sequences from multiple points of view based on the behavior of real subjects, which can be used to train and test predictive perception models. And on the other hand, they also allow to address different types of interaction studies between autonomous vehicles and real subjects, including external human-machine interfaces (eHMI), under completely controlled circumstances and with absolute safety measures in place.

In this paper, in comparison with our previous work where we already presented the hardware and software architecture [8], we have included the integration of a new motion capture system [11] and a more detailed description of the computation times and scene processing. Moreover, we have carried out a series of experiments on a novel map and we provide a consistent measure of the sense of *presence* from 18 participants who played the role of a pedestrian in a traffic scenario. Finally, we make some proposals on how to improve the user's immersive experience.

2   Virtual Reality Immersion Features

The main goal of our approach is to achieve the total immersion of real pedestrians within a simulator commonly used for autonomous driving testing. We selected CARLA, an open source simulator implemented over UE4 which provides high rendering quality, realistic physics and an ecosystem of interoperable plugins, and we added some features to support an immersive virtual reality system. The user total immersion is achieved through all the functionalities that UE4 presents, along with a virtual reality headset and a set of motion tracking sensors. CARLA is designed as a server-client system, where the server renders the scene and the client generates the agents operating within the dynamic traffic scenario. Communication between the client and the server is done via sockets.

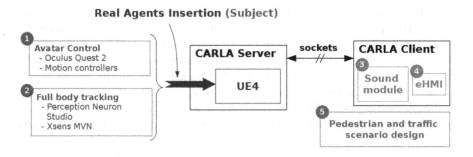

Fig. 2. System Block Diagram. Adapted from [8].

The added features to the simulator for the insertion of real agent behaviours in the CARLA server are based on the five points depicted in Fig. 2: 1) **Avatar control**: from the CARLA's blueprint library that collects the architecture of all its actors and attributes, we modify the pedestrian blueprints to create an immersive and maneuverable VR interface between the real agent and the virtual world; 2) **Body tracking**: we use a set of inertial sensors and proprietary external software to capture the subject's motion through the real scene, and we integrate the avatar's motion into the simulator via *.bvh* files; 3) **Sound design**: given that CARLA is an audio-less simulator, we incorporate positional sound into the environment to enhance the subject's immersion; 4) **eHMI integration**: in order to enable communication between autonomous vehicles and other road users to address interaction studies; 5) **Scenario simulation**: we design traffic scenarios by using the CARLA client, controlling the behaviour of vehicles and other pedestrians.

2.1   Avatar Control

CARLA's blueprints (that include sensors, static actors, vehicles and walkers) have been specifically designed to be managed through the Python client API. Vehicles that populate the scenario are actors that incorporate special internal components that simulate the physics of wheeled vehicles and can be driven by functions that provide driving commands (such as throttle, steering or braking). Walkers are operated in the same way and their behavior is directed from the client by a controller, so they are far from adopting behaviors of real pedestrians.

To support an immersive interface for a real actor, we modify a walker blueprint to make an inverse kinematics setup for full-body scale VR. The tools employed to capture the actor movement are: *a) Oculus Quest 2* (for head tracking and user position control), and *b) Motion controllers* (for both hands tracking). The Oculus Quest 2 safety distance system delimits the playing area through which the subject can move freely. The goal is to allow the subject to move within the established safety zone that purposefully corresponds to a specific area of the CARLA map.

Firstly, we modify the blueprint by attaching a virtual camera to the head of the walker whose image provided is projected onto the lenses of the VR glasses giving a first-person sensation to the spectator. The displacement and perspective of the walker are also activated, from certain minimum thresholds, with the translation and rotation of the VR headset. The skeletal mesh is another element of the blueprint that we can vary to give the walker another appearance.

That way, the immersion of a real pedestrian is achieved by implementing a head-mounted display (HMD) and creating an avatar in UE4. The subject wears the VR glasses and also controls the avatar movement throughout the preset area for the experiments.

2.2 Full-Body Tracking

On the other hand, head and hand tracking (by mean the VR headset and both motion controllers) serve to adapt the pose of the avatar's neck and hands in real time, but are not enough to represent the full pose of the subject within the simulator. There exit multiple options of motion capture (MoCap) system to do this, including vision-based systems with multiple cameras and inertial measurement units [9].

In our case, we have considered the use of two inertial wireless sensor systems: *(i) Perception Neuron Studio (PNS)* motion capture system [10], as a compromise solution between accuracy and usability. Each MoCap system includes a set of inertial sensors and straps that can be put on the joints easily, as well as a software for calibrating and capturing precise motion data. *(ii) XSens MVN*, another full body motion analysis system [11] made up of 17 inertial units (MTw). Based on a biomechanical model, MVN Analyze provides 3D information on joints, center of mass, as well as position, velocity and acceleration parameters for each of the body segments. Both systems allow integration with other 3D rendering and animation software, such as iClone, Blender, Unity or UE4. XSens MVN is a more expensive solution that includes a more sustainable calibration process over time, more exhaustive data processing, and a specific plugin to add the full avatar pose in Unreal Engine in real time.

2.3 Sound Design

Since CARLA simulator is world audio absent, the integration of a sound module is another technique to enhance the sensation of *presence* in the virtual world. Sound design and real-world isolation is also essential for interaction with the environment, as humans use spatial sound cues to track the location of other actors and predict their intentions. We incorporate ambient sounds of birds singing and wind, as well as the engines sounds of the vehicles parameterized by its throttle and brake actions. In cases where other pedestrians are involved in the scene, we propose adding other sounds such as conversation or their footsteps so that the subject can be more aware that they are present.

2.4 External Human-Machine Interfaces (eHMI)

In our experiments we include external human-machine interfaces (eHMI) to enable communication between road users. The autonomous vehicles can communicate their status and intentions to the real subject by the proposed eHMI design. As appeared in Fig. 3, it consists of a light strip along the entire front of the vehicle which changes color depending the information is desired to transmit. This allows studying the influence of the interface on decision making when the pedestrian's trajectory converges with the one followed by the vehicle in the virtual scenario.

Fig. 3. Left: vehicle with eHMI deactivated. Right: vehicle with eHMI activated [8].

2.5 Traffic Scenario Simulation

CARLA offers different options to simulate specific traffic scenarios. The Traffic Manager is a module very useful to populate a simulation with realistic urban traffic conditions. Using multiple threads and synchronous messaging, it can propitiate all vehicles to follow certain behaviors (e.g., not exceeding speed limits, ignore traffic light conditions, ignore pedestrians, or force lane changes).

The subject is integrated into the simulator on a map that includes a 3D model of a city. Each map is based on an OpenDRIVE file that describes the fully annotated road layout. This feature allows us to design our own maps as well as implement georeferenced maps taken from the real world. This opens up infinite possibilities for recreating scenarios according to the needs of the study.

3 System Implementation

The overall scheme of the system is shown in Fig. 4. In the next sections we describe the hardware and software implemented architectures, and the processes of recording and playback of the scenes.

3.1 Hardware Setup

The complete hardware configuration is depicted in Fig. 5. We employ the Oculus Quest 2 as our head-mounted device (HMD), created by Meta, which has 6GB RAM processor, two adjustable 1832 × 1920 lenses, 90Hz refresh rate and an internal memory of 256 GB. Quest 2 features WiFi 6, Bluetooth 5.1, and USB Type-C connectivity, SteamVR support and 3D speakers. For full-body tracking we use PNS or XSens solution with inertial trackers. The kit includes standalone VR headset, 2 motion controllers, 17 inertial body sensors, 14 set of straps, 1 charging case and 1 transceiver. During the experiments, we define a preset area wide enough and free of obstacles where the subject can act as a real pedestrian inside the simulator. Quest 2 and motion controllers are connected to PC via Oculus link or WiFi as follows:

- Wired connection: via the Oculus Link cable or other similar high quality USB 3.

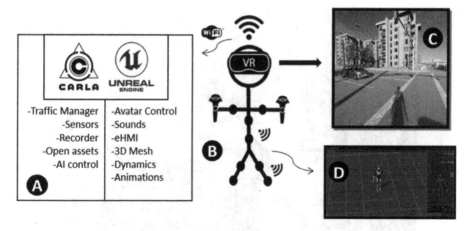

Fig. 4. System Schematics [8]. (A) Simulator CARLA-UE4. (B) VR headset, motion controllers and body sensors. (C) Spectator View in Virtual Reality. (D) Full-body tracking in Axis Studio or MVN Analyze.

– Wireless connection: via WiFi by enabling Air Link from the Meta application, or using Virtual Desktop and SteamVR.

The subject puts on the straps of the appropriate length and places the body sensors into the bases. The transceiver is attached to the PC via USB. Quest 2 enables the "VR Preview" in the UE4 editor of the build version of CARLA for Windows.

3.2   Software Setup

VR Immersion System is currently dependent on UE4.24 and Windows 10 OS due to CARLA build, and Quest 2 Windows-only dependencies. Using TCP socket plugin, all the actor locations and other useful parameters for the editor are sent from the Python API to integrate, for example, the positional sound emitted by each actor and the handling of the eHMI activation of the autonomous vehicle. "VR Preview" projects the game onto the lenses of the HMD. Perception Neuron Studio and XSens MVN work with Axis Studio and MVN Analyze software respectively, supporting up to 3 subjects at a time in the same scene.

3.3   Recording, Playback and Motion Perception

When running experiments, certain computational time constraints must be met so that the real subject introduced by virtual reality can perform a natural behavior. The *simulation step* is defined as the time of the scene that is executed at each simulator tick. Under standard conditions, this is not forced to coincide with the *rendering time*, which is the actual time that the architecture takes to process a simulation step. We face the challenge that for the actions of the

Fig. 5. Hardware setup [8]. (i) VR headset (Quest 2): transfer the image from the environment to the performer. (ii) Motion controllers: allow control of the avatar's hands. (iii) PN Studio sensors: provide body tracking withstanding magnetic interference. (iv) Studio Transceiver: receives sensors data wirelessly by 2.4 GHz.

external agent to be meaningful within the simulated scene, the simulation step and its render time must match.

The rendering time is determined by hardware limitations (i.e., the capacity of the GPU used) and by the number of tasks that are intended to be handled during the simulation. In addition, to attend the immersive sensation, the virtual environment displayed from the VR glasses must show a stable image to the performer so him/her can interact with the world of CARLA. Since the simulated sensors of the autonomous vehicles (i.e. radar, LiDAR, cameras) involve a lot of computations, the scene cannot be reproduced at more than 2 FPS, preventing a successful immersion. To overcome this difficulty, we remove the sensors blueprints, record the simulation data and play it back for later analysis. This allows us to perform the experiments in virtual reality at 18.18 FPS.

CARLA has a native record and playback system that serializes the world information in each simulator tick for post-simulation recreation. However, this is only intended for tracking actors managed by the Python API and does not include the subject avatar or motion sensors. Along with the recording of the state of the CARLA world, in our case the recording and playback of the complete body motion of the external agent is essential. In our approach we use the Axis Studio or MVN Analyze software to record the body motion during experiments. The recording is exported in a *.bvh* file which is subsequently integrated into the UE4 editor.

Once the action is recorded, the simulation is played back with all the blueprints included since the rendering time does not need to be adjusted to any constraint. Then, the simulated sensors of the autonomous vehicles perceive the skeletal mesh of the avatar and its path followed, as well as the specific pose of all its joints (i.e., body language).

4   Results

This section presents the design of some usability examples and an evaluation of the immersive experience provided by the interface for real pedestrians in the CARLA autonomous driving simulator.

4.1   Usability Examples

To attend our purposes, the implemented traffic scenario (depicted in Fig. 6) must propitiate interactions between autonomous vehicles and the user of the

Fig. 6. Simulation of Interactive traffic situations. (a) 3D world design. (b) Pedestrian matches the performer avatar. (c) Autonomous vehicle. (d) Environment sounds and agents sounds. (e) eHMI. (f) Street lighting and traffic signs.

Fig. 7. Left: real scenario, VR and motion capture setting. Right: simulated scenario and pedestrian's view.

virtual reality glasses and motion capture system who walks through the environment as a pedestrian [12]. The first step is to select a suitable map where to develop the action. We downloaded the map data of the university area from OpenStreetMap [13] and converted it to an OpenDRIVE format which can be ingested into CARLA. This allows us to obtain the geometry information of a real pedestrian crossing and replicate its same visibility conditions.

When running the scene (see Fig. 7), an autonomous vehicle circulates on the road when reaches the pedestrian crossing. The pedestrian on the edge of the sidewalk is ordered to cross the road when they consider it safe, and receives information on status and vehicle intentions through an eHMI. In addition, the pedestrian can hear the engine of the vehicle approaching, which can influence the decision to cross sooner or later. From the CARLA client, it is possible to pre-program the behavior of the autonomous vehicle so that it ignores the pedestrian and does not stop or performs a braking maneuver and gives way. To observe its impact on the pedestrian's attitude (i.e., on the interaction), more or less aggressive braking maneuvers can be applied, and the external HMI can be activated or deactivated. Lighting and weather conditions are also adjustable. Sensors attached to the vehicle capture the image of the scenario and detect the pedestrian, as shown in Fig. 8.

4.2   User Experience Evaluation

A sample of 18 experimental participants, consisted of 12 male and 6 female who ranged in age from 24 to 62, were instructed to take part in the scene in the role of the pedestrian and completed a 15-item presence scale (depicted in Appendix A) to asses the quality of immersion. *Self-presence* examines how much a user extends features of their identity into a virtual world while represented by an avatar. *Autonomous vehicle* and *environmental presence* measure how a user treats actors and environments in mediated space as if they were real. In addition, we request participants for open comments about their performance.

Fig. 8. Virtual sensors output: cameras (RGB, depth), and LiDAR point cloud (ray-casting).

As a means of assessing the test's reliability, we compute Cronbach's Afla ($\alpha = .707$) which indicates an acceptable internal consistency. Most of the participants felt a strong self-presence (M = 4.04, SD = .953) perceiving the displacement and hands of the avatar as their own. Regarding autonomous vehicle presence (M = 3.94, SD = .967), the engine noise was the main point of contention among the participants, as some found it highly helpful in identifying the vehicle, while others either didn't notice it or found it irritating. Environmental-presence (M = 4.34, SD = .627) got the highest score; the participants stated the appearance of the environment was that of a real crosswalk.

Self-presence and environmental presence were satisfactory, while most feedback was directed at improving the presence of the autonomous vehicle. Its braking maneuver did not feel threatening in the sense that was appreciated too conservative, and the vehicle dynamics did not help to anticipate the point at which it was going to stop.

5   Conclusions and Future Work

We have developed a framework to enable real-time interaction between real agents and simulated environments. The initial focus is on the integration of pedestrians in traffic scenarios, for which a virtual reality interface has been implemented in the CARLA simulator for autonomous driving. The virtual world is displayed on the glasses lenses at 18.18 FPS. The performer pose is registered by a motion capture system, generating useful sequences to train and validate predictive models to, for example, predict future actions and trajectories of traffic agents. This paper has presented some possibilities and usability cases that this system can address.

As future works, it is intended to improve some aspects of the immersive experience. XSens MVN will replace the PNS system to represent the user's full body on the avatar in real time. We will apply improvements in the dynamics of the vehicle (e.g., an inclination of its frontal part at the moment of its stop). The addition of other agents on the scene, such as vehicles traveling in the other direction, and other pedestrians, will be considered to enable different types of interaction studies. Furthermore, one of our main goals is to provide a measure of the *behavioral gap* by replicating interaction and communication studies in equivalent real and virtual environments.

Acknowledgements. This work was funded by Research Grants PID2020-114924RB-I00 and PDC2021-121324-I00 (Spanish Ministry of Science and Innovation) and partially by S2018/EMT-4362 SEGVAUTO 4.0-CM (Community of Madrid). D. Fernández Llorca acknowledges funding from the HUMAINT project by the Directorate-General Joint Research Centre of the European Commission.

Disclaimer. The views expressed in this article are purely those of the authors and may not, under any circumstances, be regarded as an official position of the European Commission.

Appendix A

Self-presence Scale Items

To what extent did you feel that... ($1 =$ not at all - 5 very strongly)

1. You could move the avatar's hands.
2. The avatar's displacement was your own displacement.
3. The avatar's body was your own body.
4. If something happened to the avatar, it was happening to you.
5. The avatar was you.

Autonomous Vehicle Presence Scale Items

To what extent did you feel that... ($1 =$ not at all - 5 very strongly)

1. The vehicle was present.
2. The vehicle dynamics and its movement were natural.
3. The sound of the vehicle helped you to locate it.
4. The vehicle was aware of your presence.
5. The vehicle was real.

Environmental Presence Scale Items

To what extent did you feel that... ($1 =$ not at all - 5 very strongly)

1. You were really in front of a pedestrian crossing.
2. The road signs and traffic lights were real.
3. You really crossed the pedestrian crossing.
4. The urban environment seemed like the real world.
5. It could reach out and touch the objects in the urban environment.

References

1. Kalra, N., Paddock, S.M.: Driving to safety: how many miles of driving would it take to demonstrate autonomous vehicle reliability? RAND Corporation, Research report (2016)
2. Fernández-Llorca, D., Gómez, E.: Trustworthy artificial intelligence requirements in the autonomous driving domain. Computer **56**(2), 29–39 (2023). https://doi.org/10.1109/MC.2022.3212091
3. Izquierdo Gonzalo, R., Salinas Maldonado, C., Alonso Ruiz, J., Parra Alonso, I., Fernández Llorca, D., Sotelo, M.Á.: Testing predictive automated driving systems: lessons learned and future recommendations. IEEE Intell. Transp. Syst. Mag. **14**(6), 77–93 (2022). https://doi.org/10.1109/MITS.2022.3170649
4. Stocco, A., Pulfer, B., Tonella, P.: Mind the gap! a study on the transferability of virtual vs physical-world testing of autonomous driving systems. IEEE Trans. Softw. Eng., 1–13 (2022). https://doi.org/10.1109/TSE.2022.3202311
5. García Daza, I., Izquierdo, R., Martínez, L.M., Benderius, O., Fernández Llorca, D.: Sim-to-real transfer and reality gap modeling in model predictive control for autonomous driving. Appl. Intell. **53**, 12719–12735 (2022). https://doi.org/10.1007/s10489-022-04148-1
6. Eady, T.: Simulations can't solve autonomous driving because they lack important knowledge about the real world - large-scale real world data is the only way (2019). https://medium.com/@trenteady/simulation-cant-solve-autonomous-driving-because-it-lacks-necessary-empirical-knowledge-403feeec15e0. Accessed 8 Apr 2022
7. Dosovitskiy, A., Ros, G., Codevilla, F., Lopez, A., Koltun, V.: CARLA: an open Urban driving simulator. In: Proceedings of the 1st Annual Conference on Robot Learning, pp. 1–16 (2017)
8. Martín Serrano, S., Fernández Llorca, D., García Daza, I., Sotelo, M.A.: Insertion of real agents behaviors in CARLA autonomous driving simulator. In: Proceedings of the 6th International Conference on Computer-Human Interaction Research and Applications, CHIRA 2022, pp. 23–31 (2022). https://doi.org/10.5220/0011352400003323
9. Menolotto, M., Komaris, D., Tedesco, S., O'Flynn, B., Walsh, M.: Motion capture technology in industrial applications: a systematic review. Sensors **20**(19), 5687 (2020). https://doi.org/10.3390/s20195687
10. Noitom (2022). https://neuronmocap.com/perception-neuron-studio-system. Accessed 22 Mar 2023
11. Movard (2023). https://www.movard.es/productos/xsens/. Accessed 22 Mar 2023
12. Serrano, S.M, Izquierdo, R., García Daza, I., Sotelo, M.Á., Fernández Llorca, D.: Digital twin in virtual reality for human-vehicle interactions in the context of autonomous driving (2023). arXiv:2303.11463
13. OpenStreetMap. https://www.openstreetmap.org/about. Accessed 23 Mar 2023

Design, Implementation, and Early Experimentation of a Music Tangible User Interface for Elderly People Rehabilitation

Helene Korsten⑩, Adriano Baratè⑩, and Luca A. Ludovico(✉)⑩

Laboratory of Music Informatics, Department of Computer Science,
University of Milan, via G. Celoria 18, Milan, Italy
helene.korsten@studenti.unimi.it,
{adriano.barate,luca.ludovico}@unimi.it
https://www.lim.di.unimi.it

Abstract. This article proposes an innovative approach for cognitive and motor rehabilitation of elderly individuals that combines tangible user interfaces, digital technologies, and musical expression. After reviewing the current literature on age-related impairments and the use of tangible user interfaces in rehabilitation, we introduce a specific MIDI controller called *Kibo* that employs geometric fiducials called tangibles. Thanks to Bluetooth connectivity and the adoption of the Web MIDI API, this device communicates with a specially-designed web framework that includes three games to facilitate the development or recovery of cognitive and motor abilities. The feedback obtained in an early experimentation phase from domain experts and a focus group underlined some strengths and weaknesses, thus driving the first revision of the interface and the gameplay. This work will describe the design and implementation of the early prototype and will shed light on the future evolution of the web platform. From the tests conducted so far, this solution based on a musical controller equipped with tangibles exhibits the potential to enhance the effectiveness and enjoyment of rehabilitation programs for elderly individuals.

Keywords: Music · Tangible user interface · Web · Elderly rehabilitation

1 Introduction

The present study focuses on the rehabilitation needs of elderly individuals who may experience cognitive or motor impairments or reduced social interactions. To this end, we conducted an analysis of common age-related changes in cognitive and motor abilities and developed a prototype that could be applied to music therapy rehabilitation sessions. As stated in a document by the American Music Therapy Association, music therapy "is the clinical and evidence-based

A. Holzinger et al. (Eds.): CHIRA 2021/2022, CCIS 1882, pp. 108–129, 2023.
https://doi.org/10.1007/978-3-031-41962-1_6

use of music interventions to accomplish individualized goals within a therapeutic relationship by a credentialed professional who has completed an approved music therapy program" [2].

The prototype's interventions can target various healthcare and educational objectives, such as promoting wellness, managing stress, alleviating pain, expressing feelings, enhancing memory, improving communication, and promoting physical rehabilitation.

Our web-based prototype incorporates a tangible user interface called *Kibo*, which facilitates intuitive interaction with musical parameters, taking advantage of haptic interaction skills with the environment. Three browser games have been designed to train rhythm, spatial, and recognition skills. The web platform was shown at the prototype stage to two user categories: i) professional caregivers and rehabilitation experts, and ii) a focus group of elderly users. We collected their opinion in order to drive a new iteration of the design phase with the final goal of improving usability and effectiveness. In this paper, after describing the hardware and software ecosystem that we have designed and implemented, we will investigate the potential of our prototype solution to enhance rehabilitation outcomes for elderly individuals and contribute to their overall well-being.

The rest of the paper is organized as follows: Sect. 2 provides the state of the art about common age impairments; Sect. 3 defines the concept of tangible user interface and explores its adoption in the fields of rehabilitation and musical expression; Sect. 4 addresses the main technologies employed in the project; Sect. 5 describes the characteristics of the web games and the gameplay; Sect. 6 reports the results of early experimentation; finally, Sect. 7 draws the conclusions.

This work is an extension of the paper presented at the 6th International Conference on Computer-Human Interaction Research and Applications (CHIRA 2022) [4].

2   State of the Art

This section focuses on a selective review of the scientific literature on age impairments, a subject that is highly pertinent to our objectives. Considering the vastness of the subject, we acknowledge that our coverage cannot be all-inclusive.

Due to changes in life expectancy, the number of elderly people has increased significantly worldwide. According to the World Health Organization (WHO), the share of the population aged 60 years and over will double from 1 billion in 2020 to 2.1 billion in 2050. The number of persons aged 80 years or older is expected to triple between 2020 and 2050, thus reaching 426 million.[1] According to the United Nations, by 2050, 1 in 6 people in the world will be over the age of 65, up from 1 in 11 in 2019.[2]

The growing demographic of older adults requires changes at the individual and societal levels. Sustainable development goals should include investment in

---

[1] https://www.who.int/news-room/fact-sheets/detail/ageing-and-health.
[2] https://www.un.org/en/development/desa/population/publications/pdf/ageing/WorldPopulationAgeing2019-Highlights.pdf.

education, health, and well-being for all, including older adults. Society will have to offer more and more products and services that meet the specific needs and desires of the geriatric age group. These people are seeking solutions to help them cope with daily life, give them the opportunity to interact socially, and find alternative ways of entertainment and learning. Moreover, health systems are dealing with the ever-increasing burden of finding solutions and cures for age-related diseases. Relevant examples embrace degenerative cognitive conditions caused by dementia and Alzheimer's disease and impaired-movement pathologies such as Parkinson's disease.

As stated in [40], while the demographic transition moves into a stage of increased longevity, attention must shift from an *aging society* to a *longevity society*. The former definition focuses on changes in the population's age distribution, the latter aims to leverage the benefits of extended lifespans by transforming the way we approach aging.

Everyone experiences changes as an inevitable part of the natural degeneration associated with aging [28]. Concerning **changes in cognitive abilities**, aging causes a decline in *spatial cognition*, which is the ability to represent spatial relationships among objects. The results of a study conducted in 2008 by Iachini *et al.* show that some spatial abilities, such as the ability to mentally rotate visual images and to retrieve spatiotemporal sequences, decline with age [23]. Elderly people also struggle more with multitasking, especially if the tasks are complex [44]. Another common age impairment is the decline in *fluid intelligence*, which refers to the processing and reasoning components of intelligence and the natural ability to learn something new [14]. Because of reduced processing efficiency, the *working memory*, which is the ability to keep information active while processing or using it, declines with age [38]. Similarly, *prospective memory*, which is the ability to remember to do something in the future, also declines with age [32]. Another issue emerging with age is the ability to select information in the environment, e.g., to attend to information on a web page. *Attention* is the ability to focus on a specific task or an object in the environment while ignoring other things. This ability changes with age and older people are slower to move their attention from one thing to another [14,22].

Another category of impairments due to aging is that of **changes in physical abilities**. Response time and accuracy of movement decline with age. Older persons' movements and reflexes are typically slower than younger persons'. This also includes reaction to stimuli [19]. The loss in the sensitivity of touch in older people reduces the ability to differentiate between shapes and textures by touch [22]. Differently from the above-mentioned normal age impairments, a disease that limits movement is Parkinson's, a neurodegenerative brain disorder that progresses slowly and worsens with age. Symptoms are involuntary shaking of the hands, arms, legs, jaw, chin, and lips. Other main symptoms include slowness of movement, stiffness of arms and legs, and trouble with balance [29].

Even if not an impairment, another phenomenon relevant to our work is **anxiety towards technology**. In a study by Czaja and Sharit dating back to 1998, elder people saw themselves as having less control over computers than younger people [15]. They had significantly less efficacy in completing computer tasks, but, surprisingly, they also perceived computers as being more useful compared to younger people. Another study revealed that older subjects reported higher levels of computer anxiety than younger persons and that the anxiety level was related to the decision time on the computer when performing a test [31]. The elderly may have a harder time using new technology, but it helps with practice [13]. These considerations pushed us to develop a solution based on a computing system but relying on a tangible interface to ease user interaction.

3   Tangible User Interfaces

Tangible user interfaces (TUIs) are interaction mechanisms that replace graphical user interfaces (GUIs), more common in computing systems, with real physical objects. The key idea is to give digital information a physical form which serves as both a representation and a control means for digital information. A TUI lets users manipulate digital information with their hands and perceive it with their senses.

One of the pioneers in tangible user interfaces is Hiroshi Ishii, a professor at MIT who heads the *Tangible Media Group* at the MIT Media Lab. His particular vision for TUIs, called *Tangible Bits*, is to give physical form to digital information, making bits directly manipulable and perceptible [26]. *Tangible Bits* pursues the seamless coupling between physical objects and virtual data. *"TUIs will augment the real physical world by coupling digital information to everyday physical objects and environments"* [27].

Currently, there are different research areas and applications related to TUIs. For instance, tangible augmented reality implies that virtual objects are "attached" to physically manipulated objects; in tangible tabletop interaction, physical objects are moved upon a multi-touch surface; moreover, physical objects can be used as ambient displays or integrated inside embodied user interfaces.

3.1   Tangible User Interfaces in Rehabilitation

Games can be used to increase the motivation of patients affected by cognitive or physical impairments in rehabilitation sessions [1,9,11,41,42]. Motivation is one of the main problems evidenced in traditional therapy sessions, often hampered by the repetitive nature of exercises. Most studies show that effective rehabilitation must be early, intensive, and repetitive [10,37]. As such, these approaches are often considered repetitive and boring by the patients, resulting in difficulties in maintaining their interest and in assuring that they complete the treatment program [37]. On the other hand, due to their nature, games can motivate and engage the patients' attention and distract them from their rehabilitation condition. On one side, they require some motor and cognitive activity, but, on the other, they have a story and can offer feedback and levels of challenge and difficulty that can be adapted to the patients' skills.

Serious games are an option that provides learning combined with entertainment. The locution "serious games" refers to playful activities that provide training and physical or mental exercise in a fun and enjoyable way [17]. These games can be not only a way to prevent the feeling of loneliness [16], but they can also enable social interaction [20]. During the last decades, digital games have become a popular leisure activity. Ijsselsteijn *et al.* claim that digital games can be considered a promise to improve the lives of seniors. To this end, it is important to develop interesting and accessible games which could provide an option to spend quality time with clear benefits [24]. Pearce reports that studies of digital games with an emphasis on older people are still rare because this need is relatively new [36]. This perception may be justified by the fact that the current elderly population did not have much access to technology at their earlier age.

Many rehabilitation games based on TUIs are already available. For example, *Handly* is an integrated upper-limb rehabilitation system for persons with a neurological disorder [43]. *Handly* consists of tangibles for training four-hand tasks with specific functional handgrips and a motivational game. The system consists of four tangible training boxes, which each present one essential grip and associated hand task: push-pull, squeezing, knob turning, and key turning (see Fig. 1). *Handly* combines tangibles specifically designed for repetitive task-oriented motor skill training of typical daily activities with serious gaming, thus offering a comprehensive approach. *Handly* focuses on therapy for various neurological disorders that can cause functional disabilities in the hands.

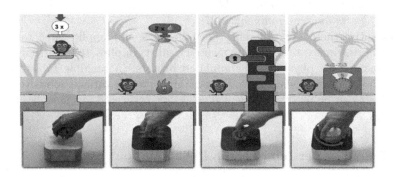

Fig. 1. User interface and activities with *Handly*. Images taken from [43].

Segara is an integrated hand rehabilitation system for patients with rheumatoid arthritis (RA) very similar to *Handly* [46]. *Segara* consists of tangibles for training six tasks with Interactive functional handgrips and a motivational serious game (see Fig. 2). It shows that a system combining games and tangibles to enhance hand rehabilitation is feasible and highly appreciated by patients.

Resonance is an interactive tabletop artwork that targets upper-limb movement rehabilitation for patients with an acquired brain injury [18]. The artwork consists of several interactive game environments, which enable artistic

Fig. 2. User interface and activities with *Segara*. Images taken from [46].

expression, exploration, and play. *Resonance* provides uni-manual and bi-manual game-like tasks and exploratory creative environments of varying complexity geared toward reaching, grasping, lifting, moving, and placing tangible user interfaces on a tabletop display (see Fig. 3). Each environment aims to encourage collaborative, cooperative, and competitive modes of interaction for small groups of co-located participants.

NikVision is a tangible tabletop based on a user-centered design approach for cognitively stimulating older people with dementia problems in nursing homes [12]. The general experiences of the users when working with the tangible tabletop were assessed and applied to the design of new cognitive and physical stimulation activities. From these experiences, guidelines for the design of tangible activities for this kind of users were extracted for the design and evaluation of tangible activities that could be useful for other researchers. *NIKIVision*'s game activities are specially designed for the elderly and have different levels of difficulty and audio feedback. The list of activities includes:

- *Clothes Activity* — Based on the daily task of getting dressed, users interact with the tabletop by using different objects with realistic drawings of pieces of clothing and letters. Fine motor skills are addressed when users have to pick up the two-dimensional objects to place them on the tabletop;

Fig. 3. User interface and activities with *Resonance*.

- *Shapes Activity* — Users have to select the indicated geometrical shapes and situate them on the box displayed on the tabletop;
- *Roads Activity* — Focusing on upper-half motor skills, users have to move the object on the tabletop surface by following a virtual road, also avoiding physical obstacles in the most difficult levels. The objects with which the users interact are different handles designed to stimulate different kinds of grabbing actions.

In conclusion, as regards their applicability to rehabilitation, one of the advantages offered by TUIs is the facilitated user experience, since the interaction occurring between the user and the interface itself is a physical rather than a digitally-mediated one. Recognizing (a cognitive task), grabbing, and moving objects (physical tasks) can be parts of the rehabilitation process. Another advantage is usability since the user intuitively understands how to manipulate the interface by knowing the function of the physical object.

3.2 Tangible User Interfaces in Music

TUIs have been used considerably in musical performances and music-therapy treatments. A tangible interface, being "real" and "concrete", offers a physical way to interact with music and sound parameters. The design is centered around the concept of tangibility, aiming to bridge the gap between physical and digital music interfaces. The underlying idea is that physical interaction with objects enhances the engagement and expressivity of users; thus, by placing importance on the tactile experience, these interfaces aim to provide more intuitive and natural means of music creation.

All physical objects can be part of a digital user interface [25]. A possibility is that an object moved or put in a specific location originates itself a digital signal to communicate position and/or movement to the surrounding system; another case is that of an external device, e.g. a camera or a pressure sensor, that senses the object.

Music TUIs can play a number of roles: synthesizers to generate sound, sequencers that perform audio samples and mix them together, remote controllers for music and sound parameters, interfaces for music-related games, and so on. Some of these devices have been reviewed or analyzed in detail in dedicated scientific works. To cite but a few references, Paradiso *et al.* reviewed TUIs based on magnetic tags [35], Newton-Dunn *et al.* described a way to control a dynamic polyrhythmic sequencer using physical artifacts [34], and Schiettecatte and Vanderdonckt presented a distributed cube interface based on interaction range for sound design [39]. Due to their availability, LEGO bricks or similar building blocks have often been employed in the control of musical parameters [6,21,33].

Several working prototypes are also available that did not originate from a scientific publication or resulted in a commercial product. Noticeable examples include the music maker device [3] designed by Lapponi *at al.* as a course project at the University of Oslo, the tangible user interface to control an audio player [4] realized by Brumley at the California College of the Arts, and the abandoned collaborative interface called *Block Jam* by Collect.Apply.

A successful case of commercially available music TUI is the *Reactable* [30], used by renowned artists such as Björk in their live performances. It provides a unique and immersive experience by combining physical objects with realtime digital audio processing and visual feedback. The *Reactable* consists of several key components that work in harmony to facilitate music composition and performance. The central element is a backlit translucent tabletop surface, equipped with a grid of light-emitting diodes (LEDs) and an underlying camerabased tracking system. This surface acts as the primary interface for interaction, allowing users to manipulate physical objects, referred to as "tangibles", placed on its surface. Each tangible object represents a distinct musical component or function, such as sound generators, audio effects, filters, or sequencers. These tangibles are typically equipped with fiducial markers, enabling the tracking system to identify and interpret their position, orientation, and other relevant parameters. The system captures the movements and configurations of the tangibles, translating them into real-time audio and visual feedback. Users can interact with the tangibles by rotating, moving, or connecting them to each other. These actions modify the musical characteristics or relationships between the elements represented by the tangibles.

Concerning our proposal, we rely on *Kibo*, another commercially available music TUI whose characteristics will be described in detail in Sect. 4.1.

In conclusion, music TUIs aim to offer a compelling user experience that blends physicality, visual feedback, and auditory output. A sense of engagement and creativity is expected to be stimulated when interacting with the system, thanks to the tangible and multisensory nature of the interface. The design of the experience should encourage exploration, experimentation, and improvisation, enabling learners, experienced musicians, and performers to discover new sonic possibilities and express their artistic ideas more intuitively.

---

[3] https://youtu.be/sKojCxcpgnk.
[4] https://youtu.be/ZQdIxQ_EOLI.

4   Employed Technologies

In this section, we will address the key technologies employed in the project: a music TUI called *Kibo* (Sect. 4.1), the way it is connected to a web application (Sect. 4.2), and the web languages and formats used to implement the browser games described later (Sect. 4.3).

4.1   *Kibo*

Kibo [5] is a wooden board produced by Kodaly that presents eight distinct, easy-to-recognize tangibles. These geometric shapes can be inserted into and removed from the corresponding slots, thus triggering events encoded in the form of MIDI messages, specifically Note On and Note Off. The device is also sensitive to pressure variations on single tangibles; individual dynamic responses are communicated via Channel Pressure messages. Additionally, the device is equipped with a knob that can be clicked and rotated and with a gyroscope, triggering Control Change messages.

Kibo can be connected via Bluetooth or USB to iOS and macOS devices running a proprietary app that acts as both a synthesizer and a configuration tool. Windows and Android operating systems are also supported via third-party drivers. As mentioned before, the communication between the controller and the app occurs by exchanging standard MIDI 1.0 messages. The MIDI engine integrated into the app supports up to 7 *Kibo* units simultaneously, without perceivable latency. This aspect is particularly interesting for collaborative experiences like those documented in [7]. Being a MIDI controller, *Kibo* can also be integrated into any MIDI setup without the intervention of the app as a mediator, and this is the approach we follow in our proposal.

The control over music parameters is mainly based on the 8 tangibles shown in Fig. 4. Each object has a different shape fitting in a single slot and presents symmetry properties so that it can be arbitrarily rotated and flipped before being inserted. Thanks to their magnetic core, tangibles can be stacked one on top of the other and interact through magnetic fields. The body of *Kibo* contains a multi-point pressure sensor able to detect the insertion and removal of tangibles. The characteristics of the sensor make the instrument extremely sensitive and, simultaneously, very resistant. For further details, please refer to [3].

Even if our proposal bypasses the native *Kibo*'s app and re-implements its functions, it is interesting to analyze the three operating modes originally conceived by *Kibo*'s manufacturer, since they inspired our initiative:

1. *Musical Instrument Mode* — In this scenario, *Kibo*'s tangibles are mapped onto pitches. Associations between shapes and notes can be customized, even triggering multiple notes through a single tangible. The device is able to detect *aftertouch*, namely the pressure variations over tangibles after note attacks;

---

[5] https://www.kodaly.app/.

Fig. 4. *Kibo*'s wooden body and tangibles. Image taken from https://www.kodaly. app/.

2. *Beat Mode* — In this scenario, each tangible is mapped onto a single percussive instrument. The pressure sensor, presenting a high level of resistance to strong mechanical stresses but also a noticeable sensitivity, allows effects ranging from hard mallet beats to delicate brush rubbing;
3. *Song Mode* — In this scenario, *Kibo* is employed as a controller to trigger already available music loops. Tangibles are associated with mutually synchronized but independent tracks, like in a multi-track environment. When a tangible is inserted, the corresponding track is activated; when it is removed, the track is muted, but it goes on running silently, so as to preserve global synchronization.

Focusing on rehabilitative and therapeutic scenarios, the reconfigurability of *Kibo* coupled with the adoption of a standard communication protocol enables heterogeneous scenarios. Multiple *Kibo* units forming an ensemble can be configured to cover distinct note ranges and timbres, or even to work in different operating modes, thus providing the therapist with great flexibility. Moreover, the standard MIDI output of *Kibo* allows the implementation of additional operating modes where other meanings, even extra-musical ones, can be assigned to user gestures. Our proposal, described in detail in Sect. 5, explores this possibility.

Even if originally conceived as a general-purpose tangible-based MIDI controller, when used in a suitable scenario *Kibo* can also be considered an *assistive* technology falling in the category of communication boards [45]. Under this perspective, it has a *therapeutic* function since it encourages upper-limb movements and challenges cognitive skills. Moreover, it is *compensatory* from both a motor point of view, being able to translate even small movements into sound, and a cognitive point of view, enabling intuitive musical expression by lowering the barriers of a traditional instrument.

4.2 Network Technologies

In our proposal, *Kibo* has to be directly connected to the computing system that hosts the browser via Bluetooth. Bluetooth is an open standard for radio-based communications in the 2.4 GHz Industrial, Scientific and Medical (ISM) band. It targets low-power, low-cost, low-range, and moderate-rate applications. A more specialized protocol, called MIDI over Bluetooth (or, simply, Bluetooth MIDI), has been conceived to exchange MIDI messages over Bluetooth connections [8].

Kibo adopts Bluetooth Low Energy (BLE), a wireless personal-area network technology that, compared to the original Bluetooth protocol, is intended to provide considerably reduced power consumption and cost while maintaining a similar communication range. BLE hardware is ubiquitous on modern devices and native driver support is available under most desktop and mobile operating systems. Once a BLE MIDI device is paired, it will transparently operate with MIDI-compatible applications on most mobile and desktop platforms with no additions.

Given its significant advantages in terms of compatibility, wireless capability, and low power consumption, BLE MIDI is an ideal choice for controllers. A potential problem in real-time scenarios could be latency, but in MIDI applications it is comparable with WiFi and, while bandwidth appears to be worse, is near to the original MIDI specifications.

4.3 Web Languages and Formats

The platform we are proposing has been implemented in the form of web pages. To this goal, we adopted W3C[6] standard languages and formats. As a result, the proposed activities can be experienced using any HTML5-compliant browser. In particular, the project was realized using HTML to structure the pages, CSS for animations and style, and JavaScript to handle and verify actions and events. With respect to HTML and CSS, whose role is descriptive, JavaScript is a programming language that can be used to modify or animate web content in response to users' actions.

A special technology adopted to bring MIDI into the web is the Web MIDI API. The main goal of such a programming interface is to allow the connection and interaction between a browser app and an external MIDI system, either physical or virtual. About 10 years from the release of the first public document, the Web MIDI API is still at the stage of a working draft and, as such, it is not fully supported by the totality of HTML5-compliant browsers. At the moment of writing, among the major browsers, only *Apple Safari* is not supporting this technology; conversely, *Google Chrome*, *Mozilla Firefox*, *Microsoft Edge*, *Opera*, and, more generally, all the browsers deriving from the open-source *Chromium*

---

[6] World Wide Web Consortium, https://www.w3.org/.

project do support the Web MIDI API. Further details on this subject have been recently discussed by Baratè and Ludovico in a dedicated scientific paper [5].

Since all technologies in use are client-side, the platform can also be enjoyed locally on the user's client, with no need to connect to a server. Nevertheless, we have publicly released the platform over the web to distribute it freely and keep it up-to-date in the case of a new release.

5   Kibo Web Games

The goal of linking music therapy, rehabilitation exercises, and technology through *Kibo* brought to the design and implementation of a web platform that proposes three serious games. The name of the platform is *Kibo Web Games*. All games are intended to foster the association between physical elements (geometric tangibles) and the concepts they represent (e.g., notes, tracks, and hit buttons).

The platform is available at https://kibogames.lim.di.unimi.it/ and its original web interface is shown in Fig. 5. *Kibo Web Games* need a *Kibo* device to be connected via BLE.

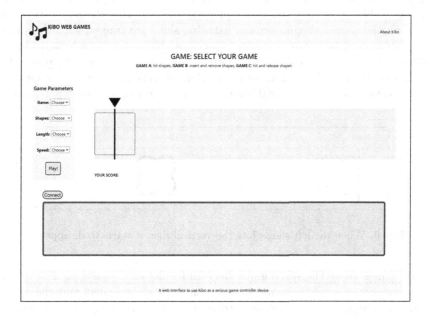

Fig. 5. The interface for *Kibo Web Games* common to the three rhythm games.

A number of game parameters have been introduced to allow flexibility in usage and adaptation to gradual improvements without causing frustration in the player. The user or therapist can set different types of activities and levels of difficulty according to the following parameters:

- The **game** to play, which is basically a rhythm-based activity where given shapes are proposed to the player and must be timely touched, inserted, removed, or continuously pressed depending on the game mode, as explained in the following;
- The **number of shapes** (1 to 8) that can randomly be involved during the game experience;
- The total **length** of the game sequence, i.e. the number of actions a user should carry out in a game session;
- The **speed** of shape generation and scroll animation.

The central part of the interface is taken by the *Game field*, which displays the moving shapes during a game session. Shapes move from right to left, and the perfect timing for the user's actions is when they hit the black vertical line. Another relevant part of the interface shown in Fig. 5 is the *MIDI message console*, namely the lower rectangle that displays Note On, Note Off, Control Change, Program Change, and Polyphonic Key Pressure messages received from *Kibo* after attaching it through the *Connect* button. Finally, the *Play* button starts the selected game with the parameters set by the user.

Concerning the gameplay, *Kibo Web Games* focus on the interactions occurring between the player and *Kibo*, i.e. simple motor movements like hitting, tapping, grabbing, holding, releasing, placing, and removing the geometrical tangibles. Furthermore, recognition and listening skills are trained with the aim to help restore or keep active cognitive functions. *Kibo* gives tactile and musical feedback to every action that is performed and allows the user to proceed in small steps. It also allows users to manipulate objects giving a clearer image of the connection between physical interaction and the response that it triggers.

Fig. 6. When the left shape hits the vertical line, it starts to disappear.

All games share the same game field and functional concepts. The system generates shapes scrolling across the screen from right to left and the goal is to timely recognize the shape by hitting, pressing, inserting, or removing the corresponding tangible from *Kibo* physical body when it reaches the vertical line in the delimiter box (Fig. 6). Specifically, the first game asks the user to timely push the tangibles, the second game expects the user to insert or remove shapes from their slots, and the third game asks the user to press and/or release multiple shapes. Games will be better explained in the following. The scores, levels of difficulty, and feedback for the players depend on their time precision in performing the actions required.

Throughout the duration of a game session, the arrow, square, and vertical line in the *Game field* animate to facilitate the game experience. Arrow and square flash when the user is supposed to perform a task. The vertical line turns either red or green according to the accuracy of the performance. The score field keeps track of the points gained while playing and remains displayed until the next game session is started.

Perfect hits are those performed in a tiny time interval around the exact timing. Good hits (see Fig. 7) occur in a slightly wider timing range. The exact values depend on the game speed set by the user, but they are in the order of tenths of a second. Score penalties for wrong shape recognition (Fig. 8) or missed hits (Fig. 9) have not been implemented to avoid frustration in players, but this feature could be easily integrated.

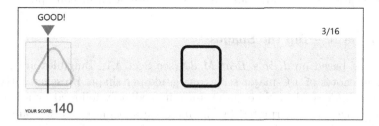

Fig. 7. A good hit for the triangle tangible. The vertical line turns green and the score is incremented. In the meanwhile, a new square-shaped tangible is approaching. (Color figure online)

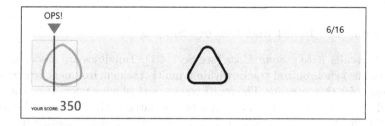

Fig. 8. Wrong shape recognition caused, e.g., by clicking a circle instead of a rounded triangle. The vertical line turns red and the score is not incremented. In the meanwhile, a new triangle-shaped tangible is approaching. (Color figure online)

Please note that *Kibo Web Games*'s interface allows users to play with *Kibo* as a simple musical controller, regardless a game session is active or not. In this scenario, only sound feedback and console messages are available. From a technical point of view, this allows the user to check the device connection, but, above all, this "sandbox mode" can help gain confidence with the controller.

Fig. 9. Wrong timing in pressing the triangle-shaped tangible. The vertical line turns red and the score is not incremented. (Color figure online)

As a final remark, please note that the three game modes do not require a music-education background nor make explicit use of music concepts.

5.1   Game A – Tap the Shapes

Game A is based on *Kibo*'s *Beat Mode* (see Sect. 4.1. Tangibles are mapped onto single notes of a C-major scale, one grade per shape. Pressing, hitting, or tapping a shape sends a Note On message immediately followed by a Note Off. MIDI messages are interpreted by the interface and played back thanks to an embedded audio synthesizer. In order to play this game, all tangibles must stay in their slots. Difficulty varies according to the speed, number of shapes involved, game length, and score precision.

The rhythm game expects the user to press the expected tangible in the right timing range, namely when the arrow and delimiter box turn yellow (see Fig. 6). The therapeutic and rehabilitative goals of this game include the ability to recognize shapes and timely activate commands.

5.2   Game B – Insert and Remove Shapes

Game B recalls *Kibo*'s *Song Mode* (see Sect. 4.1). Tangibles are associated with independent synchronized tracks within a multi-track environment realized with Pro Tools[7] for this purpose. The multi-track starts playing when the game is initialized but has no volume. Each track is associated with a shape and unmuted when the corresponding tangible is inserted into the device's wooden base. Conversely, removing the shape mutes the track. All tangibles must be removed and placed in front of the player or at a reachable distance before starting the game. The aim of *Game B* is to score points by timely inserting and extracting *Kibo*'s tangibles once the randomly generated shapes touch the hit-line or perfectly fit the delimiter box, i.e. before the animation ends and the shape disappears. The random algorithm assures that, in the case of right performance, at the end of the session no shapes are left inside *Kibo*'s body.

---

[7] https://www.avid.com/pro-tools.

This game mode solicits the development or recovery of cognitive abilities, including memory (shapes have to be quickly recognized, found in the space around *Kibo*, and inserted into the right slot) and creative reasoning (e.g., finding the most suitable layout for the pieces extracted from *Kibo*'s body).

5.3   Game C – Hold and Release Shapes

Game C recalls *Kibo*'s *Musical Instrument Mode* and takes benefits from the detection of polyphonic aftertouch. Tangibles are mapped once again onto the grades of a C-major scale. Somehow similar to *Game A*, when a shape touches the vertical line or enters the delimiter box, the user is expected not only to tap the corresponding tangible but also to keep it pressed until the same shape appears again. Consequently, multiple tangibles could be in a pressed state simultaneously.

This game mode is the most challenging one, from both a motor and a cognitive point of view. For example, some combinations of shapes require not only the ability to have them selected simultaneously but also a good strategy to have a hand free for the next insertion.

6   Early Experimentation

The design and implementation phases of *Kibo Web Games* mainly occurred between 2021 and 2022. Due to the restrictions imposed by the COVID-19 pandemic and the impact of the virus on the elderly and fragile population, at an early stage of development, it was not possible to test the web platform in a real scenario. To have feedback on our work, we had to rely on two user groups: i) experts in the fields of music therapy, physiotherapy, and cognitive rehabilitation, and ii) a focus group made of elderly people selected among family members, friends, and acquaintances.

Concerning the former group, a prototype was presented to researchers of *Fondazione Don Carlo Gnocchi*, Milan. Many useful remarks emerged about the games' structure and the user interface. *Game A* was particularly appreciated due to its simplicity. Nevertheless, its interface was considered too complex for users with impairments, above all cognitive ones. The first suggestion was to implement a back-office area so as to move the parameter configuration and the MIDI console away from the gameplay interface. In fact, side controls and console messages are not meaningful during the game; conversely, they can be a source of distraction for users. Similarly, in the experts' opinion, other aspects of the interface had to be improved. For example, the presence of colors should be limited as much as possible, using them just to differentiate some actions (e.g., "insert a tangible" or "remove a tangible"). The numeric score, too, could be too difficult to understand; rather, the level of user performance should be returned through a more direct and intuitive representation, such as a progress bar, the number of stars, or similar means.

As regards *Game B* and *Game C*, the experts' concerns focused on the graphical representation of the game field that, being currently the same as *Game A*, could sound a bit confusing for impaired users. The key difference between the former games and the latter one is that *Game A* does not present the concept of status (the symbols proposed to the user have to be clicked), whereas *Game B* and *Game C* involve persistent actions (tangibles must stay in place or must be pressed for a given time). Consequently, a differentiated layout could help, e.g. 8 scrolling areas corresponding to the 8 tangibles. Figure 10 shows the possible revisions of the current interface for *Game A* and *Game B*. Moreover, experts agreed that the last two games are more challenging and, for this reason, they suggested a step-by-step offline process before playing the web version. In the case of *Game B*, such a process could be first locating shapes with no time constraint, then physically moving shapes into their slots, and so on.

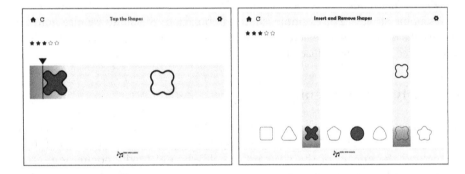

Fig. 10. Revised interface for *Game A* and *Game B*.

From the dialogue with experts, it emerged that the approach of *Kibo Web Games* could be easily generalized and adapted to other scenarios. For example, the platform could be profitably used to develop music-parameter awareness or transmit geometric concepts to young students, even at preschool age, thanks to the intuitiveness and playfulness typical of a tangible interface. Moreover, *Kibo Web Games* could help recover cognitive and motor abilities also in younger users [7].

Concerning the focus group, in general terms the *Kibo Web Games* platform was appreciated and the experience was perceived by most users as an enjoyable, yet challenging form of entertainment. The interface and the gameplay proposed to the experimental group were the original ones.

Some difficulties experienced in game sessions were particularly illuminating. For instance, some shapes have been often confused, such as in the case of the triangle and the rounded triangle, and in the case of the four-leaf clover, the five-pointed star, and the rounded cross. The occurrence of these tangibles caused a significantly higher miss rate in all games, which suggests that: i) in early game sessions, only one tangible in the set of confusingly similar shapes could be used, and ii) users must gradually get acquainted with distinguishing between them, possibly accompanied by therapists. An issue experienced by one of the participants, absolutely unexpected for us, was due to what we considered a strength of *Kibo*: the user prepared to press the next button by gently placing her finger on the tangible, but the extreme sensitivity of the pressure sensor detected such a gesture as an event and triggered a new note at the wrong timing.

Game A was perceived as intuitive and most users were able to play with little or no explanation at all. Conversely, *Game B*, whose starting scenario is having all shapes out of the board, had to be prepared and carefully explained. In general terms, users learned how to play only after a number of game sessions, and even the slowest game speed was perceived as challenging. It was interesting to observe the different strategies employed when tangibles had to be removed; in particular, a user left tangibles almost in place by moving them out from their slots and placing them on the wooden board, which is a very clever strategy indeed. *Game C*, when set to use all 8 shapes randomly, was considered extremely demanding from a physical and cognitive point of view. As a result of the focus group, the gameplay for this scenario must be rethought in order to avoid challenging combinations that would undermine even the performances of non-impaired users.

To obtain subjective feedback, ad hoc questions were mediated by the interviewer and transformed into 5-point Likert scales. All participants in the focus group partially (4 points) or strongly (5 points) agreed with the idea to play *Kibo Web Games* again. They found *Game A* and *Game B* simple from a physical (1 to 2 points in the Likert scale) and a cognitive (1 to 2 points in the Likert scale) point of view. However, it must be noted that the focus group was composed of elderly people with no certified physical or cognitive impairments. In this sense, only clinical experimentation under expert supervision can return significant results.

7   Conclusions and Future Work

In this project, we investigated the suitability of music TUIs in general, and a specific device called *Kibo* in particular, to compensate for age impairments. To this goal, we designed, implemented, and tested an early release of a web platform proposing three games based on the same concept, namely the timely interaction with tangibles. The games aimed at developing or reactivating different cognitive functions, physical abilities, and soft skills. Examples include the recognition of shapes, press/insert/remove actions, and the choice of a best-fitting strategy to solve a problem, respectively.

Due to *Kibo*'s 8-voice polyphony, multiple participants have the opportunity to operate the same interface simultaneously. Consequently, a game session can be played in a collaborative way. This could be advantageous for seriously disabled individuals needing assistance from caregivers. However, it is worth noting that the current release of the web platform is not designed to fully benefit from this opportunity.

The possibility to choose parameters and set levels allows users to proceed in small steps and progress at their own pace. Therapists, caregivers, or users themselves can suitably configure game sessions based on the players' attitudes and abilities. Moreover, no game penalties were implemented with the purpose of not discouraging elderly users who are often not technology savvy and likely to be afraid of making mistakes or getting stuck.

The adoption of a standard communication protocol between the controller and the web platform virtually supports a number of generalizations for the proposed approach. For instance, the web platform could be operated through any MIDI-compatible device connected via BLE and sending the same set of MIDI commands (Note On and Note Off on given channels, Control Change with specific CC numbers, etc.). Anyway, it is worth remarking that only tangible-based controllers offer the benefits described in this paper. Moreover, the graphical interface of *Kibo Web Games* was tailored to the physical layout of *Kibo*, proposing the same number and type of shapes. This does not prevent the adoption of a DIY approach to create a low-cost device capable of emulating the interaction of *Kibo*, e.g. by using an Arduino board, pressure sensors, and a 3D-printed case.

The inspiration for future work mainly comes from the observations and remarks by experts and early users reported in Sect. 6. Short-term improvements for the web platform include:

- the creation of a different game field for each specific game, keeping the interface's aspect as clean and simple as possible to avoid distractions during the gameplay;
- the implementation of a dedicated page to set game parameters;
- methodologies to record game performances and track specific parameter values (e.g. pressure variations) as a support tool for rehabilitation experts.

Further developments are expected to be inspired by thorough experimentation in clinical environments, thus extending the number of participants as it regards both patients and rehabilitation experts.

Our expectation is that *Kibo Web Games* will constitute an effective and engaging way to stimulate declining cognitive abilities and reignite strained motor skills in elderly people.

Acknowledgements. The authors are grateful to *Kodaly S.r.l.*, the manufacturer of *Kibo*, for the support. The authors also wish to thank the experts of *Fondazione Don Carlo Gnocchi, Milan* for their help in the early evaluation of the prototype and all elderly people participating in the focus groups.

References

1. Adlakha, S., Chhabra, D., Shukla, P.: Effectiveness of gamification for the rehabilitation of neurodegenerative disorders. Chaos, Solitons Fractals **140**, 110192 (2020)
2. American Music Therapy Association: About music therapy & AMTA. https://www.musictherapy.org/about/ (2022) Accessed May 27 2021

3. Amico, M.D., Ludovico, L.A.: Kibo: A MIDI controller with a tangible user interface for music education. In: International Conference on Computer Supported Education, pp. 613–619. SCITEPRESS (2020)
4. Baratè, A., Korsten, H., Ludovico, L.A.: A music tangible user interface for the cognitive and motor rehabilitation of elderly people. In: Constantine, L., Holzinger, A., Silva, H.P., Vanderdonckt, J. (eds.) Proceedings of the 6th International Conference on Computer-Human Interaction Research and Applications (CHIRA 2022), pp. 121–128. SCITEPRESS - Science and Technology Publications, Lda. (2022). https://doi.org/10.5220/0011395900003323
5. Baratè, A., Ludovico, L.A.: Web MIDI API: State of the art and future perspectives. J. Audio Eng. Society **70**(11), 918–925 (2022). https://doi.org/10.17743/jaes.2022.0028
6. Baratè, A., Ludovico, L.A., Malchiodi, D.: Fostering computational thinking in primary school through a LEGO®-based music notation. Procedia Comput. Sci. Knowledge-Based and Intelligent Information & Engineering Systems: Proceedings of the 21st International Conference, KES 2017, 6–8 September 2017, Marseille, France **112**, 1334–1344 (2017). https://doi.org/10.1016/j.procs.2017.08.018
7. Baratè, A., Ludovico, L.A., Oriolo, E.: An ensemble of tangible user interfaces to foster music awareness and interaction in vulnerable learners. In: Proceedings of 5th International Conference on Computer-Human Interaction Research and Applications, pp. 48–57. SCITEPRESS (2021)
8. Bartolomeu, P., Fonseca, J., Duarte, P., Rodrigues, P., Girao, L.: Midi over bluetooth. In: 2005 IEEE Conference on Emerging Technologies and Factory Automation. vol. 1, pp. 8–102 (2005). https://doi.org/10.1109/ETFA.2005.1612507
9. Berton, A., et al.: Virtual reality, augmented reality, gamification, and telerehabilitation: psychological impact on orthopedic patients' rehabilitation. J. Clin. Med. **9**(8), 2567 (2020)
10. Burke, J., McNeill, M., Charles, D., Morrow, P., Crosbie, J., McDonough, S.: Augmented reality games for upper-limb stroke rehabilitation. In: 2010 Second International Conference on Games and Virtual Worlds for Serious Applications, pp. 75–78 (2010). https://doi.org/10.1109/VS-GAMES.2010.21
11. de Castro-Cros, M., et al.: Effects of gamification in BCI functional rehabilitation. Front. Neurosci. **14**, 882 (2020)
12. Cerezo, E., Bonillo, C., Baldassarri, S.: Therapeutic activities for elderly people based on tangible interaction. In: ICT4AWE, pp. 281–290 (2020)
13. Chu, R.J.c.: How family support and internet self-efficacy influence the effects of e-learning among higher aged adults-analyses of gender and age differences. Comput. Educ. **55**(1), 255–264 (2010)
14. Czaja, S.J., Lee, C.C.: The impact of aging on access to technology. Univ. Access Inf. Soc. **5**(4), 341–349 (2007)
15. Czaja, S.J., Sharit, J.: Age differences in attitudes toward computers. J. Gerontol. B Psychol. Sci. Soc. Sci. **53**(5), P329–P340 (1998)
16. De Carvalho, R.N.S., Ishitani, L., Nogueira Sales De Carvalho, R., et al.: Motivational factors for mobile serious games for elderly users. In: Proceedings of XI SB games, pp. 2–4 (2012)
17. Dörner, R., Göbel, S., Effelsberg, W., Wiemeyer, J. (eds.): Serious Games. Springer, Cham (2016). https://doi.org/10.1007/978-3-319-40612-1
18. Duckworth, J., et al.: Resonance: an interactive tabletop artwork for co-located group rehabilitation and play. In: Antona, M., Stephanidis, C. (eds.) UAHCI 2015. LNCS, vol. 9177, pp. 420–431. Springer, Cham (2015). https://doi.org/10.1007/978-3-319-20684-4_41

19. Farage, M.A., Miller, K.W., Ajayi, F., Hutchins, D.: Design principles to accommodate older adults. Global J. Health Sci. **4**(2), 2 (2012)
20. Fonseca, X., Slingerland, G., Lukosch, S., Brazier, F.: Designing for meaningful social interaction in digital serious games. Entertain. Comput. **36**, 100385 (2021)
21. Gohlke, K., Hlatky, M., de Jong, B.: Physical construction toys for rapid sketching of tangible user interfaces. In: Proceedings of the Ninth International Conference on Tangible, Embedded, and Embodied Interaction, pp. 643–648. TEI '15, Association for Computing Machinery, New York, NY, USA (2015). https://doi.org/10.1145/2677199.2687900
22. Huppert, E., et al.: The development of children's preferences for equality and equity across 13 individualistic and collectivist cultures. Dev. Sci. **22**(2), e12729 (2019)
23. Iachini, T., Borghi, A.M., Senese, V.P.: Categorization and sensorimotor interaction with objects. Brain Cogn. **67**(1), 31–43 (2008)
24. Ijsselsteijn, W., Nap, H.H., de Kort, Y., Poels, K.: Digital game design for elderly users. In: Proceedings of the 2007 Conference on Future Play, pp. 17–22. Future Play '07, Association for Computing Machinery, New York, NY, USA (2007). https://doi.org/10.1145/1328202.1328206
25. Ishii, H.: Tangible bits: Beyond pixels. In: Proceedings of 2nd International Conference on Tangible and Embedded Interaction, pp. xv–xxv. TEI '08, Association for Computing Machinery (2008). https://doi.org/10.1145/1347390.1347392
26. Ishii, H.: The tangible user interface and its evolution. Commun. ACM **51**(6), 32–36 (2008). https://doi.org/10.1145/1349026.1349034
27. Ishii, H., Ullmer, B.: Tangible bits: towards seamless interfaces between people, bits and atoms. In: Proceedings of the ACM SIGCHI Conference on Human Factors in Computing Systems, pp. 234–241 (1997)
28. Iversen, T.R.: Exploring tangible interaction: Alternative interfaces for assisting elderly users. Master's thesis, Department of Informatics, University of Oslo (2015)
29. Jankovic, J.: Parkinson's disease: clinical features and diagnosis. J. Neurol., Neurosurgery Psych. **79**(4), 368–376 (2008)
30. Jordà, S., Geiger, G., Alonso, M., Kaltenbrunner, M.: The reacTable: exploring the synergy between live music performance and tabletop tangible interfaces. In: Proceedings of 1st International Conference on Tangible and Embedded Interaction, pp. 139–146 (2007)
31. Laguna, K., Babcock, R.L.: Computer anxiety in young and older adults: implications for human-computer interactions in older populations. Comput. Hum. Behav. **13**(3), 317–326 (1997)
32. Maylor, E.A.: Prospective memory in normal ageing and dementia. Neurocase **1**(3), 285–289 (1995)
33. Miotti, B., Bassani, L., Cauteruccio, E., Morandi, M.: Musicblocks: An innovative tool for learning the foundations of music. In: Proceedings of CSME 2022, pp. 475–484 (2022). https://doi.org/10.5220/0011152100003182
34. Newton-Dunn, H., Nakano, H., Gibson, J.: Block jam: a tangible interface for interactive music. J. New Music Res. **32**(4), 383–393 (2003)
35. Paradiso, J.A., Hsiao, K.y., Benbasat, A.: Tangible music interfaces using passive magnetic tags. In: Proceedings of the 2001 Conference on New Interfaces for Musical Expression, pp. 1–4. NIME '01, National University of Singapore, SGP (2001)
36. Pearce, C.: The truth about baby boomer gamers: A study of over-forty computer game players. Games and Culture **3**(2), 142–174 (2008). https://doi.org/10.1177/1555412008314132, https://doi.org/10.1177/1555412008314132

37. Rego, P.A., Moreira, P.M., Reis, L.P.: Architecture for serious games in health rehabilitation. In: Rocha, Á., Correia, A.M., Tan, F.B., Stroetmann, K.A. (eds.) New
Perspectives in Information Systems and Technologies, Volume 2. AISC, vol. 276,
pp. 307–317. Springer, Cham (2014). https://doi.org/10.1007/978-3-319-05948-
8_30
38. Salthouse, T.A.: Mediation of adult age differences in cognition by reductions in
working memory and speed of processing. Psychol. Sci. **2**(3), 179–183 (1991)
39. Schiettecatte, B., Vanderdonckt, J.: Audiocubes: A distributed cube tangible interface based on interaction range for sound design. In: Proceedings of 2nd International Conference on Tangible and Embedded Interaction, pp. 3–10. TEI '08,
Association for Computing Machinery, New York, NY, USA (2008). https://doi.
org/10.1145/1347390.1347394
40. Scott, A.J.: The longevity society. Lancet Healthy Longevity **2**(12), e820–e827
(2021)
41. Steiner, B., Elgert, L., Saalfeld, B., Wolf, K.H., et al.: Gamification in rehabilitation
of patients with musculoskeletal diseases of the shoulder: scoping review. JMIR
Serious Games **8**(3), e19914 (2020)
42. Tuah, N.M., Ahmedy, F., Gani, A., Yong, L.N.: A survey on gamification for health
rehabilitation care: applications, opportunities, and open challenges. Information
12(2), 91 (2021)
43. Vandermaesen, M., De Weyer, T., Feys, P., Luyten, K., Coninx, K.: Integrating
serious games and tangible objects for functional handgrip training: A user study
of handly in persons with multiple sclerosis. In: Proceedings of the 2016 ACM
Conference on Designing Interactive Systems, pp. 924–935 (2016)
44. Wecker, N.S., Kramer, J.H., Hallam, B.J., Delis, D.C.: Mental flexibility: age effects
on switching. Neuropsychology **19**(3), 345 (2005)
45. World Health Organization, United Nations Children's Fund: Global report on
assistive technology. World Health Organization (2022), https://apps.who.int/iris/
rest/bitstreams/1424204/retrieve
46. Zhao, X., et al.: Segara: Integrating serious games and handgrip for hand rehabilitation in rheumatoid arthritis patients. In: The 9th International Symposium of
Chinese CHI, pp. 101–104 (2021)

An Extended Study of Search User Interface Design Focused on Hofstede's Cultural Dimensions

Karen Chessum[1]([✉]) [iD], Haiming Liu[2] [iD], and Ingo Frommholz[3] [iD]

[1] University of Bedfordshire, Luton, England, UK
karen.chessum@beds.ac.uk
[2] University of Southampton, Southampton, UK
[3] University of Wolverhampton, Wolverhampton, UK

Abstract. Geert Hofstede's classic cultural model has been studied and applied to website design for a number of years. In this paper we examine if Geert Hofstede's six cultural dimensions can also be applied to search user interface design. Two user studies have been conducted to evaluate the culturally designed search user interfaces, and the findings are reported in this paper. Our first study comprised of 148 participants from different cultural backgrounds. The second study was smaller with 25 participants, also from different cultural backgrounds. The results from these studies have been analyzed to ascertain if Hofstede's cultural dimensions are suitable for understanding users' preferences for search user interface design. Whilst the key findings from these studies suggest Hofstede cross-cultural dimensions can be used to model users' preferences on search interface design, further work is still needed for particular cultural dimensions to reinforce the conclusions.

Keywords: Cross-cultural information retrieval · Cross-cultural theory · Website design · Human-Computer Information Retrieval (HCIR) · Hofstede's cultural dimensions · Human-Computer Interaction (HCI)

1 Introduction

A form of 'localisation' is offered by search engines (SE). This is achieved by displaying the search results related to a particular country and location within that country. Geographical location only offers a basic or a surface pointer of the user's culture or ethnic identity.

Considerable research has been undertaken regarding the necessity for the localisation of websites and software applications to meet cross cultural requirements. This paper refers to the term localisation as tailoring the user experience (UX), both affective and cognitively. Examples are given in Smith et al., [1] Singh [2] Alcántara-Pilar et al., [3] and Benaida [4] to name but a few. However, research is limited with regards to cross cultural search engine user interface (UI) design, such as Taksa and Muro Flomenbaum [5] and Hover [6].

© The Author(s), under exclusive license to Springer Nature Switzerland AG 2023
A. Holzinger et al. (Eds.): CHIRA 2021/2022, CCIS 1882, pp. 130–152, 2023.
https://doi.org/10.1007/978-3-031-41962-1_7

This research paper looks at the gap that exists between cross cultural website design and search engine user interface design. The chief idea and motivation behind this research is to incorporate an extant cultural model into search engine user interface design. This paper is an extension to our first paper by Chessum et al., [7] that examines different cultural models and how they can be utilised to enhance the user experience. This paper reports the additional findings of the second experiment and compares them to the findings of the first experiment.

Several cultural models are talked about in the field of Human Computer Interaction (HCI) for example, Hall [8], Nisbett [9], Trompenarrs & Hampden-Turner [10] and Hofstede et al., [11]. These cultural models are described in more details below.

1.1 Edward Hall

The anthropologist, Edward Hall, became a pioneering person for cross-cultural business communication. Hall [8] gave a definition of culture as, 'high context' (HC) and 'low context'(LC).

The high-low framework relates to how information is stored and flows. Smith et al., [1] describe a high context communication as being when 'little has to be said or written because most of the information is either in the physical environment or within the person, while very little is in the coded, explicit part of the message'. Liu [12] describes 'people from high-context cultures prefer face-to-face communication' and continues by saying high-context cultures, 'look for both less-direct verbal and subtler nonverbal cues during the communication'.

Conversely, with a low context culture, little is hidden and the information in the message is explicit. Oshlyansky [13] notes examples of low context cultures are: USA, Germany and Switzerland, and examples of high context cultures would be Japan and China.

Hall was also responsible for creating 'elements of units of culture'. This allowed projects to be measured against each other. Oshlyansky [13] notes Hall also encouraged others to identify universal measures of culture. One of the responses to this call from Hall, was from Trompenaars & Hampden-Turner [14], their contribution is described later in Sect. 1.2.

Hall created the Primary Message Systems (PMS), this is non-lingual communication made by humans to one another. Hall advocates, that to understand a culture, the individual needs to understand how the culture relates to the PMS system. Hall recognized 10 PMS, each one he related to a facet of human activities [15].

Hall's 10 PMS are; Interaction, Association, Subsistence, Bisexuality, Territoriality, Learning, Play, Defence and Exploitation. Despite Hall's work on PMS, it is his work on 'high-context' and 'low-context' that is utilised the most from a perspective of Human Computer Interaction (HCI).

1.2 Trompenaars and Hampden-Turner

Trompenaars & Hampden-Turner viewed culture at a dimensional level, where the dimensions can be considered as units, and like Hall's PMS, can be used for comparison. Trompenaars & Hampden-Turner defined seven dimensions. As noted by Chessum et al., [7] they took Parson's five relational orientations [16] as a starting point. These seven dimension are; Universalism vs Particularism, Individualism vs Communitarianism, Specific vs Diffuse, Neutral vs Emotional, Achievement vs Ascription, Sequential time vs Synchronous time and Internal direction vs Outer direction.

1.3 Richard Nisbett

Social psychologist Richard E. Nisbett, looks at the culture differences from Eastern and Western cultures.

Oshlyansky [13] notes, Nisbett examines the 'processes of thought, perception, attention, organisation of knowledge, understanding' along with and other mental processes. Oshlyansky [13] continues to say, Nisbett uses what he refers to as, 'holistic' and 'analytic' thought patterns or mental processes, to make a distinction between Eastern and Western cultures. This is where Western cultures would be on the analytics side and East/Asian cultures would be on the holistic side.

As noted by Nisbett and Miyamoto [17] with regards to differences in attention and perception, "the evidence indicates that people in Western cultures focus on salient objects and use rules and categorization for purposes of organizing the environment. By contrast, people in East Asian cultures, focus more holistically on relationships and similarities among objects when organizing the environment."

Regarding East Asian cultures, Oshlyansky [13] continues to say, 'there is a continuity and a relationship among objects and events that cannot be broken down into constituent parts, for it is meaningless to do so', conversely for western cultures, it is seemingly 'important to categorise and find rules that govern the world so that predictions and control can be established'.

1.4 Geert Hofstede

Geert Hofstede, a Dutch anthropologist, conducted in-depth surveys/questionnaires from 117,000 IBM employees spanning over 50 countries, as noted in [18]. Hofstede analysed the responses and identified four cultural dimensions initially, with an additional fifth dimension for Long Term Time Orientation, identified from work conducted by Michael Harris Bond with the support of Hofstede. This dimension was added in 1991 [19].

Later a new sixth dimension, Indulgence versus Restraint (IND), was added and published by Hofstede et al., [11]. This followed the analysis by Michael Minkov of the World Value Survey (WVS) data, obtained from the World Values Survey Organisation; this data was from 93 countries. Details of all six dimensions can be found in Hofstede et al., [11]. Hofstede's dimensions are as follows: Power Distance (PD), Individualism vs. Collectivism (IDV), Masculinity vs. Femininity (MAS), Uncertainty Avoidance (UA), Long-term Time Orientation (LTO) and Indulgence versus Restraint (IND). These dimensions are described further from Sect. 2.1 to 2.6 inclusive.

1.5 Why Choose Hofstede's Cultural Model?

Hofstede's cultural research has been selected for this research due to it being, as observed by Chessum et al., [7] likely the most well-known of the cultural models and the most widely accepted and acknowledged metric set for cross cultural studies, as described by Ghemawat & Reiche [20] and also the most widely used.

Hofstede's work also has its critics. One of the more well-known being Mc Sweeny, [21, 22]. However, notwithstanding this, as noted by Chessum [23] Hofstede's research provides us with a set of recognizable metrics, that can be used to quantify and objectively reason.

Dimitrov [24] looked areas where Hofstede's cultural model has been applied and notes it 'has attracted the attention of different social actors – scientists, managers, politicians, administrators, opinion leaders, and other agents' [24].

Geert Hofstede's eldest son, Gert Jan, says his father has written 244 journal publications [25]. As noted by Chessum [23] a number of books have been published by Hofstede, among the publications are 'Culture's consequences: Comparing values, behaviors, institutions, and organizations across nations', Hofstede [26] 'Cultures and Organizations: Software of the Mind' [11, 19] and 'Cross-Cultural Analysis: The Science and Art of Comparing the World's Modern Societies and Their Cultures' Minkov and Hofstede [27].

As noted by Chessum [23], Hofstede's work has been widely used in a number of areas, including global branding and advertising, Mooij and Hofstede [28]. Oshlyansky [13] notes with regards to cross cultural models used in Human Computer Interaction (HCI), 'By far the most popular of these models is Hofstede's',

Pogosyan [29] describes Hofstede's work as being used in international management, marketing, inter cultural communications, cross cultural psychology and negotiation. Pogosyan [29] continues to say, 'he is among the most widely cited social scientists in the world'.

To conclude, Hofstede created six dimensions by which cultures can be compared, Reid [30] and as noted by Chessum [23] fulfils the requirement for scientific research, 'to be able to quantify and objectively reason a set of recognisable metrics'. [23].

2 User Interface Design

Using Hofstede's six cultural dimensions described below in Sect. 1.4, twelve prototype user interfaces have been designed. These prototypes consist of two user interfaces designed for each dimension, with one interface representing the lower end and one representing the higher end of each dimension, making twelve user interfaces in total, as described in Chessum et al., [7][1].

The design of the user interfaces, has been based upon the following attributes of Hofstede's dimensions and have been applied to user interfaces as shown below. These attributes have also been published in Chessum et al., [7].

2.1 Power Distance (PD)

Power Distance within a culture refers to the extent members of that culture are willing accept or expect an unequal distribution of power, [31]. It is noted by Hofstede, that

---

[1] Examples of UI 1 to UI 12 can be seen at https://github.com/ifromm/cross-cultural-ui-designs/.

high Power Distance governments are generally more centralised, with substantial pay differences for people with higher and lower positions, and have taller hierarchical company structure, [31]. High Power Distance culture and country members would expect, and could even have a preference for inequality [11]. As noted by Traquandi [32] the inequality is defined from the bottom and not from the top. This suggests, that within a society, the amount of inequality can be approved by the countries members, as well as the country's leaders. The following user interface design features are shown in Chessum et al., [7].

User Interface 1 High (PD) exemplar site population features, are as follows:

- Images of Experts, official buildings, official logos, prominence given to security and restrictions [31].
- Structured website design [33].
- "Older people are both respected and feared" use images of older people for wisdom and credibility [34].

User Interface 2 Low (PD) exemplar site population features, are as follows:

- Status is displayed to leaders rather than the population, staff or consumers. Information hierarchy is shallow [31].
- Use a looser structure to allow users to explore your site for themselves [31, 35].
- Use earned evaluations e.g., ratings, testimonials, likes, to promote your goods or services [35].
- "Older people are neither respected nor feared" Show images of younger or youthful people [34].

2.2 Individualism (IDV)

With this dimension, Hofstede looked at the Individualism and Collectivism within cultures, that is to say how much individuals are integrated into groups [32]. Within Individualism cultures, an individual person is only expected to care for 'one's self or immediate family' [31]. As opposed to a collectivism culture, where the members from birth are 'integrated into strong, cohesive in-groups, often extended families' [32]. The following user interface design features are shown in Chessum et al., [7].

User Interface 3 High (IDV) exemplar site population features, are as follows:

- "High text-to-image ratio". Avoid cluttered graphics. Show positive images of goal achievement [36].
- "Create competitions and challenges to engage your customers". "Give visitors a sense of personal achievement to motivate actions". Have content that has 'novelty' and 'difference' in order to 'attract attention' [37].
- Have their own personal goals. Follow their likes and dislikes [38].
- "Speaking one's mind is healthy" [34].

User Interface 4 Low (IDV) exemplar site population features, are as follows:

- "High image-to-text ratio" [36].
- Transparency, give users full disclosure, for example how their data would be used. "Show that you respect privacy and security of personal info". "Engage the community – 'we' not 'me'" [37].

- Emphasis on social and organisational goals. An individual's goals are less important [36].
- Members of a collective society, aspire to achieve their in-groups' goals [38].
- "Harmony should always be maintained' [34].

2.3 Masculinity (MAS)

As noted by Chessum et al., [7], this dimension does not refer to physical gender but to gender roles. Traquandi [32] describes Hofstede's analysis of the IBM questionnaires showed women's (feminine) values are more consistent across countries than male values. The male (masculine) values can vary from assertive and competitive, to being modest and caring. Traquandi [32] continues to say within feminine cultures both women and men have the same caring values. Whereas in masculine cultures, women also show assertive and competitive values, however, this is less than males show. Traquandi [32] concludes, there is a gap shown between male and female values. The following user interface design features are shown in Chessum et al., [7].

User Interface 5 High (MAS) exemplar site population features, are as follows:

- User attention obtained by games and competitions. Work tasks, roles, and skills, quick results obtained for limited actions. Navigation focused on exploring but also on control [31].
- Masculine societies are competitive. Motivated by achievement, heroism, assertiveness, and materialism [39].
- "Admiration for the strong" [34].
- Bright contrasting colours [40, 41].

User Interface 6 Low (MAS) exemplar site population features, are as follows:

- User attention is obtained by the use of poetry, aesthetics, and appealing to uniting values [31].
- Provide contact information and be prepared for feedback and questions. "This group is very cooperative and if they want to give feedback, they don't hesitate to get in contact with you". [39].
- "Feminine societies are consensus-oriented". With a preference for values, corresponding to cooperation, modesty, care for the weak, and quality of life [39].
- "Sympathy for the weak" [34].
- Pastel colours, low saturation [40, 41].

2.4 Uncertainty Avoidance (UA)

Hofstede's Uncertainty Avoidance dimension, is related to what extent members of a culture tolerate unknown situations or uncertainty [31]. Members from an uncertainty avoidance culture tend to reduce uncertainty, in unknown, or novel situations, by having 'strict laws' within the country and formal rules in business [32]. The following user interface design features are shown in Chessum et al., [7].

User Interface 7 High (UA) exemplar site population features, are as follows:

- Tries to show/predict the results or effects of actions before the user acts. Navigation structures are designed to help prevent users from becoming lost. Any ambiguity can be decreased by the use of "Redundant cues", e.g., design, sound visual aids [33].

- Simplicity, with clear metaphors, restricted options, and limited volume of data [31].
- "The uncertainty inherent in life is felt as a continuous threat that must be fought". "Need for clarity and structure" [34].

User Interface 8 Low (UA) exemplar site population features, are as follows:

- Information is maximised by the use of colour coding, typeface, font, and sound. Use multiple links but not redundant cueing. Limited control over navigation e.g. Links could open content in new windows that lead away from the original webpage(s). Complexity with maximum content and options. Acceptance of exploring and risk (can even be encouraged), with a stigma on "over- protection." [31].
- "The uncertainty inherent in life is accepted and each day is taken as it comes", "Comfortable with ambiguity and chaos" [34].

2.5 Long-Term Time Orientation (LTO)

Long-term Time Orientation, is also known as Long Term Orientation versus Short Term Normative Orientation (LTO).

This fifth dimension was recognized later and described in [42] Hofstede & Bond (1984), when Michael Bond and Hofstede conducted a study using a re-designed questionnaire Bond called the Chinese Value Survey, (CVS). This survey was conducted in 23 countries. A Long Term Time Orientation culture member values long term gain over short-term gain, [31]. As observed by Traquandi [32] Long-term Time Orientation values, both negative and positive, are found in the teachings of Confucius who lived in about 500 B.C. The following user interface design features are shown in Chessum et al., [7].

User Interface 9 High (LTO) exemplar site population features, are as follows:

- Offer ways for the user to save browsing history, e.g., wish lists. Together with means of sharing on social media. Persons with long-term orientation decisions are comprehensive and grounded "for the future" [39].
- Patience shown in attaining results and reaching goals. "Relationships as a source of information and credibility" [31].
- "Perseverance in achieving results" [43].
- "Thrift and perseverance are important goals". "Large savings quota, funds available for Investment" [34].

User Interface 10 Low (LTO) exemplar site population features, are as follows:

- Users require quick results that are consistent with known values and traditions. Persons with a short-term orientation would appear "to live more in the past and in the present than in the future" [39].
- Persons from a very short-term oriented culture e.g., Spain have a tendency "to live in the moment" [44].
- A wish for instant results and achieving goals. "Rules as a source of information and credibility" [31].
- "Focus on achieving quick results" [43].
- "Service to others is an important goal". "Social spending and consumption" [34].

2.6 Indulgence vs Restraint (IND)

This last sixth dimension, refers how happy a societies members are, how much they feel in control of their own life, and how much they value freedom of speech. [33].

As noted by MacLachlan [45] the indulgence dimension is partly based on the work carried by Bulgarian sociologist Michael Minkov, who created the World Values Survey.

Nickerson [46] observes, the indulgent vs restraint dimension, looks at what degree and inclination a particular culture has to satisfy their desires or to control them. Nickerson [46] continues to say, a high indulgence culture has comparative freedom with regards to satisfy their desires and enjoy the 'good life'. Whereas restraint within a culture, is where its members have a tendency to control the fulfilment of its needs and desires, and these are regulated 'through social norms'.

High indulgent societies have a 'higher importance of leisure', and restraint societies have a 'lower importance of leisure', as described in [34]. The following user interface design features are shown in Chessum et al., [7].

User Interface 11 High (IND) exemplar site population features, are as follows:

- Use and encourage user-generated content. "Make interactions fun". "Reflect loose gender roles by using a range of models" [47].
- People from an Indulgent culture have a tendency to put an emphasis on individual happiness and wellbeing. Their leisure time is more significant and people experience more freedom and "personal control" [45].
- Maintaining order in the nation is not given a high priority. A perception of personal life control. Freedom of speech is seen as important [34].

User Interface 12 Low (IND) exemplar site population features, are as follows:

- Frugal, show how they can save money. "Emphasise how you serve the community". "Strict, cultured gender roles" [47].
- People from a restrained culture do not display positive emotions as easily, with freedom, happiness and leisure time not assigned the same significance [45].
- Higher number of police officers per 100,000 population. A perception of helplessness: what happens to me is not my own doing. Freedom of speech is not a primary concern [34].

3   Experiment One Set-Up

An on-line survey was conducted asking participants to select one from each of the six pairs of user interfaces, i.e., one from each dimension. This allowed the participant to select six user interfaces in total. As discussed in Chessum et al., [7] this survey was completed by 148 participants. The number consisted of 101 participants currently residing in the UK and 47 who reside overseas. The survey attracted 97 participants who identified as male, and 51 who identified as female. The 148 participants are from 33 countries, however, a number of countries only had 1 to 2 participants and it was decided not to include these results. The countries without a Hofstede index score have also been excluded.

A set of hypotheses for experiment one have been created using all six Hofstede's cultural dimensions. There are six hypotheses in total, with one relating to each dimension, as shown below in Table 1. These hypotheses have also been used for experiment two.

Table 1. Hypotheses for experiments one and two [7, 23].

Hofstede's Cultural Dimensions	UI Design Number	Hypothesis
Power Distance (PD)	PD High UI 1 PD Low UI 2	H1: Higher PD Countries will show a preference for UI design number 1 and Lower PD Countries will show a preference for UI design number 2
Individualism (IDV)	IND High UI 3 IND Low UI 4	H2: Higher IDV Countries will show a preference for UI design number 3 and Lower IDV Countries will show a preference for UI design number 4
Masculinity (MAS)	MAS High UI 5 MAS Low UI 6	H3: Higher MAS Countries will show a preference for UI design number 5 and Lower MAS Countries will show a preference for UI design number 6
Uncertainty Avoidance (UA)	UA High UI 7 UA Low UI 8	H4: Higher UA Countries will show a preference for UI design number 7 and Lower UA Countries will show a preference for UI design number 8
Long-term Time Orientation (LTO)	UA High UI 9 UA Low UI 10	H5: Higher LTO Countries will show a preference for UI design number 9 and Lower LTO Countries will show a preference for UI design number 10
Indulgence (IND)	IND High UI 11 IND Low UI 12	H6: Higher IND Countries will show a preference for UI design number 11 and Lower IND Countries will show a preference for UI design number 12

The findings from the data have been analysed using standard statistical software, Microsoft Excel. The data has been analysed according to the participant preferences for each user interface selected from a pair, then grouped into nationality.

These findings are then measured against Hofstede's index scores and rankings tables, available in Hofstede et al., [11] and lastly compared to the six hypotheses, in order to ascertain if the hypotheses have been supported. This work has been published in Chessum et al., [7] where the results show potential to inform search user interfaces, although further research was found to be required to understand why several of the results showed some inconclusive findings.

4 Experiment One Results

Table 2. Experiment one results [7, 23].

Hypotheses	H1	H2	H3	H4	H5	H6
Dimension Country	Power Distance (PD)	Individualism (IDV)	Masculinity (MAS)	Uncertainty Avoidance (UA)	Long-term Time Orientation (LTO)	Indulgence (IND)
U.K.	Not Con	Not Con	Con	Not Con	Not Con	Con
Germany	Not Con	Not Con	Con	Con	Not Con	Not Con
Poland	Con	Not Con	Con	Con	Con	Con
Pakistan	Con	Con	Partial	Con	Partial	Con
Nigeria	Con	Con	Not Con	Not Con	Not Con	Con
Bangladesh	Not Con	Not Con	Partial	Con	Con	Not Con
Ethiopia	Con	Not Con	Con	Con	N/A	N/A
China	Con	Con	Not Con	Not Con	Not Con	Not Con
Nepal	Con	Con	Con	Con	N/A	N/A
Sri Lanka	Con	Con	Con	Not Con	Not Con	N/A
India	Con	Not Con	Con	Not Con	Partial	Not Con

Key: Con = Confirmed   Not Con = Not Confirmed
        Partial = Partially Confirmed   N/A = Not Applicable

4.1 Hypothesis 1 (H1) Power Distance (PD)

The UK and Germany both have a Hofstede index score of 35, and would be considered as low Power Distance countries. This index score indicates a culture supporting any inequalities within society to be kept to a minimum. Consequently, the expected result for Hypothesis1 would be for these countries to show a preference for user interface 2. This was not found to be case, with 12% for the UK and 14% for Germany showing a preference for user interface 2.

With a Hofstede index score of 55, Pakistan would be just above the centre point for Power Distance. This would indicate just over half of the survey participants would show a preference for user interface 1. We would consider this to be partially supported with 80% of users showing a preference for user interface 1.

Other countries with a high Power Distance index scores, such as Poland, Nigeria, Ethiopia, China, Nepal, Sri Lanka and India, showed a preference for user interface 1 as would be expected. Unexpectedly, participants from Bangladesh, showed a preference for user interface 2. It should be noted these countries were only represented by a few participants.

4.2 Hypothesis 2 (H2) Individualism (IDV)

The UK, Germany, and Poland, with a high Individualism score, would be considered as high Individualism countries. This would indicate they would show a preference for user interface 3.

This prediction for Poland was supported, however, it was not supported for the UK and Germany.

India would be just below the centre point with a Hofstede index score of 48. This would indicate just over half of the survey participants would show a preference for user interface 4, however, this is not the case with 86% of users showing a preference for user interface 4, and only 14% for user interface 3.

From Hofstede index scores, Pakistan, Nigeria, Bangladesh, Ethiopia, China, Nepal, and Sri Lanka would be considered to be low Individualism countries. As such the expectation would be for participants to show a preference for user interface 4. Our survey data has confirmed this for Pakistan, Nigeria, China, Nepal, and Sri Lanka, however not for Bangladesh and Ethiopia.

4.3 Hypothesis 3 (H3) Masculinity (MAS)

Hofstede's Index scores, for the UK, Germany, Poland, Nigeria, Ethiopia and China would indicate they are high masculine countries, and as such would show a preference for user interface 5. This expectation has been confirmed for the UK, Germany and Ethiopia, with mixed preferences shown for China and India. Nigeria preference for user interface 5 has not been confirmed.

Pakistan, Bangladesh and India would be considered to be close to the centre point for Masculinity. As such we would expect no clear preference to be shown for this pair of user interfaces.

A low Hofstede index score is reported for Nepal and Sri Lanka, and as such would indicated a preference for user interface 6. Our survey data, although not conclusive for this hypothesis, does show a slight preference for use interface 6.

4.4   Hypothesis 4 (H4) Uncertainty Avoidance (UA)

This hypothesis (H4), indicates higher Uncertainty Avoidance countries will show a preference for user interface 7, and lower Uncertainty Avoidance countries will show a preference for user interface 8.

Poland, Pakistan, Germany and Bangladesh, with a higher Hofstede index score would be considered to be high uncertainty avoidance countries. This has been confirmed with the participants indicating a preference for user interface 7.

Middle range countries with regards to the Uncertainty Avoidance index score, such as Sri Lanka, Nigeria and Ethiopia, would be expected to show no clear preference for either user interface from this pair. This has not been confirmed for Nigeria or Sri Lanka. With a Hofstede index score of 55, Ethiopia did show a preference for user interface 7.

In the case of the UK, China, Nepal and India, all countries with a low Uncertainty Avoidance index score, with the exception of Nepal, our results do not agree with anticipated user interface 8 preference.

4.5   Hypothesis 5 (H5) Long-Term Time Orientation (LTO)

As noted by Chessum et al., [7] virtuous behaviour, perseverance and having patience for achieving goals and results, are qualities valued by Long-term time orientation cultures. Our hypothesis 5 (H5), indicates higher Long-term time orientation countries would show a preference for user interface 9, whilst lower Long-term time orientation countries would show a preference user interface 10.

Hofstede index score would show Germany and China are high Long-term orientation countries and as such, would show a preference for user interface 9, however this was not the case.

The UK, Pakistan, Bangladesh, India and Sri Lanka would be considered to be middle range countries regarding Long-term time orientation. As expected, there is no clear preference shown for either user interface, although Pakistan did show a slight preference for user interface 9.

Poland and Nigeria would be considered as low Long-term time orientation countries. Their preference for user interface 10 has been confirmed. Hofstede does not report an index score for Ethiopia and Nepal.

4.6   Hypothesis 6 (H6) Indulgence (IND)

With regards to this final dimension and hypothesis, we expect higher Indulgence countries to show a preference for user interface 11 and lower Indulgence countries to show a preference for user interface 12.

The UK and Nigeria would be considered as high Indulgence countries, this has been confirmed with both countries showing a preference for user interface 11.

Hofstede's index score show Germany, Bangladesh, India and China, to be low Indulgence countries. Our data shows mixed results for these countries, and as such, would not be considered to be confirmed.

However, our final hypothesis for Poland, a low Indulgence country, would be considered to be a confirmed country. Hofstede had not reported an Indulgence index score for Ethiopia, Nepal and Sri Lanka.

5   Experiment Two Set-Up

The six hypotheses developed for experiment one, have also been used in experiment two, and are shown with their corresponding user interface number in Table 2.

The user interface designs have been updated[2], based upon feedback collected from a subsection of the survey conducted for experiment one, this is reported in [23]. The updated prototype web based search user interfaces, as with experiment one, comprise six pairs of user interfaces, one pair for each of Hofstede's six dimensions. One user interface designed for the low end and one for high end of each dimension, making twelve in total. The participants can only choose one user interface from each pair as the responses are mutually exclusive.

As noted in Chessum [23] the survey for the second experiment was conducted over a shorter time span, and as a consequence, attracted fewer participants, with 25 in total from eleven countries. Many of the eleven countries had fewer than four respondents. Therefore, the respondents have been grouped with respondents from another country in the same region as defined by Hofstede et al., [11]. However, it was decided in the case of Germany and Greece, categorised by Hofstede et al., [11] as 'Europe N/NW Anglo World' (Europe North and North West, and Anglo World) and 'Europe S/SE' (Europe South and South East) respectively, would be re-classified as 'European' for the purpose of the results of this experiment. As such for analysis, the arithmetic mean average of both countries Hofstede indices have been used.

5.1   Regional Grouping

The countries are given below with the number of participants shown in brackets.

UK (11), Germany (1), Nigeria (1), Greece (1), Russia (1), Venezuela (1), Zimbabwe (2), Congo (1), China (4), Romania (1), and Uzbekistan (1).

The following countries have been grouped together using Hofstede's region 'Europe C/E Ex-Soviet'. (Europe, Central and East, and Ex-Soviet), Romania, Russia, and Uzbekistan. (Hofstede does not report an index for Uzbekistan, consequently, the index for Russia has been used.)

Hofstede's region 'Muslim World M.E. & Africa' (Muslim World, Middle East and Africa) for Nigeria, Zimbabwe and the Congo (DRC). (Hofstede does not report an index for Zimbabwe and Congo, DRC (Democratic Republic of the Congo), consequently the index for Nigeria has been used).

As explained above, Germany and Greece have been grouped together, and are referred to as 'Europe'. The index scores for all six of Hofstede's dimensions, [11]

---

[2] Updated UIs https://github.com/ifromm/cross-cultural-ui-designs/tree/main/UIDesignImages.

(Hofstede, 2010) for both countries have been averaged, thus creating an arithmetic mean average index score. The index scores used are shown in Table 3 below.

Table 3. Regional grouping [23].

Region or Nationality	PD Index	IDV Index	MAS Index	UA Index	LTO Index	IND Index
China	80	20	66	30	87	24
Europe	47	51	61	82	64	45
Europe C/E Ex-Soviet	91	34	39	92	66	20
Muslim World M.E. & Africa	80	30	60	55	13	84
United Kingdom	35	89	66	35	51	69
Venezuela	81	12	73	76	16	100

6 Experiment Two Results

As with experiment one, the findings from the data have been analysed using standard statistical software, Microsoft Excel. The data has been analysed according to the participant preferences for each user interface selected from a pair, then grouped into nationality or regional grouping.

Hofstede's countries index scores Hofstede et al., [11] have been compared to the experiment two results for analysis. The results, as displayed in Table 4, showed mixed outcomes, with some hypotheses being confirmed and partially confirmed, whilst others being unconfirmed.

6.1 Hypothesis 1 (H1) Power Distance (PD)

With a Hofstede index score of 80, China would be considered to be a high Power Distance country, therefore, the results for H1 would expect to show that participants show preference for user interface 1. This is the case, with 75% (3), participants indicating this preference.

The author generated 'Europe' combined index scores for Germany and Greece, as described in Sect. 4 above, and Table 3 have been calculated as 47 for Power Distance [23]. The expected result would be for Europe to show a preference for user interface 2. However, this is not the case, with both participants showing a preference for user interface 1.

Hofstede's region of 'Europe C/E Ex-Soviet', has a Power Distance index score of 91. With this score it would be expected a preference to be shown to user interface 1, this indeed the case.

Table 4. Experiment two results [23].

Hypotheses	H1	H2	H3	H4	H5	H6
Region or Nationality	Power Distance (PD)	Individualism (IDV)	Masculinity (MAS)	Uncertainty Avoidance (UA)	Long-term Time Orientation (LTO)	Indulgence (IND)
China	Con	Con	Con	Not Con	Con	*Partial*
Europe	Not Con	Not Con	*Partial*	*Partial*	*Partial*	*Partial*
Europe C/E Ex-Soviet	Con	Con	Not Con	Con	Not Con	Not Con
Muslim World M.E.& Africa	Con	Con	Not Con	Not Con	Con	Not Con
United Kingdom	Not Con	Not Con	Con	Not Con	*Partial*	Con
Venezuela	Not Con	Con	Not Con	Not Con	Con	Con

Key: Con = Confirmed   Not Con = Not Confirmed   *Partial* = Partially Confirmed

The Hofstede region of 'Muslim World M.E. & Africa', has a Power Distance index of 80; this would indicate that a preference for user interface 1 would be expected. This was confirmed.

The UK is placed in the lower part of Power Distance index with a score of 35. This would suggest the UK participants would show a preference for user interface 2. However, the result showed a preference for user interface 1.

For completeness we are reporting the results for our one Venezuelan participant.

We also fully acknowledge once participant cannot be representative of any culture.

However, this one participant, as expected, showed a preference for user interface 1.

6.2 Hypothesis 2 (H2) Individualism (IDV)

China has a low Hofstede Individualism index score of 20. Consequently, it would be expected the participants show a preference for user interface 4. This was confirmed with 75% (3), of participants showing a preference for user interface 4.

The author created 'Europe' grouping for Germany and Greece, have a mean averaged Hofstede index score of 51 as shown in Table 3. It would be expected to see the result to be showing a 50/50 split preference, alternatively, a possible marginal preference for user interface 3 to be shown. This is not the case with a preference being shown for user interface 4.

Regarding Hofstede's region for 'Europe C/E Ex-Soviet', which has an Individualism index score of 34, user interface 4 is the expected participant preference. This outcome has been confirmed.

Similarly, the Hofstede region for the 'Muslim World M.E. & Africa', which has an index score of 30, has also been confirmed, with participants showing a preference for user interface set 4.

The UK has a high Hofstede Individualism score of 89. This would indicate the participants would show a preference for user interface 3. However, the UK is reporting only one participant (9%), is reported as showing a preference for user interface 3. Subsequently, this hypothesis 2 for the UK has not been confirmed.

Likewise for Venezuela in Hypothesis 1, the results for Hypothesis 2 are also reported for completeness. With a low Hofstede index score of 12, it would be expected a preference for user interface 4 to be shown, for this one individual and this was indeed the case.

6.3 Hypothesis 3 (H3) Masculinity (MAS)

China has a Hofstede index score of 66 for the Masculinity. This would suggest participants would show a preference for user interface 5. This has been confirmed for China with 75% (3), of the participants selecting their preference as user interface 5.

The author created 'Europe' with a mean average index score of 61, as shown in Table 3, show a split preference of 50%, for user interface 5 and 50% for user interface 6. Consequently, this Hypothesis is being considered as partially supported.

The region grouping by Hofstede for the 'Muslim World M.E. & Africa', showing an index score of 60, participants would be expected to show a preference for user interface 5. All four participants reported a preference for user interface 6, therefore this Hypothesis 3 has not been supported.

The UK's Hofstede index score for Masculinity is 66, and as such the expected preference is for user interface 5 to be shown. With 55 (6)% of participants identifying user interface 5 as their preference, Hypothesis 3, has been confirmed.

Similarly, as with the hypotheses 1 and 2, the results for Venezuela are being reported for completeness. Conversely, our one participant did not show a preference for user interface 5, as we expected.

6.4 Hypothesis 4 (H4) Uncertainty Avoidance (UA)

Hofstede reports an index score of 30 for China with regards to Uncertainly Avoidance. As such it would be expected the participants would show a preference for user interface 8. However, 75% (3), participants indicated a preference for user interface 7, consequently, Hypothesis 4, for China has not been confirmed.

The results for 'Europe' as shown in Table 3, with 50% of participants showing a preference for user interface 7, would be considered to be partially supported.

Hofstede's region of 'Europe C/E Ex-Soviet', has an index score of 92, this would indicate a preference for user interface 7 to be shown. This has been confirmed.

Hofstede's 'Muslim World M.E. & Africa' region has an index score of 55, this would suggest participants would show a preference for user interface set 7. This hypothesis is unconfirmed with 75% (3), of the participants showing a preference for user interface 8.

The UK has a Hofstede index score of 35 and would be considered to be low, a preference for user interface 8 would be expected. This was not shown to be the case, with 55% (6) participants showing a preference for user interface 7.

As with previous hypothesis, the results for Venezuela are being reported for completeness. A preference for user interface 7 would be expected, however this was not the case, with our one participant preferring user interface 8.

6.5 Hypothesis 5 (H5) Long-Term Time Orientation (LTO)

The Long-term Time Orientation index score for China is 87, and is considered as high. Consequently, the anticipated result for China would be to show a preference for user interface 9. This was indeed the case for hypothesis 5, with 75% (3), participants showing a preference for user interface set 9.

The results for the region of 'Europe' for Hypothesis 5, are considered to be partially supported, with a result of a 50/50 split. With one participant showing a preference for each of the two user interfaces.

The Long-term Time Orientation Hofstede index score for the region of 'Europe C/E Ex-Soviet' is 65, and therefore would indicate participants would show a preference for user interface 9. This is not confirmed with 66% or (2), participants showing a preference for user interface set 10.

Hofstede's grouping region of the 'Muslim World M.E. & Africa', has an index score of 13. This would be considered to be low Long-term Time Orientation, therefore, it would be anticipated results for this region would show a preference for user interface10. Our results support this with 75% (3), participants indicating this preference.

The UK, with a Long-term Time Orientation Hofstede index score of 51, would be considered to be the central point. A 50/ 50 split result would be expected to be returned. Due to the odd number of participants being 11, this would be mathematically impossible, therefore the result the result of 45% (5), has considered as partially supported.

As with the other previous hypotheses, the results for Venezuela are being reported for completeness. The Venezuelan Hofstede index score is 13, and would be considered to be low. This preference has been echoed with our one participant showing a preference for user interface 10.

6.6 Hypothesis 6 (H6) Indulgence (IND)

China has a low Hofstede index score of 24 for Indulgence, and as such the expected participant user interface preference would be for 12. This has been partially supported with the 50% (2), participants, showing a preference for user interface 12.

Likewise, the 'Europe' region has an index score of 45, as shown in Table 3. This result would also be considered to be partially supported, with 50% (1), participant showing a preference for user interface 12.

The 'Europe C/E Ex-Soviet' Hofstede region has an index score of 20. This score would be considered to be low, therefore, the participants for the region would be anticipated to show a preference for user interface 12. However, the results do not support this, with only 1 participant showing a preference for user interface 12.

The Hofstede region for 'Muslim World M.E. & Africa' with an index score of 84, would be considered to be high Indulgence. Consequently, an expected preference for user interface 11 would be given. However, this is not the case with 1 participant showing a preference for user interface 11.

The UK with an Indulgence Hofstede index score of 69, would be expected to show results indicating a preference for user interface 11. Our results for this hypothesis would be considered to be supported by the UK with 64% (7), participants showing a preference for user interface 11.

As a final point, as previously, the results for Venezuela are being reported for completeness. The Hofstede index score of 100 for Venezuela would be considered to be very high, hence a preference for user interface 11 would be shown. This has been supported by our one participant.

Thirty six results have been recorded, this consists of the number of Hofstede's dimensions, being six, multiplied by the number of nations and regions also, and being six in this instance. As shown in Table 4 above, fifteen results are confirmed, six results are considered to be partially confirmed and fifteen results not confirmed.

7 Discussion and Conclusion

7.1 Experiment One

The results shown for experiment one, show support for four of Hofstede's cultural dimensions. There are a possible 11 confirmations, (one for each country) for each of the six dimensions with the exception of Long-term Time Orientation (LTO) where there are 9 possible confirmations, and Indulgence, where there are 10. This is due to Hofstede not reporting an index score for Ethiopia and Nepal for both of these dimensions and with Sri Lanka being reported for Indulgence.

These are as follows:

- Power Distance (PD) 8/11 confirmed
- Masculinity (MAS) 7/11 confirmed and 2/11 partial confirmations
- Uncertainty Avoidance (UA) 6/11 confirmed
- Indulgence (IND) 4/8 confirmed

The least supported dimension in this experiment, is Long term time orientation with 2/9 confirmed and 2/9 partial confirmations.

We Offer the Following Observations for Experiment 1. As noted in Chessum et al., [7] the findings for this experiment show 33 of a possible 61 results support the Index scores from Hofstede et al., [11] and our hypotheses. We found 12 results difficult to catagorise fully, and as such, these are considered to be partially confirmed. We also found 16 results that do not correspond with their anticipated hypothesis.

First, we would like to say Hofstede's dimensions and index scores original use, was not for web design or search user interface design. However, we consider this to be our contribution to ascertain the degree to which these dimensions and index scores can be applied to search user interfaces. The data collected from this experiment, indicates there is potential for Hofstede's dimensions and index scores to be used to inform the design of search user interfaces. These results also show further research is needed to understand why some of our results did not match our hypotheses, and how cultural awareness can better inform search user interfaces. As observed in Chessum et al., [7] 'we consider our study as an important contribution to triggering this discussion.'

Our second observation is we have a limited number of participants for some of the countries within our study. Our study involved numerous participants with UK (51), Germany (21) and Pakistan (10).

Our data shows the dimension with the most confirmations is Power Distance, with 8 from 11. Masculinity having 7 confirmations, and 2 partial confirmations, and Uncertainty Avoidance, with 6 from 11 confirmations.

7.2   Experiment Two

The results given for experiment two also show the support for four of Hofstede's cultural dimensions. There are a possible 6 confirmations, being one for each regional grouping or country, for each of the six dimensions.

As follows:

- Power Distance (PD) 3/6 confirmed
- Individualism (IDV) 4/6 confirmed
- Long Term Time Orientation (LTO) 3/6 confirmed, 2/6 partial confirmations
- Indulgence (IND) 2/6 confirmed and 2/6 partial confirmations

The least supported dimension in this experiment is Uncertainty Avoidance, with 1/6 confirmed and 1/6 partial confirmations.

We Offer the Following Observations for Experiment 2. As noted by Chessum [23] the sample size for experiment two being twenty five, would be considered as small, particularly for a cross cultural study. The twenty five participants are made up from eleven different countries and identify with a number of cultural backgrounds.

An attempt has been made to overcome some of the challenges of the small sample size and those countries having under four participants, by grouping these respondents with respondents from another country but from the same region as defined by Hofstede et al., [11].

Every care has been taken to ensure the grouping of the countries are as closely linked as possible, this has been achieved by using Hofstede's own regional groupings, [11]. However, in the case of Germany and Greece, this was not possible, and they have been grouped together as 'Europe'. This author created grouping, may well explain the unexpected results of four partially confirmed and two non-confirmed results, and is the only result to contain no confirmations.

The sample size for this experiment could be considered as being small, particularly when compared to experiment one, which attracted 215 participants. In view of this, every effort has been made to use all 25 participant's results. One of the 25 participants identified as Venezuelan. We acknowledge one participant cannot be considered to represent Venezuelan culture; however, for completeness, this individual's results are also reported.

Our findings indicate the results from Chinese participants show the most confirmations. The results in Table 4 show four confirmations, one partial confirmation and only one non-confirmation. All four of the participants identify as Chinese, comprising one participant who identified as male, and three identifying as female.

Three of the four participants self-classify as living for less than one year in the UK, therefore, these respondents, due to their limited length of stay in the UK, may not have assimilated much British culture, as a result their answers maybe Chinese in nature.

In conclusion it would seem we have varying results from the two experiments. However, it would seem the Power Distance dimension has performed well in the first experiment, and fairly well in the second experiment. Hofstede's last identified Indulgence dimension coming in fourth out of a possible six in both experiments. One explanation for this could be there has been considerably fewer research studies undertaken that include this last dimension, therefore the design features for this user interface design, shown in Sect. 2.6 have been taken from a somewhat limited number of studies. This indicates further research needs to be carried out with this dimension from a cross cultural HCI prospective.

With our first experiment the results indicated the most support shown was for three of Hofstede's original four dimensions. However, the second experiment indicates support for two of Hofstede's original four dimensions, along with his fifth dimension, Long Term Time Orientation.

Although these results are a little mixed, we believe, there is potential for Hofstede's dimensions to inform search user interface design and to enhance the user experience. We consider further research is required to ascertain how best this can be achieved.

References

1. Smith, A., French, T., Dunckley, L., Minocha, S., Chang, Y.: A Process Model for developing Usable cross-cultural websites. Interact. Comput. Spec. Ed. Glob. Human-Comput. Syst. Cult. Determ. Usabil. **24**(1), 63–91 (2004)
2. Singh, N., Dumar, V., Baack, D.: Adaptation of cultural content: evidence from B2C e-commerce firms. Eur. J. Mark. **39**(1/2), 71–86 (2005)
3. Alcántara-Pilar, J.M., Armenski, T., Blanco-Encomienda, F.J., Del Barrio-García, S.: Effects of cultural difference on users' online experience with a destination website: a structural equation modelling approach. J. Destin. Mark. Manag. **8**, 301–311 (2018)
4. Benaida, M.: Cross-cultural web design and education: a comparison between Arab Universities and US Universities based on hofstede cultural dimensions. IJCSNS Int. J. Comput. Sci. Netw. Secur. **18**(10), 1–9 (2018)
5. Taksa, I., Flomenbaum, M.J.: An integrated framework for research on cross-cultural information retrieval. In: 2009 Sixth International Conference on Information Technology: New Generations, Baruch College, City University of New York, 27–29 April 2009, pp. 1367–1372 (2009)

6. Hover, P.: Egyptian and American internet-based cross-cultural information seeking behavior. Part I: research instrument (2006). https://www.webology.org/data-cms/articles/202005150 34658pma31.pdf. Accessed 12 Apr 2023

7. Chessum, K., Liu, H., Frommholz, I.: A study of search user interface design based on hofstede's six cultural dimensions. In: Proceedings of the 6th International Conference on Computer-Human Interaction Research and Applications, pp. 145–154 (2022). , ISBN 978–989–758–609–5, ISSN 2184–3244. https://doi.org/10.5220/0011528700003323

8. Hall, E.T.: Beyond Culture. Doubleday, Garden City (1976)

9. Nisbett, R.E.: The Geography of Thought: How Asians and Westerners Think Differently …and Why. The free press (2003)

10. Trompenaars, F., Hampden-Turner, C.: Riding the Waves of Culture: Understanding Cultural Diversity in Business, 3rd edn. Sonoma/Nicolas Brealey Publishing Ltd., London (2012)

11. Hofstede, G., Hofstede, G.J., Minkov, M.: Cultures and Organizations: Software of the Mind: Intercultural Cooperation and its Importance for Survival. The McGraw Hill Companies, New York (2010)

12. Liu, F.: Modify Your Design for Global Audiences: Crosscultural UX Design. Nielson Norman Group (2021). https://www.nngroup.com/articles/crosscultural-design/. Accessed 18 Mar 2023

13. Oshlyansky, L.: Cultural Models in HCI: Hofstede, Affordance and Technology Acceptance. PhD Thesis, Swansea University (2007). http://cronfa.swan.ac.uk/Record/cronfa 42813. Accessed 12 Apr 2023

14. Trompenaars, F., Hampden-Turner, C.: Riding the Waves of Culture: Understanding Cultural Diversity in Business, 2nd edn. Nicholas Brealey Publishing Limited, London (1998)

15. Hall, E.T.: The Silent Language. Anchor Books, New York (1990)

16. Parsons, T.: The Social System. The Free Press, New York (1951)

17. Nisbett, R.E., Miyamoto, Y.: The influence of culture: holistic versus analytic perception. Trends Cogn. Sci. **9**(10), 467–473 (2005)

18. Social Science Space. Geert Hofstede, 1928–2020: The Engineer of Cross-Cultural Psychology (2021). https://www.socialsciencespace.com/2021/08/the-engineer-of-cross-cul tural-psychology-geert-hofstede-1928-2020/. Accessed 12 Apr 2023

19. Hofstede, G.: Cultures and Organization: Software of the Mind, pp. 77–85. HarperCollins-Business, An imprint of HarperCollinsPublishers (2021)

20. Ghemawat, P., Reiche, S.: National Cultural Differences and Multinational Business, Globalization Note Series (2011). https://www.hbs.edu/rethinking-the-mba/docs/iese-globe-note-national-cultural-differences-and-multinational-business-2011.pdf. Accessed 12 Apr 2023

21. McSweeney, B.: Hofstede's model of national cultural differences and their consequences: a triumph of faith—a failure of analysis. Human Relat. **55**, 89–118 (2002). https://doi.org/10.1177/0018726702055001602LastAccessed23/4/12

22. McSweeney, B.: Collective cultural mind programming: escaping from the cage. J. Organ. Chang. Manag. **29**(1), 68–80 (2016). https://doi.org/10.1108/JOCM-12-2015-0229LastAccessed23/4/12

23. Chessum, K.: A Conceptual Framework to Support Cross-cultural User Experience Design for Web Search. PhD thesis. University of Bedfordshire (2021). https://uobrep.openrepositoryt.com/handle/10547/624931

24. Dimitrov, K.: Geert Hofstede et al's set of national cultural dimensions - popularity and criticisms. Econ. Altern. (2), 30–60 (2014)

25. Hofstede, G. .: Geert Hofstede. https://geerthofstede.com/geert-hofstede-biography/publicati ons/. Accessed 11 Sept 2019

26. Hofstede, G.: Culture's Consequences: Comparing Values, Behaviors, Institutions, and Organizations Across Nations, 2nd edn. Sage Publications, Thousand Oaks (2001)

27. Hofstede, G., and Minkov, M. (2013) Value Survey Module 2013 Manual. https://geerthofs tede.com/wp-content/uploads/2016/07/Manual-VSM-2013.pdf. Accessed 9 Apr 2023
28. Mooij, M., Hofstede, G.: The Hofstede model Applications to global branding and advertising strategy and research. Int. J. Advert. **29**(1), 85–110 (2010)
29. Pogosyan, M.: Geert hofstede: a conversation about culture. beyond cultural dimensions. Psychol. Today (2017). https://www.psychologytoday.com/us/blog/between-cultures/201702/geert-hofstede-conversation-about-culture. Accessed 12 Apr 2023
30. Reid, L.: The Importance of Hofstede's Dimensions of Culture (2015). https://sites.psu.edu/global/2015/04/25/the-importance-of-hofstedes-dimensions-of-culture/. Accessed 18 Mar 2023
31. Marcus, A., Gould, E.: Crosscurrents cultural dimensions and global web user-interface design. Interactions **7**(4), 32–46 (2000). http://dl.acm.org/citation.cfm?doid=345190.345238. Accessed 12 Apr 23
32. Traquandi, L.: The three classic schools for intercultural management The western, Indian and Chinese vision of the world (2016). https://my.liuc.it/MatSup/2016/A86047/3%20Mult icultural%20schools.pdf. Accessed 10 Apr 2023
33. Burgmann, I., Kitchen, P., Williams, R.: Does culture matter on the web? Mark. Intell. Plan. **24**(1), 62–73 (2006)
34. Hofstede, G.: Dimensionalizing cultures: the hofstede model in context. Online Read. Psychol. Cult. **2**(1) (2011). https://doi.org/10.9707/2307-0919.1014. Accessed 10 Apr 2023
35. Nahai, N.: How to sell online to different cultures: power distance. Psychol. Today (2013). https://www.psychologytoday.com/gb/blog/webs-influence/201306/how-sell-online-different-cultures-power-distance. Accessed 3 Apr 2023
36. Gould, E., Zakaria, N., Yusof, S.: Applying culture to website design: a comparison of Malaysian and US websites. In: Paper Presented at the Proceedings of IEEE Professional Communication Society International Professional Communication Conference and Proceedings of the 18th Annual ACM International Conference on Computer Documentation. Technology and Teamwork, pp. 162–171 (2000)
37. Nahai, N.: How to sell online to individualist vs collectivist cultures. Psychol. Today (2013). https://www.psychologytoday.com/gb/blog/webs-influence/201307/how-sell-online-individualist-vs-collectivist-cultures. Accessed 3 Apr 2023
38. Sinha, J.B.P. (2014) Psycho-Social Analysis of the Indian Mindset, 2 edn, p. 27. Springer, Heidelberg (2014). https://doi.org/10.1007/978-81-322-1804-3
39. Idler, S.: How to Design for a Cross-Cultural User Experience (part 2/2) 23 April 2013 (2013). https://usabilla.com/blog/designing-for-a-cross-cultural-user-experience-part2/. Accessed 18 Mar 2023
40. Voehringer-Kuhnt, T.: Kulturelle Einflüsse auf die Gestaltung von Mensch-Maschine Systemen. GRIN Verlag, Munich (2002)
41. Dormann, C., Chisalita, C.: Cultural values in web site design. In: Proceedings of the 11th European Conference on Cognitive Ergonomics, Catania, Italy (2002)
42. Hofstede, G., Bond, M.: The need for synergy among cross-cultural studies. J. Cross Cult. Psychol. **15**(4), 417–433 (1984)
43. Makkonen, E.: Cultural differences and localization in user interfaces. Thesis for Bachelor of Engineering (B.E.), Media technology. Central Ostrobothnia University of Applied Sciences (2012)
44. Nahai, N.: How to sell online to short vs long-term cultures. Psychol. Today (2013). https://www.psychologytoday.com/gb/blog/webs-influence/201308/how-sell-online-short-vs-long-term-cultures. Accessed 3 Mar 2023
45. MacLachlan, M.: Indulgence vs. Restraint – the 6th Dimension (2013). https://www.communicaid.com/cross-cultural-training/blog/indulgence-vs-restraint-6th-dimension/. Accessed 18 Sept 2023

46. Nickerson, C.: Hofstede's Cultural Dimensions Theory & Examples (2023). https://simply psychology.org/hofstedes-cultural-dimensions-theory.html. Accessed 12 Apr 2023

47. Nahai, N.: How to sell online to indulgent vs restrained cultures. Psychol. Today (2013). https://www.psychologytoday.com/us/blog/webs-influence/201308/how-sell-online-indulgent-vs-restrained-cultures. Accessed 3 Apr 2023

48. Pixabay. Stunning free images & royalty free stock (2018). https://pixabay.com/. Accessed 15 Jan 2021

survAIval: Survival Analysis
with the Eyes of AI

Kamil Kowol[1]([✉]), Stefan Bracke[2], and Hanno Gottschalk[3]

[1] School of Mathematics and Natural Sciences, IZMD, University of Wuppertal,
Gaußstraße 20, Wuppertal, Germany
kowol@math.uni-wuppertal.de

[2] Chair of Reliability Engineering and Risk Analytics, IZMD,
University of Wuppertal, Gaußstraße 20, Wuppertal, Germany
bracke@uni-wuppertal.de

[3] Institute of Mathematics, Technical University Berlin, Straße des 17. Juni 135,
Berlin, Germany
gottschalk@math.tu-berlin.de

Abstract. In this study, we propose a novel approach to enrich the
training data for automated driving by using a self-designed driving simulator and two human drivers to generate safety-critical corner cases in a
short period of time, as already presented in [12]. Our results show that
incorporating these corner cases during training improves the recognition
of corner cases during testing, even though, they were recorded due to
visual impairment. Using the corner case triggering pipeline developed
in the previous work, we investigate the effectiveness of using expert
models to overcome the domain gap due to different weather conditions
and times of day, compared to a universal model from a development
perspective. Our study reveals that expert models can provide significant benefits in terms of performance and efficiency, and can reduce the
time and effort required for model training. Our results contribute to the
progress of automated driving, providing a pathway for safer and more
reliable autonomous vehicles on the road in the future.

Keywords: Driving simulator · Corner case · Human-in-the-loop ·
Semantic segmentation · Survival analysis

1 Introduction

If automotive manufacturers want to put autonomous vehicles higher than level
2 on the road, they should ensure that safety-critical driving situations are registered and that a safe solution for all road users is found as quickly as possible.
One way to achieve this is to provide a large amount of diverse data to the
model during training to increase the robustness and performance of AI algorithms. However, large amounts of annotated data alone may not ensure safe
operation in those rare situations where road users are exposed to significant

© The Author(s), under exclusive license to Springer Nature Switzerland AG 2023
A. Holzinger et al. (Eds.): CHIRA 2021/2022, CCIS 1882, pp. 153–170, 2023.
https://doi.org/10.1007/978-3-031-41962-1_8

risk. For this reason, we introduced the A-Eye method [12] to apply an accelerated testing strategy that exploits human risk perception to capture corner cases and thereby achieve performance improvements in safety-critical driving situations. To this end, a self-designed driving simulator was developed that detects safety-critical driving situations in real-time based on poor AI predictions. With the help of this driving simulator and a further driving campaign, the domain shift will be investigated on different weather domains. Closing the gap of domain shifts due to different weather conditions requires targeted data generation from multiple domains to achieve a good performance. Even if using more data and the best models leads to overcoming the domain gap, the question is whether this is the most efficient way from the manufacturer's point of view. In this regard, we investigate whether overcoming the domain gap in different weather conditions with specialized models works as well as or even better than a universal model in the sense that all weather modalities are covered during training. This involves training a baseline model on sunny and daytime images, and then measuring in 600-second drives how long it takes for a corner case to occur in one of the following conditions: rain, fog or night. An expert model is then trained for each weather condition, which retrains the baseline model for that domain. Finally, a universal model is trained, which is exposed to all weather parameters during training. The expert and universal models are also tested using the same scheme as the baseline model to measure the duration of a corner case in case one occurs.

Outline. Section 2 introduces the self-designed driving simulator with the software and hardware used, followed by a corner case definition. A corner case triggering pipeline is then presented and used in test field. Section 3 discusses the basics of survival analysis to evaluate the drives from the weather-driving campaign. Finally, we present our conclusions and give an outlook on future directions of research in Sect. 4.

2   Driving Simulator

There is an increased interest in human-in-the-loop (HITL) and machine learning approaches, where humans interact with machines to combine human and machine intelligence to solve a given problem [19]. For this purpose simulators were used to improve AI systems by means of human experience or to study human behavior in field trials. We have therefore developed a test rig in which two human drivers can control a vehicle in real-time, with the visual output of a semantic segmentation network displayed on one driver's screen, while the other driver sees the untouched original image.

By evaluating the same driving situation differently due to visual perception, we are able to find and save safety-critical driving situations in the shortest possible time, which can subsequently be used for training. This kind of targeted enrichment of training data with safety-critical driving situations is essential to increase the performance of AI algorithms. Since the generation of corner cases in the real world is not an option for safety reasons, generation remains in the synthetic world, where specific critical driving situations can be simulated and recorded. For this purpose, the autonomous driving simulator CARLA [6] is used. It is open-source software for data generation and/or testing of AI algorithms. It includes various sensors to describe the scenes such as cameras, LiDAR as well as RADAR and provides ground truth data. CARLA is based on the Unreal Engine game engine [17], which calculates and displays the behavior of the various road users with consideration of physics and thus enables realistic driving. In addition, with the Python API, the world can be modified and adapted to one's own use case. Therefore, we added another sensor, the inference sensor, to the script for manual control from the CARLA repository which evaluates the CARLA RGB images in real-time and outputs the prediction of a semantic segmentation network on the screen, see Fig. 1. By connecting a control unit that includes a steering wheel, pedals and a screen, it is possible to control a vehicle with 'the eyes of the AI' in the synthetic world of CARLA. Furthermore, we connected a second control unit with the same components to the simulator, so that it is possible to control the same vehicle with 2 different control units, see Fig. 1. The second control unit, therefore, has control over the CARLA clear image and can intervene at any time. It always has priority and saves the past 3 seconds of driving, which are buffered, on the hard disk. In order for the semantic driver to follow the traffic rules in CARLA, the script had to be modified to display the current traffic light phase in the top right corner and the speed in the top center.

View of the semantic driver (top) and the safety driver (bottom).

Test rig including steering wheels, pedals, seats and screens.

Fig. 1. Harware and visual outputs of the A-Eye approach.

2.1 Test Rig

The test rig consists of a workstation with dual Intel Xeon Gold 6258R as CPUs, 3x GPUs Quadro RTX 8000 and 1TB of RAM, which provides both high access speeds and sufficient memory swap calculations to meet the requirements of CARLA version 0.9.10. The test rig also includes 2 driving seats, 2 control units (steering wheel with pedals), one monitor for each control unit as well as two monitors for the control center. The control unit represents the interface between humans and machines. It enables the human to control a vehicle in CARLA freely via the steering wheel and the brake or throttle pedals. The device of choice was the Logitech G29 [13], which is also pre-implemented in CARLA's control script and can therefore be used as a controller almost without any problems.

2.2   Corner Cases

When thinking about autonomous vehicles that move safely through traffic, it is necessary to perceive the environment correctly in order to provide safe driving. Especially the detection of atypical and dangerous situations is crucial for the safety of all road users. In order to improve the ability of today's models to handle such critical situations, datasets are required that allow for targeted training and, more importantly, testing with such critical situations. While there is no standard definition for the term *corner case* in the context of autonomous driving, most definitions in the literature refer to rare but safety-critical driving situations. These scenarios can include, for example, extreme weather conditions, as well as unexpected road obstacles that are uncommon but still need to be considered to ensure safe vehicle operation.

According to [1], a corner case for camera-based systems in the field of autonomous driving describes a *"non-predictable relevant object/class in relevant location"*. This means that the unpredictable happens to moving objects (relevant class) interacting with each other on the road (crossing trajectories). Based on this definition, a corner case detection framework was presented to calculate a corner case score based on video sequences. The authors of [2] subsequently developed a systematization of corner cases, in which they divide corner cases into different levels and according to the degree of complexity. In addition, examples were given for each corner case level. This was also the basis for a subsequent publication with additional examples [3]. Due to the camera-based approach in the referenced works, a categorization of corner cases based on sensors was employed in [8], which also included radar and LiDAR sensors. The authors defined four overarching layers - *Sensor, Content, Temporal, and Method* - that incorporated the previously defined levels. As this definition is scientifically grounded and takes into account different sensor modalities, we would like to adopt it.

While *Sensor, Content* and *Temporal Layer* describe corner cases from the perspective of the human driver, the *Method Layer* specifies corner cases in machine learning models due to lack of knowledge. Accordingly, epistemic uncertainty comes into play, which can be addressed by targeted data generation. Therefore, our focus is on this type of layer to increase safety.

2.3   Triggering Corner Cases

Two test operators drive across the virtual world of CARLA and record scenes in our specially designed test rig, where one subject (safety driver) gets to see the original virtual image and the other (semantic driver) receives the output of the semantic segmentation network (see Fig. 1). The test rig is equipped with controls such as steering wheels, pedals and car seats and connected to CARLA to create a simulated environment for realistic traffic participation.

The corner cases were generated as shown in Fig. 2, using the real-time semantic segmentation network Fast-SCNN where visual perception was limited by intentionally stopping training early. This is sufficient to move in the virtual streets, but is poor enough to enhance corner cases of the *Method Layer*. We note that, according to [18], there were 128 accidents involving autonomous vehicles on the road during test operations in 2014–2018, at least 6% of which can be directly linked to misbehavior by the autonomous vehicle. It follows that at least every 775335 km driven, a wrongful behavior of the autonomous vehicle occurs. Using a poorly trained network as a part of our accelerated testing strategy, we were able to generate corner cases after 3.34 km on average between interventions of the safety driver. We note however that the efficiency of the corner cases was evaluated using a fully trained network. Figure 3 shows two safety-critical corner cases where the safety driver had to intervene to prevent a collision.

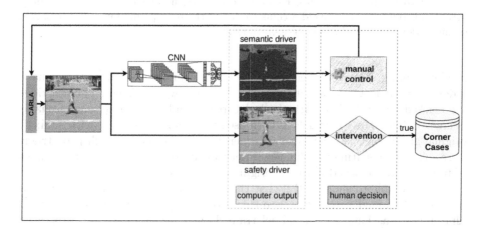

Fig. 2. Two human subjects are able to control the ego-vehicle. Thereby, the semantic driver primarily controls the vehicle while following the traffic rules in the virtual world seeing only the output of the semantic segmentation network. The safety driver, who only sees the original image, takes on the role of a driving instructor and intervenes in the situation as soon as a dangerous situation arises. Intervening in the current situation indicates poor situation awareness of the segmentation network and represents a corner case, which simultaneously terminates the ride. The figure was already published in [12].

In the event of a corner case being triggered by the safety driver, the test operators are required to label the scenario with one of four options (overlooking a pedestrian or a vehicle, disregarding traffic rules, intervening out of boredom) and provide comments. In addition, the duration and the kilometers driven until the corner case appears are registered. The test drivers were instructed to obey traffic rules and not exceed 50 km/h during the test drives. Over time, the drivers became more familiar with the system, leading to a decrease in driving errors and

Fig. 3. Two examples of a corner case with pedestrians included, where the safety driver had to intervene to avoid a collision due to the poor prediction of the semantic segmentation network (both images on the right).

sudden braking. However, a learning effect also occurred where drivers may have hidden situations where objects were not detected by the system. The test rides are tracked and recorded, with the last three seconds of a corner case scenario being saved at 10 fps. This data is then used to retrain the system, with a mix of original and corner case images. 50 corner cases in connection with pedestrians were collected, resulting in 1500 new frames for retraining, with an equal number of frames being removed from the original training dataset.

We were able to show in [12] that the occurrence of a corner case situation in a model trained with about two-thirds of *Method Layer* corner cases took almost twice as long as in a model trained with the original dataset or with more pedestrians included, see Table 1. The latter was checked because using corner cases with pedestrians results in more pedestrian pixels being available in the data. To allow a fair comparison the additional model was trained with the same average number of pedestrian pixels per scene.

Table 1. Corner case appearances on Fast-SCNN trained with 3 different datasets. The table was already published in [12].

dataset	distance d [km]	time t [min]	#CC [-]	$\text{mean}_{d_{CC}}$ [km/CC]	$\text{std}_{d_{CC}}$ [km/CC]	$\text{mean}_{t_{CC}}$ [min/CC]	$\text{std}_{t_{CC}}$ [min/CC]
natural disritbution	121.32	411	13	7.73	14.25	25.93	39.60
pedestrian enriched	163.09	500	21	7.52	10.47	23.25	28.72
corner case enriched	153.38	528	11	**13.84**	8.68	**47.47**	31.87

We have therefore demonstrated the benefits of our method for generating corner cases, especially for safety-critical situations. We were also able to show that adding safety-critical corner cases recorded by intentional perceptual distortions improves performance, so future datasets should include such situations. Next, with this test rig setup we investigate whether a single network is required to overcome the so-called domain gap, which describes the difference in data during training and deployment, or whether, for cost and performance reasons, different networks should be used depending on the task. This will be investigated using different weather conditions and survival analysis.

3   Survival Analysis

Survival analysis is the study of lifespans, also survival times, and their influencing factors [15]. It uses statistical methods to investigate time intervals between sequential events. Groups, but also individuals can be considered as the unit of study when an expected event happens during a considered time period like the time from birth until death, the time from entry a clinical trial until death, the time from buying a vehicle until an accident happens, or other use cases. The basic goals of survival analysis are [11]:

- estimation and interpretation of survivor or hazard functions
- comparing survivor and/or hazard functions
- relationship determination of explanatory variables to lifespans

First, some typical terms of survival analysis are introduced with an overview in Table 2.

Table 2. Terms in Survival Analysis.

Term	Explaination
observation time	observation period for which start and end points are known
entity	single object or individual of the observed study
event	change in status (e.g. life to death, accident-free to accident)
entry	starting state (e.g. birth, date of vehicle purchase)
failure time T	exit time of a subject
risk set	all test objects in the study
censoring	incomplete information about either entry before or/and event after the observation time
truncation	non-observable data that either does not exist or whose entry and exit state have not been observed
lifespan	duration until an event occurs
hazard	probability that an observed entity has a certain event at time t

The observation time period is described by a beginning point $t_{start} = 0$ and an end point $t_{end} > 0$ defined by a failure condition due to a special event [9]. An event implies a change in status, e.g., from alive to dead, from healthy to sick, or from accident-free to accident and is usually easy to find. However, defining the exact failure event is a more difficult task in some cases [14]. Although it is desirable to know each the beginning and end point of an individual observed in the study, one or both are not always observed which is known as censoring. Figure 4 provides an overview of some typical observation types, where white circles describe the entry state. Using our experiments with the driving simulator, the beginning point of pedal pressing may describe the entry state. A cross represents a change of state, such as the occurrence of a corner case due to an impaired perception, while black circles refer to a change of state that was triggered by unexpected reasons like an intervention out of boredom rather than a corner case as cause of impaired perception. Observations 1 and 9 describe a *truncated state*, which is non-observable data that either does not exist or whose entry and exit state have not been observed. Observations 2, 7, 8 characterize *left-censored* data as their starting points are not identifiable as they occurred prior the observation start. In addition, observations 5 to 8 escape the observation time unchanged, so they are referred to as *right-censored* as their exit event could not be observed. In addition, the events of observations 2–4 are observed during the observation time, with only 3 being *uncensored* since both start and end times are known. Although an event was detected at observation 4, the expected event did not occur and/or there were other causes for this condition.

Parts of the theory of survival analysis are taken from [11], unless otherwise stated. The continuous random variable T describes the time of occurrence of an event, which denotes the time of death of a subject, the time of failure of a machine, start of a disease or similar. t denotes a particular time of interest, which can be used to describe the probability that T has not yet occurred at time t, i.e., that the entity has survived. Accordingly, the survival function $S(t)$ represents the probability that the event of an entity at time t did not occur in the observed time period, and can be formulated as follows:

$$S(t) = Pr(T > t) \tag{1}$$

Two ways to describe a survival distribution are survival and hazard functions. As a survival function, the so-called Kaplan-Meier [7] estimator is often used, which estimates the probability that an event for an entity does not occur within a certain time interval. It is defined as follows:

$$\hat{S}(t_j) = \prod_{i=0}^{j} \frac{n_i - d_i}{n_i} \tag{2}$$

The observation time t_j is therefore divided into j-parts, each of which considers a time interval $\Delta t = (t_i, t_{i+1}]$. With n being denoted by the number of entities which are alive at Δt and d the number of entities which already left the observation at Δt.

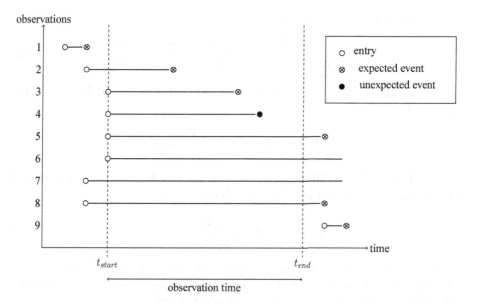

Fig. 4. Examples of different observation types. Circles mark the beginning of an observation, while crosses or black circles mark an event. When there is no information about either the entry and/or the event state, this is referred to as censoring.

Since T is a continuous random variable, it is necessary to work with the probability density function $f(t)$, which describes the probability, that an event occurs in a time interval. The cumulative density function $F(t)$, which is the area under the density function up to the value t, describes the probability, that the event occurs at time $T \leq t$:

$$F(t) = \int_{-\infty}^{t} f(u)\, du \qquad (3)$$

On the other hand, if we consider the probability that an event will not occur until a given time, which is what the survival function means, we can also write the following:

$$S(t) = 1 - F(t) \qquad (4)$$

In many situations, it is crucial to know how an individual risk for a particular outcome changes over time due to other events. For example, weather conditions can negatively affect the lifespan of a semantic driver when the model was not trained with such data. In addition, the use of multiple unknown weather variables can lead to interactions, which in turn can alter a semantic driver's lifespan. For those cases the hazard rate $h(t)$ indicates the probability that an observed entity experiences a failure event the next short time interval Δt [10]. It describes the risk of actual failure rate corresponding as a function over time.

The hazard rate is defined as:

$$h(t) = \lim_{\Delta t \to 0+} \frac{Pr(t \le T < t + \Delta t | t \le T)}{\Delta t} = \frac{f(t)}{S(t)} \tag{5}$$

The cumulative hazard $H(t)$ is used to estimate the hazard probability which is defined as follows:

$$H(t) = -\log(S(t)) = \int_0^t h(s)\, ds \tag{6}$$

The Hazard Ratio (HR) is a measure of the relative survival experience of two groups (A or B) and is defined as follows:

$$HR = \frac{O_A/E_A}{O_B/E_B} \tag{7}$$

The ratio O/E describes the relative death rate of a group, where O is the observed number of deaths and E the number of expected number of deaths. The HR is useful to compare two individuals or groups.

The Cox PH model, introduced in 1972 [4], uses the hazard function as a function of the influencing variables and looks as follows:

$$h(t, \mathbf{Z}) = h_0(t) \exp(\sum_{i=1}^{p} \beta_i Z_i), \quad \mathbf{Z} = (Z_1, Z_2, \ldots, Z_p), \tag{8}$$

where h_0 describes the baseline hazard, which depends only on time and is therefore equivalent to the Kaplan-Meier estimator. $\mathbf{Z}$ denotes the influence variables, which are time-independent and β the regression coefficients of the influence variables to be estimated.

The Cox model is often called proportional hazards model since the ratio of the risk for 2 entities with covariates $\mathbf{Z}$ and $\mathbf{Z}^*$ is proportional. The relative risk, also known as the hazard ratio (HR), describes that an individual with risk factor $\mathbf{Z}$ will experience an event proportional to an individual with risk factor $\mathbf{Z}^*$. The relative risk is defined as follows: [10]

$$HR = \frac{h(t, \mathbf{Z})}{h(t, \mathbf{Z}^*)} = \frac{h_0(t) \exp(\sum_{i=1}^{p} \beta_i Z_i)}{h_0(t) \exp(\sum_{i=1}^{p} \beta_i Z_i^*)} \tag{9}$$

$$= \exp[\sum_{i=1}^{p} \beta_i (Z_i - Z_i^*)] \tag{10}$$

It becomes noticeable that HR is independent of time.

Additionally, probabilities about the occurrence of an event can be calculated with the hazard function so that the influence of different parameters can be taken into account. Furthermore, events that have already occurred are included in the calculation so that at a time d_i the probability of an event occurring in the next time step can be predicted. This can be done with the partial likelihood, including a risk set $R(t_d)$ and an index set of death times D:

$$L(\beta) = \prod_{d=1}^{D} \frac{\exp(\sum_{i=1}^{p} \beta_i Z_{di})}{\sum_{j \in R(t_d)} \exp(\sum_{i=1}^{p} \beta_i Z_{ji})} \tag{11}$$

To optimize the regression coefficients we can maximize the Log-Likelihood:

$$\beta^* = \text{argmax} \log(L(\beta)) \tag{12}$$

This is done by computing:

$$\nabla_\beta \log(L(\beta)) = 0 \tag{13}$$

which can be solved numerically.

3.1   Experimental Design

After learning the basics of survival analysis, we will use it to find factors that affect survival while driving in the driving simulator. We will use the setup presented in Sect. 2 and observe how long it takes for a corner case to occur under different weather conditions. For this study, the previously used semantic segmentation network Fast-SCNN [16] is trained on good weather data, which we refer to *clear*, and serves as a baseline before being fine-tuned with different weather conditions, namely *rain*, *fog* and *night*. Figure 5 gives an overview of the different weather conditions. In addition, a further model is re-trained on all 3 weather conditions, referred to as *mix*, resulting in a total of 5 models available for the experiments. For post-training, 2100 additional images per weather setting (300 per map) are provided for training and 420 for testing.

In the following, we refer to each of the weather conditions *rain*, *fog* and *night* as expert models, since they are specifically trained on one domain. In contrast, all 3 weather settings are available to the *mix* model during training, which we refer to universal model. The baseline and universal models are tested

| rain | fog | night |

Fig. 5. Overview of the used weather conditions. The grayish sky, falling water drops as well as water puddles on the road are characteristic for *rain*. In the case of *fog*, fine water droplets cover the image, and it is especially tough to see in depth. *Night* images are characterized by many dark areas, with streetlights and vehicle lights illuminating the scenes.

on all five test datasets, whereas the expert models are tested on the respective trained conditions as well as on the *clear* ones. Table 3 gives an overview of the performance of all models on the particular test data.

Table 3. Test data performance for all 5 models.

model	test data									
	clear		rain		fog		night		mix	
	IoU_{ped}	$mIoU$	IoU_{ped}	$mIoU$	IoU_{ped}	$mIoU$	IoU_{ped}	$mIoU$	IoU_{ped}	$mIoU$
clear	0.487	0.759	0.368	0.586	0.024	0.207	0.063	0.191	0.123	0.321
rain	0.379	0.606	0.485	0.718	-	-	-	-	-	-
fog	0.074	0.130	-	-	0.301	0.596	-	-	-	-
night	0.292	0.302	-	-	-	-	0.402	0.655	-	-
mix	0.451	0.657	0.471	0.734	0.326	0.644	0.369	0.694	0.402	0.682

The evaluation of the initial model shows a significant decrease of all IoU values in any weather conditions, with the safety-critical class human below 0.1 for fog and night being awful. In contrast, the performance of the universal model remains largely the same. Additionally, compared to the mix model, the expert networks perform better in rain and night and worse in fog for the human class. In the mIoU, the universal model always outperforms the experts. This comparison has already shown the tendency for the expert models to perform at least as well or even slightly better than the universal model in the human class, while the overall performance in the mIoU is best for the universal model in all weather conditions. The next step is to conduct the weather driving campaign, where each model is also tested under these weather conditions in order to obtain a reliable statement about its performance in test.

The experiments are conducted as described in [12], so that two drivers drive freely on the roads of CARLA. During the rides, the semantic driver has full control over the vehicle, while the safety driver observes the rides and should intervene in the scene only in safety-critical driving situations using the brake pedal or the steering wheel. Intervention indicates incorrect assessment of the scene, which is a corner case of the *Method Layer*. Differences from the previous driving campaigns include the number of maps and the duration of the rides. This time, the focus is only on Town01 and Town03, since they have a high variability and due to their moderate size the number of vehicles and pedestrians does not need to be set excessively high in order to consistently see some, which relieves the traffic manager and thus computations on the CPU. In addition to the reduced number of maps, the drives will be limited to 600 s. If no corner case occurs during this time, the drive is stopped, which corresponds to a right-censored observation. In addition, the drivers didn't know what data the network had been trained on during the experiments as well as what weather condition they were driving in. The baseline and universal models are tested for 120 min on each weather setting (*clear, rain, fog, night*). In addition, the expert models

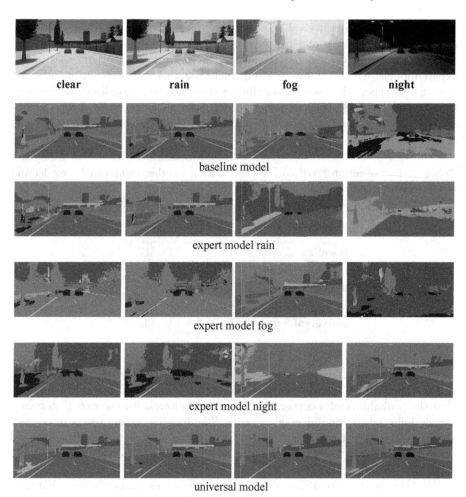

Fig. 6. Model outputs on each weather setup. Under the baseline model, it would be still possible to drive in rain, whereas fog and night would become a risk. The expert models perform well in their domain but quite worse in the other ones. On the other hand, the universal model performs sufficiently well in all weather conditions.

are tested on the respective weather condition, also for 120 min each. In total, this results in 1320 min with 11 different combinations.

3.2 Results

A total of 160 drives with a maximum length of 600 s were performed. If no corner case occurs in this time, the drives are aborted so that we have a right-censored data point. Therefore, the number of rides per combination varies, as models in which a corner case appears more quickly can also be driven more frequently.

The software used for survival analysis is lifelines [5]. Table 4 presents the total number of corner cases registered with respect to the trained model and the weather conditions driven. As we can see, there are barely corner cases in the expert models, which is why we group them together in their own model type, the experts type. All observations during the study are visualized in Fig. 7(a). In total, we have 48 observations of corner cases that can be used for survival analysis. Furthermore, the two students drove 406.838 km on the virtual streets of CARLA.

Table 4. List of all observed corner cases during weather campaign by model and tested weather condition.

model type	trained	tested			
		clear	rain	fog	night
baseline	clear	4	5	13	17
	rain	-	0	-	-
experts	fog	-	-	0	-
	night	-	-	-	1
universal	mix	1	3	1	3

As a first step, we consider the plot for the Kaplan-Meier estimation in Fig. 7(b) for the 3 model types *baseline, universal* and *experts*, which shows that the probability of a corner case occurring is lowest for the expert network, closely followed by the universal network. The baseline model seems to be very sensitive to different weather conditions, which is why there is only a survival probability of 63.24% after 300 s and at the end of the observation period only 42.65%.

We then use the Cox PH model to obtain the regression coefficients. For this, the input variables must first be preprocessed. For the weather parameter *rain* the values can range from 70 to 100 and for *fog* from 50 to 100. The parameter *night* is assigned to a Boolean variable and the value 1 is set as soon as the sun position parameter ($\in [-90, 90]$) is < 0. Additionally, we distinguish on which model we are driving, for this we use also a Boolean variable and set a 1 for either the expert model or the universal model.

Table 5 shows the evaluations of the Cox-PH. The analysis demonstrates that 3 covariates can be classified as significant, as their confidence interval is below 0.05. Fog is significant with 92% and rain even only with 58%.

The hazard rate is calculated using the expert model as an example. Since this value is a boolean variable, it can be calculated as follows:

$$HR_{expert} = \frac{h_{expert=1}(t)}{h_{expert=0}(t)} = 0.02 \tag{14}$$

Driving with an expert model reduces the hazard rate by 98% with a low ranging confidence interval.

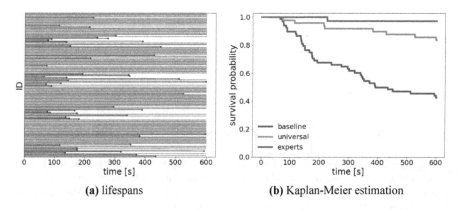

(a) lifespans   **(b)** Kaplan-Meier estimation

Fig. 7. (a) Lifespans of all observations during the study. Red lines show the occurrence of a corner case, whereas blue lines are right-censored. The majority of the drives, approx. 70%, did not lead to a corner case. (b) Kaplan-Meier estimation for all model types. The probability that no corner case occurs is highest in the expert models, followed by the universal model. The poor generalizability in bad weather provides that the survival probability in the base model decreases significantly over time. (Color figure online)

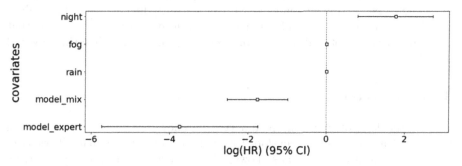

Fig. 8. The comparison of the hazard ratios shows that the night ensures that a corner case is more likely to occur. If an expert or universal model is used instead, a corner case occurs less frequently, which is also evident from the Kaplan-Meier estimate.

Table 5. Cox PH model.

covariate	Hazard Ratio HR	95% confidence interval for the hazard ratio	confidence level p
rain	1.01	0.99 - 1.02	0.42
fog	1.01	1.00 - 1.02	0.08
night	5.83	2.23 - 15.22	< 0.005
experts	0.02	0.00 - 0.17	< 0.005
universal	0.17	0.08 - 0.38	< 0.005

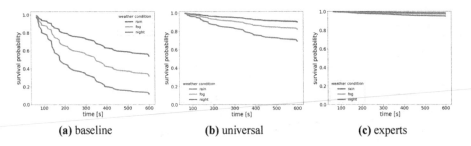

Fig. 9. The survival probabilities for rain, fog and night clearly show that the baseline model struggles with all bad weather settings. The universal model seems to be more robust, but the probability of survival at night also drops to 69% at the end of the study, whereas the expert model assures a survival of 95%.

Next we have a closer look to the probabilities for all models in different weather conditions. Figure 9 shows the performance for all models over time and for the weather conditions *rain, fog, night*. The baseline model has the biggest problems when driving on unseen weather conditions, with the highest probability of a corner case occurring at *night*. It also appears to be the most problematic for the universal and expert models, with significantly higher survival probabilities. The comparison between the universal and the expert models indicates that the latter perform noticeably better on their trained domains than the universal models.

4   Conclusion

Due to the lack of explanation and transparency in the decision-making of today's AI algorithms, we developed an experimental setup that allows visualizing these decisions and thus allows a human driver to evaluate the driving situations while driving with the eyes of AI, and from this to extract data that includes safety-critical driving situations. Our self-developed test rig provides two human drivers controlling the ego vehicle in the virtual world of CARLA. The semantic driver receives the output of a semantic segmentation network in real-time, based on which she or he is supposed to navigate in the virtual world. The second driver takes the role of the driving instructor and intervenes in dangerous driving situations caused by misjudgments of the AI. We consider driver interventions by the safety driver as safety-critical corner cases which subsequently replaced part of the initial training data. We were able to show that targeted data enrichment with corner cases created with limited perception leads to improved pedestrian detection in critical situations. In addition, we continue the further development of AI by means of human risk perception to identify situations that are particularly important to humans and thus train the AI precisely where it is particularly challenged by a human perspective.

The experimental setup with its components, the software used and the inference sensor have already been described in detail in [12], as well as the proof that corner cases occur less frequently when they are generated by a driving simulator with weak perception and then used for training. Based on this, survival analysis was used to investigate whether universal models could be replaced by expert models trained for specific domains only, in order to save development time for the application. Although the validity of such a few data points must be treated with caution, a trend does seem to emerge, namely that the use of expert models indeed seems to be more appropriate, as an omniscient model has to find a balance to perform well in each domain. Therefore, it may be useful to focus on some basic data and add other models for special cases that are temporarily responsible for prediction. Examples of use would be driving in left-hand traffic or in snowy winter regions, so that an appropriately trained model could be used. It would also be conceivable to have a separate trained model for each country that may be used when crossing borders. This solution might be based on the vehicle's GPS coordinates and would not require an additional upstream classification network.

Acknowledgements. The research leading to these results is funded by the German Federal Ministry for Economic Affairs and Climate Action within the project KI Data Tooling under the grant number 19A20001E. We thank Matthias Rottmann for his productive support, Natalie Grabowsky and Ben Hamscher for driving the streets of CARLA.

References

1. Bolte, J.A., Bar, A., Lipinski, D., Fingscheidt, T.: Towards Corner Case Detection for Autonomous Driving. In: 2019 IEEE Intelligent Vehicles Symposium, IV 2019, Paris, France, June 9–12, 2019, pp. 438–445. IEEE (2019)
2. Breitenstein, J., Termöhlen, J.A., Lipinski, D., Fingscheidt, T.: Systematization of Corner Cases for Visual Perception in Automated Driving. In: IEEE Intelligent Vehicles Symposium, IV 2020, Las Vegas, NV, USA, October 19 - November 13, 2020, pp. 1257–1264. IEEE (2020)
3. Breitenstein, J., Termöhlen, J.A., Lipinski, D., Fingscheidt, T.: Corner Cases for Visual Perception in Automated Driving: Some Guidance on Detection Approaches. CoRR abs/2102.05897 (2021)
4. Cox, D.R.: Regression models and life-tables. J. Roy. Stat. Soc.: Ser. B (Methodol.) **34**(2), 187–202 (1972)
5. Davidson-Pilon, C.: Lifelines: survival analysis in Python. J. Open Source Softw. **4**(40), 1317 (2019)
6. Dosovitskiy, A., et al.: CARLA: an open urban driving simulator. In: 1st Annual Conference on Robot Learning, CoRL 2017, Mountain View, California, USA, November 13–15, 2017, Proceedings. Proceedings of Machine Learning Research, vol. 78, pp. 1–16. PMLR (2017)
7. E. L. Kaplan and Paul Meier : Nonparametric estimation from incomplete observations. J. Am. Stat. Assoc. **53**(282), 457–481 (1958)
8. Heidecker, F., Breitenstein, J., Rösch, K., et al.: An Application-Driven Conceptualization of Corner Cases for Perception in Highly Automated Driving. In: 2021 IEEE Intelligent Vehicles Symposium (IV). Nagoya, Japan (2021)

9. Hosmer, D., Lemeshow, S., May, S.: Applied Survival Analysis: Regression Modeling of Time-to-Event Data. Wiley Series in Probability and Statistics, Wiley (2008)

10. Klein, J.P., Moeschberger, M.L.: Survival Analysis, 2nd edn. Statistics for Biology and Health, Springer, New York, NY (2003)

11. Kleinbaum, D.G., Klein, M.: Survival Analysis. Springer, New York (2012)

12. Kowol., K., Bracke., S., Gottschalk., H.: A-Eye: Driving with the Eyes of AI for Corner Case Generation. In: Proceedings of the 6th International Conference on Computer-Human Interaction Research and Applications - CHIRA, pp. 41–48. INSTICC, SciTePress (2022)

13. Logitech International S.A.: G920/G29 - Racing wheel for Xbox, PlayStation and PC. [Online] https://www.logitechg.com/en-us/products/driving/driving-force-racing-wheel.941-000110.html (2015). Accessed Feb 15 2023

14. Machin, D., Cheung, Y.B., Parmar, M.: Survival Analysis - A Practical Approach. John Wiley & Sons Inc, 2 edn. (2006)

15. Moore, D.F.: Erratum. In: Applied Survival Analysis Using R. UR, pp. E1–E13. Springer, Cham (2016). https://doi.org/10.1007/978-3-319-31245-3_13

16. Poudel, R.P.K., Liwicki, S., Cipolla, R.: Fast-SCNN: Fast Semantic Segmentation Network. In: 30th British Machine Vision Conference 2019, BMVC 2019, Cardiff, UK, September 9–12, 2019. pp. 289. BMVA Press (2019)

17. Sweeney, T.D.: Unreal Engine. [Online] https://www.unrealengine.com (1998)

18. Wang, J., Zhang, L., Huang, Y., Zhao, J., Bella, F.: Safety of autonomous vehicles. J. Adv. Transp. **2020**, 1–13 (2020)

19. Wu, X., et al.: A survey of human-in-the-loop for machine learning. Futur. Gener. Comput. Syst. **135**, 364–381 (2022)

Author Index

A. Holzinger et al. (Eds.): CHIRA 2021/2022, CCIS 1882, p. 171, 2023.
https://doi.org/10.1007/978-3-031-41962-1

Printed in the United States
by Baker & Taylor Publisher Services